The
AUTHORITATIVE
and the
AUTHORITARIAN

The
AUTHORITATIVE
and the
AUTHORITARIAN

JOSEPH VINING

THE UNIVERSITY OF CHICAGO PRESS
Chicago and London

Joseph Vining is Harry Burns Hutchins
Professor of Law at the University of
Michigan. He is the author of *Legal
Identity: The Coming of Age of Public Law.*

The University of Chicago Press, Chicago 60637
The University of Chicago Press, Ltd., London
© 1986 by The University of Chicago
All rights reserved. Published 1986
Printed in the United States of America

95 94 93 92 91 90 89 88 87 86 5 4 3 2 1

Library of Congress Cataloging-in-Publication Data

Vining, Joseph,
    The authoritative and the authoritarian.

    Bibliography: p.
    Includes indexes.
    1. Law—Philosophy.   2. United States.   Supreme
Court.   I. Title.
K237.V56   1986   340'.1   85-21018
ISBN 0-226-85663-1

A., S., G.
qui cognoverunt

Accordingly it would be strange indeed if the study of jurisprudence were not well adapted to throw light on the mind and its workings. That study was formerly regarded as an essential element in a liberal education. . . . It is perhaps a pity that this respectful attitude to legal studies has long since been abandoned; a pity both on general grounds and because the vast change in man's idea of himself wrought by the new notions of evolution and development, and by the comparatively recent birth of historical imagination, have opened up rich new fields of speculation both in language and in law.

—Owen Barfield

Fatalism and progress were as closely linked as the Heavenly Twins and like them invincible. Their victory, however, implied the banishment of all anthropomorphic ideas, and since mind was the most anthropomorphic thing in man, it must be driven from the field, first in the form of God or Teleology, then in the form of consciousness or purpose. These were explained away as illusions; those were condemned as superstition or metaphysics.

—Jacques Barzun

I order you, in the name of the law. . . .

—Everyman

CONTENTS

ACKNOWLEDGMENTS   xv

PROLOGUE   xvii

1. INTRODUCTION
   The Name of the Law   3

PART I
AUTHORITY AND PRESUPPOSITION   7

2. MIND
   The Presupposition of Mind in Legal Analysis   9

3. NATURE
   Rule without Eyes or Voice   16

4. METHOD
   The Creation of Authority   27

5. AUTHENTICITY
   Connecting the Speaker and the Spoken   41

PART II
AUTHORITY AND INSTITUTIONAL ARRANGEMENT   61

6. HIERARCHY
   Law without a Supreme Court   63

7. FOCUS
   The Function of a Center in a Search for the Authoritative   76

8. TIME
    The Achievement of Freedom   89

9. ILLUSION
    The Mysterious Example of the Legislature   110

10. DEMOCRACY
    The Democratic Connection   132

PART III
THE AUTHORITATIVE AND THE AUTHORITARIAN   143

11. DILEMMA
    Faith and Failure   145

12. IMAGE
    The Self-Imposed Dilemma   161

13. FAITH
    Evolution of Legal Descriptions of Mind   172

14. RECOGNITION
    The Neglected Metaphor   187

EPILOGUE   203

AMPLIFICATIONS   205

WORKS QUOTED IN TEXT   239

INDEX OF WORDS AND PHRASES   243

GENERAL INDEX   257

AMPLIFICATIONS

MIND
A Small Example of the Elision of Time 205
Word Definition 205
Points of Departure 206

NATURE
The Proposal of a Heaven without Law 206
Positivism in Social Science 208
Sociobiology 209
Paradigms in Thinking about Law 209
Public and Private Purposes 209
Forms of the Authoritarian 210
Ambiguities of Free Enterprise 210

METHOD
The Name of Science 211
A Note on Observations about Legal Analysis 212
The Literary Canon 212
Majority Rule 212
Hermeneutics 213
A Note on the Objectivity of Language 213
Connection to the Past 213

NOTE: Superscript numbers in text refer to Amplifications (see pp. 205–37) written to be read in conjunction with the text, or not, as the reader chooses. These anticipate or recall discussions in the text (for readers who read partially or intermittently), help mark departures in the text from what some readers may take to be the received approach to a matter, respond to additional questions some readers may have, and provide examples or extend examples where emphasis in the text, and what is communicated by emphasis, would be too much obscured if a note were not used.

Legal Method and Clear Meaning   213
An Example of Legal Method Outside Law   215

AUTHENTICITY
Critics' Choices   216
Games   216
A Note on Constitutional Free Speech   217
Monumentality   217
Legal Rules   217
The Relation between Obedience and Understanding   218
Movies   218
The Law of Agency   219
Intimations in Action   219
Statements as Things   219
Ghostwritten Philosophy   219

HIERARCHY
Closed Systems and Relativism   220
A Further Note on Hierarchical Statements   220
Superior Texts of Inferior Authors   221
The Theory of a Case   221

FOCUS
Counterthrusts toward Irresponsibility   221

TIME
A Note on Limits to Infinite Regress   221
Objets Trouvés   222
A Further Note on Conversation and Consistency   222

ILLUSION
Commitment and Acceptance in Joint Writing   223
Court and Administrative Agency   224
An Example of the Demand for the Actual   225
Jokes   226

DEMOCRACY
Law and Politics   226
Organizing Mechanisms and the Process of Speech   227
The Effect of Size   228
Vetoes   228

DILEMMA
System and Process   229
Examples of Legal Method   229

Legislation and Lawyers 230
Impersonal Criteria 230

IMAGE
Consequences of Metaphor 230
Anti-Summary 230
Other Institutions 231

FAITH
Doing and Saying 233
Commands and Categories 234
A Note on Escape and the Problem of Punishment 235
Contractual Relations and Relations of Duty 236
A Further Note on Form and the Recognition of Entities 236
Death 237

ACKNOWLEDGMENTS

I am grateful to colleagues, Jacques Barzun, Owen M. Fiss, Thomas A. Green, Donald H. Regan, E. Philip Soper, Cass R. Sunstein, Richard A. Stewart, and James Boyd White, and to the Reverend Philip J. Lee, the Reverend John L. McCausland, Sanford G. Thatcher, Alice Williams Vining, and Thomas H. Wright, Esq., for reading and commenting upon drafts of the manuscript. Each has been more than generous in his or her own fashion; James Boyd White has suffered my impositions perhaps most of all.

For the last several years I have been stimulated not only by the talk but by the example of two of my readers, John L. McCausland and Philip J. Lee. I am conscious that their influence appears at various points in ways that defy acknowledgment. Over a decade ago James Boyd White published *The Legal Imagination* and William R. Bishin and Christopher D. Stone published *Law, Language, and Ethics*, teaching materials that were based upon a sensitive appreciation of the relationship between law and language and that were notable for their departure from the prevailing images of law. In the early stages of thinking about this work I had the benefit of teaching from Bishin and Stone's materials.

The Cook Fund of the University of Michigan Law School has provided support from time to time since 1979. A fellowship from the National Endowment for the Humanities permitted me to complete the book.

I shall also note here three acknowledgments of a general kind.

First, I write from within the experience of law.

Lawyers look out from law to other disciplines, all the while unself-consciously engaging in the practice of their own, to the point where many have come to entertain the thought there may be nothing in legal study that is not a pale reflection of some other discipline. Certainly those working in law should consult those working on similar problems in other disciplines, and we shall be doing so in the discussion that follows. But there is a prior question, namely, which disciplines to consult, and it is this prior question we shall be considering throughout. Those in other disciplines are not well served if, when they consult what goes on in the practice of law, they find standing between them and the discipline of law a pale reflection of themselves.

Second, I write from within the experience of American law, which, like the experience of law itself, is less a limitation than a debt that may be properly mentioned in acknowledgments. Law in the United States may be seen at work in individuals' lives more by itself, as it were, than in British, Continental, Middle Eastern, Asian, or other societies; this I think true notwithstanding the legacy of class and slavery in the United States.

Third, I wish to acknowledge, because so few do, that I write from within the experience of life and thought amidst widespread material plenty, affluence indeed beyond the experience of anyone reflecting upon these matters in an earlier age. The presuppositions of law, together with law's demand for good faith and law's condemnation of resistance, look to the ideal and always have. The present situation in the West does not limit an exploration of the authority of law. Quite the reverse: while openness, sincerity, and responsibility are found among the poor and desperate and understood by them, these are not thought to be the characteristics of a poor, hungry, and desperate society.

But this last acknowledgment must have in it also elements of an apology. The world is not ideal and the United States is not ideal, and acting as if the world is an ideal world and delicately refining the principles that would apply in an ideal world is difficult to be proud of when there is so much else to do. Lawyers—and I do not exclude myself—must confront the question of how they can continue work in a nonideal world without giving up that which makes them lawyers. I can only suggest that if the world became worse than it is and reverted to barbarism everywhere, as it can in the blink of an eye, the authoritative would still be what the lawyer would be working toward, albeit with so much farther to go. Just as we would seek to play music again, so would we seek true authority, and such true authority as there was would still be what held together such society as there might then be.

PROLOGUE

Temple columns process along;
Trees in forests lead nowhere.
Temple columns one after another,
Arch after arch,
In ordered lines they march,
Soft drum beats in the silence
Or reconstructed for the ear in stately music,
Leading,

Where? Where do they go,
Those rows of columns that lead the eye and foot along?

In a great garden's finest moment,
Somewhere in every planted park,
You enter long allés of trees
That make your walk processional.
Stately music plays among them,
Not loudly, unless you act a part,
But even at your truest you cannot shake the dignity from your step
As the columns pass by two by two on either side
Leading on

Where? Where do those columns
At the center of a forest tamed to garden
Full of beauty to delight the eye, and dignity, and meaning,
As fit for man to live in as man can make it,
Where do those naves and rows of columns lead?
To an urn?
Consider the gardener's plight.
To an open door? an arch?

Opening on what?
Another allé?

Stately music cannot go on and on.
No one supposes that it will.
Journeys must have destinations.
It is enough, when young,
That something new be around each corner,
And that there be another corner after that.
But when age appears, it lifts the corner of the painted backdrop
Before which Adventure plays.
There must be more.

Process along, they say. To what? you say.
No matter, they say. The process is enough.
March with dignity, meaning, like the soldier on parade.
Listen to the stately music. It is enough.
The soldier though,
So proud and full of circumstance,
Marching for us all as we watch caught up in what he does,
Turns around and marches back again.

Or the soldier stops, and the music stops,
And the guns and swords and flutes and bows are put in boxes.
We cannot do that in our lives, we cannot just stop.
Do we then just go round and round?

Journeys must have destinations,
Else the march with stately music is foolish;
Else stately music with the march deep within, is foolish;
Else the guiding row of columns leads only to its end, the last column;
Else the temple is like the forest, its columns leading nowhere,
A place where one finds oneself eventually lost,
The place where one is lost.

Consider what the gardener does in his plight.
It is what the builders of cathedrals do with great allés within,
And builders of temples, with their rows of golden columns glowing:
They end with a view beyond which one cannot hope to go,
The sea or distant mountain peak, or an altar.
If the gardener has no sea or mountain peak to end the processional way,
His garden can serve to recall those that do,
And every temple-builder can set up an altar at the end.

The largest view, the view beyond,
Where one cannot think of going with one's feet,
The sea, the sky, the peak beyond the gulf,
Is this a destination?
Is there a difference between a temple and the forest dark?

The
AUTHORITATIVE
and the
AUTHORITARIAN

1

INTRODUCTION
The Name of the Law

Frazer's *Golden Bough* ends with a striking image. Human thought is a fabric woven of three threads, a black one of magic, a red one of religion, and a white one of science, and Frazer sees it being unrolled in history, black at the beginning and gradually acquiring a crimson center, which then begins to be interwoven with white. At the time he wrote, in the early part of this century, the fabric was for him still stained crimson at the center but becoming increasingly white, and he wondered hopefully whether the fabric would become whiter and whiter as the decades passed.

Frazer was writing at the high water mark of the romance of science, and things did become almost as he had hoped. The fabric of thought did become white, very white, bloodless, featureless. Law, however, never did become scientific. At the same time law could not possibly be dismissed. The structure of another world, the world of the theologian, might be thrown away, but not the structure of this world, the world of the lawyer.

This is a book about the dilemma of being a lawyer. It is one dilemma, because its parts are related. Lawyers know that theirs is a discipline not like those which have been at the center of twentieth century thought, but they have great difficulty in saying just what it is. This is one part of the dilemma. The other is that the method central to a lawyer's training, which has much to do with setting them apart and defining who they are, is used to search for meaning; yet they as lawyers profess to be willing to do without meaning.

Now doing without meaning is a form of despair and carries its own measure of pain. But when a man in despair is sentenced to purposeful action, there is worse pain than dull despair. That is the lawyer's pain. I think it can be alleviated, even if not wholly cured.

What makes our era new is not technology, or anything else outside us, but rather that we seem today to have no way of thinking that will order our wants. The way in which we have been accustomed to order or to have ordered for us that range of wants within our focus—speed, for instance; mobility; elimination of labor; meat—will not do. We cannot rank our wants now in any mathematical and manipulative way, as if they were outside us. We falsify and know we falsify whenever we try. For a human life, a green field, work that is not toil, leisure that is not empty, for any of these the usual time frames and units of reference blur and dissolve.

We think actively about our wants. That of course is not new. We have been thinking actively about wants, means and ends, ends that are means and means that are ends, since the fading away of sanctified hierarchy and traditional differences between men. But now wants do not fall into place. The way we have been thinking has no place for them, and we cannot go back to the order of tradition. The idea of equality has done its work, and individuals are not given wants, given identities, and ranked accordingly. We cannot step back into places now long forgotten. So we are left, actively thinking, yet with apparently no way of thinking.

The law offers a way of thinking that orders our thoughts in a non-mathematical way, a way not external and manipulative. It uses hierarchy and has echoes of tradition. It is not new. It predates, in its form if not its focus, the era just past in which a quite different form or way has been dominant. It has persisted beside the dominant way of thinking up to the present, affected by the dominant way but never absorbed, but it is not simply an intractable atavism. In fact it was and is still associated with the dissolution of the old order and differences between individuals as different sorts of being, and with the rise of each man and woman to an equal dignity.

We shall now have to look carefully at this other way of the law, for we must order our wants and our thoughts. We are lost if we do not—mad, incoherent, in hell: there are many words for what we face. I do not know that this other way will do. But at least it is at hand. At the end of our look at it in this book we may be in a better position to judge whether it might do.

A SHAKING AT THE FOUNDATIONS

The book is an argument in part. The argumentative part of the discussion is muted, but an argument in part the discussion must be, not just a description of the territory, simply because for so many years there has been even among lawyers an effort to deny what law affirms.

Law has not accepted the spirit of the age that (in Keats's words) would clip an Angel's wings and empty the haunted air. Perhaps other fields have not really done so either, and there is not so much a gulf between fields as gulfs within fields and a shaking at their foundations. But the refusal to accept the spirit of the age is most evident in law, to the point that law can be said to affirm that to which the spirit of the age points by contrast.

Yet we must acknowledge the history of denial by lawyers themselves of what law affirms, the long effort to see and make law a machine. And so there must be something of an argument. It is really an argument with ourselves, because if we affirm we must still be open to doubt when so many others seem to deny.

OUTLINE OF THE BOOK

The discussion will be divided into three parts. Together they form an introduction to the problem of legal authority, which may be described in a phrase as the problem of perceiving the difference between the authoritative and the authoritarian. Chapter headings running through the Parts indicate different aspects of lawyers' experience of the world, but in the end it is one experience. So too with the larger division into parts: the problem of authority cannot be separated from the problem of method; the problem of method, in turn, cannot be separated from institutional arrangements; and the dilemma of professional life in the law is bound up with them all. We divide not to emphasize distinctions between these matters but to trace their connections more easily. It is possible that the very perception of such connections may allow some alleviation of the lawyer's pain to come of its own.

Chapters are meant to be read in order. For the reader who reads only particular chapters in a book, or, if he reads them all, reads them out of order, there will be occasional notes anticipating what is to come or recalling previous discussion. In the final chapter the reader will find it argued that modern theology is a neglected source of aid in the study of law and the solution of legal problems, including problems involving the structure of legal institutions. Indeed I suggest that theology, rather than social science or literary criticism, is the sister discipline of law. I am not writing there from any particular ecclesiastical or religious position. I am working instead from methodological affinities between law and theology. The book may be read without the final chapter. Its object is substantially complete, as a preface to the study of law and to acceptance of being a lawyer, at the end of Chapter 13. But I hope the reader will continue through the final chapter. It is itself a preface to further work and serves, in addition, as a summary of much that will have gone before.

Sometimes lawyers, judges, officials, and citizens say they speak "in the name of the law." When they say this they invoke the authority of the law. It is not too literal to ask what the law's name is and whether it can have a name. That in a way is what we will be asking now as we proceed. Our inquiry is guided, as will be seen, by a question that can be raised today about the American Supreme Court: whether it will become a bureaucratic institution, and if so what that will mean. The implications of the internal bureaucratization of American courts for the presuppositions of legal method provide the subject of Chapters 2 through 5. We begin with the presupposition of mind in legal analysis and then inquire whether there can be rule without eyes or voice, what is involved in the making of an authoritative statement of law, and how speakers are connected to the spoken with which lawyers work. Chapters 6 through 10 turn to the institutional arrangements serving method and the ends for which method is practiced. Chapters 6, 7, and 8 take the implications of bureaucratization to their limit and consider what the effects upon lawyers and law would be of actually eliminating the Supreme Court as a source of law. This will lead us to address the phenomenon of hierarchy, which is such a distinctive part not just of American but of Western law, and the reasons why a center might be thought attractive in a search for the authoritative. Chapters 9 and 10 place beside courts as they exist today the other grand institutions of law that modern lawyers face, legislatures and electorates. Here we will approach law's use of illusion and tricks and lawyers' experience of them. The last four chapters consider what we have seen and point beyond. Chapter 11 recalls and restates our dilemma. Chapters 12 and 13 explore the hope that the lawyer's dilemma is in part self-imposed, and Chapter 14 looks forward to the aid that may be hoped for from others in sister disciplines who also hover between the authoritative and the authoritarian. The problem of an internally bureaucratized Supreme Court fades as a thread and is replaced by that for which it has all along been a surrogate: impersonal system, impersonal process itself.

PART I
AUTHORITY
and
PRESUPPOSITION

2

MIND

The Presupposition of Mind in Legal Analysis

T HE METHOD OF CHOICE in standard legal analysis is close reading and full discussion of a text. In the United States the texts of
choice are the opinions of the federal Supreme Court. Most American
lawyers gravitate toward them, with important and untraced effects upon
the substance of American law. The prominence of federal constitutional
law, for example, in the curricula of law schools, in the strategies of litigating lawyers, and in the thinking of judges, may be quite as much a product
of its methodological congeniality as of its substantive importance.

The attractions of Supreme Court texts for lawyers are powerful indeed.
The forms of speech adopted in the Supreme Court opinions themselves,
and in analysis of them, imply the existence of a single mind, that of "this
Court." It is not quite so easy to postulate a single mind lying behind other
legal texts. There is also a wonderful elision of time. Time is very nearly
transcended. The Court of men long dead is still "this Court." If one
listens to the way an American lawyer talks, what John Marshall said in
1803 is as important and relevant as what any contemporary justice says.[1]
And the texts produced by the Supreme Court are presumptively authoritative throughout the geographic jurisdiction of the United States.
Although geographic reach is not necessary to a text's relevance to the
task of determining what the law is on this or that question, the breadth of
the Supreme Court's jurisdiction at least mitigates the lawyer's ever-present worry that what he is so carefully parsing and arguing from may be an
aberration and of little moment, no real evidence of anything larger and
more meaningful. Working with other opinions—of state supreme courts,
or federal appeals courts or district judges, or Canadian or British courts—

9

an American lawyer is open to the challenge "So what? That's *their* opinion, but why do you pay such attention to it?" Indeed, whenever lawyers set about legal analysis of such opinions they feel they must be ready to answer the question "Why pay attention?" even if it is never asked. In preparing to respond lawyers appeal, rather more than they would like to think, to a primitive assertion that each judge speaks as an oracle of the law. It is possible for lawyers to think themselves less exposed to a charge of primitivism if they work with statements of the Supreme Court.

But legal habits in the United States are threatened. There is a sense among serious analysts that the Supreme Court is failing them and that the texts of choice for American legal analysis are wanting. Extraordinary open complaints are underscored by a general tone of comment and criticism which is unhappy and disrespectful. There is not contempt so much as there is distress, of the kind associated with deprivation: if one listens, one can hear a general murmur of dissatisfaction punctuated by sharp cries.

Complaint about imperfection is of course perennial, as is some undercurrent of disrespect. The Court of the 1950s and 1960s was criticized for poor craftsmanship, and it could hardly be said that all lawyers in the southern states respected that Court. Pre–World War II realists were certainly contemptuous of the then-traditional legal forms, and the late nineteenth century was spent fighting the foolishness of those legal fictions that are the subject of Dicey's most entertaining pages. But the restlessness of the late twentieth century is different. It points to a change of a sort not experienced before.

There is more to the complaint than that the Court's opinions too often treat other legal texts in a perfunctory way, do not engage points made in dissent, are inconsistent or poorly articulated—as if the writer of the opinion were sleepy, or hurried, or dull. Now opinions too often seem things written by no one at all: they are very long, much too long to be written by judges struggling with an enormous increase in caseload: they are things of patchwork which seem, on their face, to express the institutional process of their making rather than the thinking, feeling, and reasoning of the author and those persuaded with him. Poor craftsmanship, if that were the problem, could be cured by gradually replacing the authors of opinions with better craftsmen. The writing of opinions by no one, bureaucratic writing, is not so easy to change once it has taken hold. Bureaucratic writing is a structural matter; there may in fact be a quality of irreversibility about it to be feared as much as we fear the irreversibility of environmental change or genetic manipulation.

The bureaucratization of the Supreme Court is also reflected in the elaboration of the Court's institutional organization. The Court is no longer nine judges in dialogue with one another, trying to come to common ground and setting out in writing their agreements and disagreements with a special sense of the representative quality of their thinking. Each of the nine is acquiring a staff, developed from the legal secretary or research assistant of old. As the staff has grown there are indications that it is becoming layered. Some clerks may be detailed to a central pool for special tasks. Chief clerks, senior clerks, and junior clerks are beginning to appear. One clerk may help regulate access by other clerks to a justice. Clerks may interview the flood of applicants for clerkships.

Within a single generation the justices have quadrupled the number of their law clerks. Some justices are now asking their clerks to stay a longer time. The short stint by the bright, young, just-graduated law student, who moved into an intimate relationship with an old justice, kept him fresh, and then moved quickly on into a separate life and career, has already begun to be replaced by a job description and a job. It appears that the nine staffs communicate directly with one another. They may be horizontally connected and reach agreements among themselves—or they may operate more by bargain than persuasion: that they do not act for themselves puts them in a role to which persuasion is not immediately pertinent. And there may be reciprocal relationships vertically. Justices may be loyal to staff or to the expectations that make possible complex organizations of individuals.

The actual operations of the Court have always been veiled and still are, and what is revealed is often dismissed as gossip or self-aggrandizement. But clerks routinely now say in private that they wrote one or another important opinion and that it was published with hardly a change, while studies of lower court procedures suggest that an institutional practice of assigning to staff the reading of briefs and the drafting of opinions is becoming well established. However veiled the actual operations of the Supreme Court may be, we know that a large professional staff must have something to do. All are working to produce a product. And the products they are producing are the texts of choice to which American lawyers turn when they undertake legal analysis.

As lawyers become aware of this, their confidence that through reading an opinion or sequence of opinions they can reach a mind behind it must begin to fail within them.

THE METHODOLOGICAL PROBLEM POSED BY BUREAUCRACY

Think for a moment how differently lawyers treat opinions issued by one or another of the great federal administrative agencies, for example, the

Interstate Commerce Commission or the Federal Trade Commission, with their many employees, many layers, and complex organization charts. There is no such governing assumption in reading and analysis, no such faith where opinions of administrative agencies are concerned.

When commissioners decide a case after argument and briefing (if indeed there is oral argument, and if they rather than their staff assistants read the briefs), they vote, and the vote is frequently, perhaps typically, transmitted to an opinion-writing section of the agency, one among the many offices on the agency's organization chart. The opinion-writing section prepares a justification and explanation to accompany the result. If the vote had gone the other way, the same office would still write the opinion. It would simply say different or opposite things. The opinion is then sent back to the commissioners or their staffs, who may read it, may amend it, may return it, or may approve it. Once approved, it is promulgated on behalf of the agency.

Would it be too harsh to say that no good lawyer would ever spend the time analyzing these opinions that he lavishes on Supreme Court opinions? Certainly he would not look for nuance and image, or examine the structure of thought revealed, or work out developments and transformations over time. He would not do what American lawyers do with Supreme Court opinions. He would not think of doing it, and would feel foolish if he found himself engaged in such an intense and delicate reading—as if, fresh from an immersion in Milton, he caught himself reading a corporate advertisement in the same way he had been reading *Paradise Lost.*

The reason is not that the decisions of such agencies are unimportant. They are often of vast importance. The reason is that the texts produced by agencies in this way offer no access to a mind. They are not evidence of the workings of a mind. The texts are evidence of what kinds of evidence it was thought necessary to produce for the purpose of giving the appearance of the workings of a mind. One knows how commissioners voted. One knows of their action. But one cannot listen in on them. One does not know whether there was dialogue that produced a decision that can be said to be a common decision. One does not know whether there is any mutual influence over time. One can be sure that the commissioners themselves would not read opinions written by an opinion-writing section several floors below to discover what their colleagues present or past actually thought. They would look at letters, memoranda, or notes of conversation. Those would be their texts.[2]

Lawyers who challenge administrative action in court in the United States will initially try to show, if they can, some ex parte influence upon what is written or some forbidden consultation among investigatory, prosecutory, and opinion-writing officials within the agency. In this part of their analysis or brief, the administrative opinion will be viewed and portrayed as if it were the product of a machine, rather like one of the credit card letters churned out by computers and mailed to us so frequently. The search is for circuits that went awry, "inputs" that were wrong. But if defending lawyers build a good enough wall around the process to keep the challengers from seeing into it, or successfully defend its working in the particular instance, the challengers will shift and will indeed portray the opinion as if it were a judicial opinion. The argument will then be about the nature and adequacy of the reasoning set forth, connection between basis and conclusion, consistency with prior decisions, distinction between what was essential and what peripheral in prior decisions, and interpretation of majority writings in light of points made in dissents. Both challenger and defender will use these and all the other techniques of textual analysis used by lawyers to establish what the law is and to criticize and defend particular statements of it.

Such an activity does imply a search for a unifying mind. But here it does not mean there is on the part of lawyers a belief in such a mind, even what might be called a working belief. It does not mean that the text is actually viewed as something other than the product of a machine. The use of these techniques of textual analysis in working with bureaucratic texts is conventional and strategic. It is a conventional prelude to argument about matters of policy that could be discussed regardless of the existence of an opinion; it is a kind of salutation, like the beginning of a letter.

It is strategic in that lawyers do it because it might just work. A showing of breaks in the chain of reasoning might lead judges, under an illusion that they were dealing with the workings of a mind, to reverse and remand as they would if they were reviewing a lower court. Lawyers need not be committed here to the conventions of their discourse, for there are many ways to challenge decisions of administrative agencies other than legal argument. Negotiation with the agency is always possible, as is delay, appeal to congressional committees, influencing the agency's budget, and involvement in electoral politics. Because argument from texts is but one string to the bow, lawyers can afford to think of what they say and do as simply strategic.

But if the text, the opinion, was all there was—as is almost the case on the judicial side—could lawyers afford to be strategic? To the extent that they are strategic, they are dealing with nothing that has authority or meaning for them. Can lawyers do without authority? Can any of us? Suppose lawyers decided to give the text authority. Could they pretend that the opinion is something it is not, that this product of many hands is the speech of a mind that can command their attention? Can lawyers live without authority and meaning, or supply it by pretense and presumption? Can any of us?

The Nature of Our Inquiry

Now some may think that this is simply a concern taken too far, that what I have said about the problem posed by the possibility of a bureaucratized Supreme Court applies to any written document: to any piece of legislation, papal bulls, histories, even standard philosophical works. Anyone who has had anything to do with the publication of books will have been struck by the extent to which books can be the product of many hands, of research assistants, friendly critics of the manuscript, professional readers, editors, copyeditors. One look at the facsimile of Ezra Pound's editorial work on *The Waste Land* tells us how endemic this is: poetry itself is not exempt. The question could be asked then, Must we not always jump over how a work is produced and treat it as an integrated whole that can stand on its own?

I do not think so. In the case of a poem or an essay or a book, we ordinarily assume that there is a guiding mind controlling its creation. Pound sent the changed *Waste Land* back to T. S. Eliot, not on to the printer. Sentences, forms of expression, even ideas that are not originally an author's own become his by adoption, because he actually considers them, sentence by sentence, phrase by phrase, thought by thought, comma by comma, and makes them his own after deliberation. To the extent that he does not, they mar the piece, and the process of reading, close reading, will involve pruning them away, putting them aside, and not hearing them. To be sure, there is legislation with its special claim to our respect. But other pieces of writing—and perhaps legislation too—exert their authority over us and command our respect and serious attention only to the extent that we hear a person speaking through them. Their authority rests upon the sense of mind behind them. The Ancient Mariner exerted power over the wedding guest. He held him "with his glittering eye." Writings do the same with us, if they hold us at all.

What then are we to do in the United States if the Supreme Court no longer looks at us with a glittering eye? How will legal analysis be done if Supreme Court opinions come to resemble the opinions of a large administrative agency? The question is important, certainly in the United States, and I think it is one that should now be pursued. I hope it will engage us and keep us engaged. I propose to pursue it as one might follow after a butterfly in a great forest of oaks, as a lure, for it will lead us to the dilemma of being a lawyer and the dilemma at the center of law itself.

Even if one takes to a forest purely to experience its darkness and grandeur, face it and fathom it, one wants a present and proximate goal. This must be half the reason for hunting, to have something specific to do as one moves through landscape and the wild, some reason to go this way rather than that, around this tree, down that path. The question with which we will begin is both quarry and guide. Fully worth the time and trouble of pursuit, it is yet but a means.

The courts are among the last of the great voices to be rationalized, detached from substance and reduced to process, as a result of that pursuit of objectivity outside ourselves which has produced both the radical individualism and the impersonal bureaucracy we know today. They are among the last, and in the United States their bureaucratization has not been consummated. The bureaucratization of courts may not in the end come to pass. That the possibility is real may jolt us all into more attention to the underpinnings of law.[3] There may be in fact a choice to be made between the authoritative and the authoritarian, and when we or those who come after us look back it may be clear that it is we who have made the choice. No doubt we will move incrementally in institutional change, and what emerges will not be conceived by any of us now alive. But growth in a particular direction is not inevitable.

Thus when you, the reader, pick these pages up, the problem of bureaucratization may have begun to fade and be no longer the contemporary problem it is as I write. But that is not the end of the book. Our object is to understand authority and its shadow, authoritarianism. We shall want to see woven together method, institutional structure, authority, and personification, for they are in fact woven together and together link our minds to the sensible and even material world. The place of hierarchy in a society in which obedience for its own sake has no value, the place of illusion in a discipline rooted in the actual and devoted to truth, speech divorced from speaker, beings beyond individuals, the disappearance of all into process—these will be our subjects. We shall be exploring the lawyer's world.

3

NATURE
Rule without Eyes or Voice

The Mute Result of Description

How would we go about doing legal analysis if Supreme Court opinions came to resemble the opinions issued by a bureaucratic organization such as the Interstate Commerce Commission? To answer this question we must ask what lawyers think they are doing when they construct an authoritative statement of law. That is a question of methodology—what the method of legal analysis can be said to be—and to understand it fully we must look at the connections and distinctions between lawyers and the practitioners of other disciplines.

Legal analysts, by and large, no longer think they are engaged in a scientific enterprise in the tradition of the mathematical and physical sciences. This was once the dominant professed conception, and we still live in its shadow. The central building in the monumental law complex at the University of Michigan, begun in the 1920s, is named the Legal Research Building. The central building at Harvard Law School is Langdell Hall, named for the late nineteenth-century Dean whose legacy to American legal education was the proposition that the utterances of judges were raw data from which law might be objectively induced as laws of science might be induced from the data presented by nature. Lawyers are still taught from descendants of the casebooks introduced by those who propagated the scientific metaphor. The American Law Institute, established to carry out the scientific enterprise by restating the law in a formulaic way, with its condensed black-letter taking the place of the pregnant equations of physics, still functions.

And yet it is all only a shadow. None but the benighted believes in the method. To take one small example, an assertion that this one formulation is the "majority" rule followed by more than 50 percent of state or federal courts, but that other is the "minority" rule, does not move a modern student to say the "majority rule" is the law. In fact, from its very beginning the method was pretense. The casebooks and treatises emphasized the opinions of some judges and not others; they reflected the law of chosen jurisdictions, notably Massachusetts, New York, and England. Was one to treat as equivalent an opinion of Holmes in Massachusetts and an opinion of what's-his-name in Wyoming? Of course not. Some judges spoke truer doctrine than others, a New York opinion on a commercial matter had more weight than one from Maine. The opinions themselves were presented in heavily edited form. A person seeking to state the law did not in fact go about finding it empirically.[1]

Claims about the method of social science, however, are still very much with us. It was an early and enthusiastic vision of a science of society that first influenced legal thinking; and legal thinking, like the ocean, retains the heat of an idea longer than the atmosphere around it. In contrast to the nineteenth-century view of the divination of law as a science, social science turns from what lawyers and judges say and therefore from analysis of doctrine, and looks instead to what judges and other officials do, to behavior and patterns of behavior, with discovery of correlations leading to assertions of causality. Partly as a result of the scientific ethos generally, partly as a result of the realist movement in law particularly and the recognition of what is called administrative law (emanating from official agencies in addition to courts and legislatures), lawyers today all act as naturalists or positivists from time to time, and with some conviction.[2]

A strain of this can be found in the old common law. Students are told at the very beginning of traditional legal training that in analyzing a case a distinction should be drawn between what the judge says and what the judge does. What he says can be put aside if it is not necessary to what he does. It is then idle talk, speculation. There are, as might be expected, enormous difficulties in establishing criteria for determining necessity and even what exactly it is that the judge does. There is also a core of psychological truth in treating as more seriously reflective of actual belief the making of decisions that have perceptible consequences. But I shall not go further into this aspect of common-law analysis. I want only to note it, to recall how familiar the distinction is toward which such analysis tries to point, and upon which the standard method of social science is built. It is the distinction between speaking and acting.

The distinction as we know it in ordinary life is most vividly perceived in the difference between a friend and an enemy. With friends we pay attention to what they say as well as what they do. The phrase that so often comes to the mind of the agonized parent, and that is sometimes said out loud to everyone's embarrassment, "This hurts me more than it hurts you," is not always a lie. With enemies, on the other hand, we look *only* to what they do, and treat what they say as something that they are *doing*. We assume that their language is strategic, not authentic, their words counters in a game like a boxer's banter in the ring, and that the only pressure within them toward truthfulness is their fear of getting caught and losing the credibility that makes possible successful distortion and omission.

Disentangled from the experience of everyday life and raised to the level of theory or method, the distinction is that between nature and man, that between the outside and the inside, and, to a large degree, that between what is objective and what is not.

Teachers, scholars, and practitioners of law often consider themselves social scientists when they do not take at face value what a judge says and instead ask what is really going on. But an interest in the actual and the real, in what is really going on, does not make one necessarily a scientist. When in search of law one asks, "What does this speaker really mean?" one has not crossed the line between man and nature. When one speaks in causal terms and asks "What caused this speaker to say what he said?" one has crossed that line. And for the lawyer it is a most dangerous line to cross. Once over it, we know, the lawyer is in danger of being picked up and swept bumpety-bump over the horizon and into a breakfast theory of justice—the theory of the 1930s that what a judge does is determined by what breakfast he eats in the morning. When at the end of one's search for law one finds oneself deposited in a small white room staring at a fried egg, one has the choice of giving up the enterprise, for one really has nothing useful or interesting to say and no one to say it to; or one can come out of the room and creep back to one's fellows.

One might think, however, that one could go outside and cross the line without exposing oneself to the risk of that lonely little room, if one confined oneself to description. Although description is the first step in scientific analysis, it does not necessarily involve the pursuit of causes that carry us away. One can say to a friend, "Look at what you are doing to yourself," without going on and saying, "You are doing this *because* of this and that and the other"; one can say, "Let me describe this painting or this piece of music to you," without undertaking to explain it away.

But when we describe we make implicit causal statements, at least in the sense that we describe something rather than everything: we draw a line around that which we focus our attention upon. A painting has a frame around it. A piece of music has a beginning and an end in time. Within the thing we are describing and have drawn a line around, there is a hanging together of parts and pieces because they are connected in some fashion. They are organized into the entity to which we point. They have been given structure. In any good description one can see the parts *pushing* this way and that and resulting in a perceivable form, rather as one can see the parts of a skyscraper pushing this way and that to produce the sky-scraper and continuously *cause* it to be a skyscraper and a thing that can be described.

In the course of legal analysis we certainly do describe. Careful, ex-haustive description is part of legal method. Just think how rich a cultural, social, historical, and economic context lawyers build up around a case if they are trying to draw law from it in a way that will excite the professional admiration of their colleagues. Felix Frankfurter's early course in admin-istrative law, which was called Public Utilities, was nicknamed the Case-of-the-Month Club. American law students are amazed at how much time a contracts professor can spend on *Hadley* v. *Baxendale,* an English deci-sion of 1854. The working over of cases in questions from the bench, the memoranda of clerks to their judges, and the arguments in good briefs may be more in the way of sketches of such full analysis, owing to limits of space and time, but their object is the same. Good lawyers today are all practitioners of sociological jurisprudence. Exhaustive investigation and description, as the product of an urge, indeed a necessity to know what is really going on if we are to engage in legal analysis, does give the study of law a kinship with science.

So, if we want to know what the law of probation is in an American jurisdiction, we go beyond conclusory judicial statements about public safety and dangerousness, and examine what factors are being taken into account in decisions to grant probation or to institutionalize juveniles or convicts. If we want to know what the law is in a field regulated by an administrative agency, we are instructed by the Administrative Procedure Act not to limit ourselves to the rules the agency has designated as the law, but to examine also the internal policies and guidelines that organize the agency and govern the decisions of agency officials. Those, too, are defined as agency rules. In short, we see sources of law as systems. As we explore, investigate, probe, collect, categorize, and arrange the data, we more and more have before us a process, a set of moving relationships that form a pattern; and with the process brought out and set down on paper, the legal products—the texts and statements to which our attention is initially directed—become parts of the process, outcomes of the process. The decisions and the statements of rules become, in a way, transparent, as a living cell becomes transparent upon investigation, and what we see instead is a system, a structure—

—As if we were scientists of a descriptive bent.

But here again we are in terrible difficulty, not quite so severe or quite so obvious as if we were to be presented with a fried egg whenever we asked for law, but severe enough. The difficulty in saying that description and perception of process is all, or even the major part, of legal analysis is that when we are done we have nothing that need be obeyed, nothing that we need respect. What we have discovered to be really going on has no authority over us, and for the same reason that nature has no authority over us. Since we have from the first been searching for what is authoritative and to be obeyed, we cannot say that we have found the law at all.

THE AUTHORITY OF NATURE

It may not be self-evident that nature has no authority over us. *Of course* nature has authority over us, you may say. It has the most powerful authority of all. We are physically limited, mentally structured. Our passions rise in us despite ourselves. The art of happiness consists in the acceptance of these limitations and these drives, our sexual nature and our social nature particularly. How can it be said that nature has no authority over us? Why, nature has the *only* authority over us that we must accept.

In truth, however, when we accept, let us say, the sexual part of ourselves, and feel we ourselves are at the center of it rather than it outside us and we the victims or playthings of it, then we have to that extent transcended nature. You cannot be the slave of *your* passions, for if you felt that, they would not be *your* passions. We need not accept the sexual urge, and insofar as men and women do not accept it and fight and struggle against it, it is something apart from them, over and against them, a cause they can resist, manipulate, and trick, with cold baths and repression. We never accept the limitations of time and space. We have no wings, but we want to fly. We steady the body against old age. We seek to escape in art the rush of time. The nature we think of as good and an extension of ourselves is just that, an extension of ourselves. The authority of beauty is the authority of our own perceptions. We could *say* that a row of hills is not beautiful when in fact we felt it was, but we would not be disobeying any command or even disassociating ourselves from the object that had enthralled us.

Nature is sometimes said to be that which we actually do. But what we actually do is not what we must do: our entire effort over centuries may be directed against what we actually do. What we must do is not what we ought to do or want to do. Again, our entire effort may be directed against what, *for the time being,* we must do. For, really, we do not know our limits. Nature, real nature, about which we have no say, does not, in itself, have legitimacy or justify what we do or fail to do. Nature, that which is, just goes on.

I have called the difference between nature and man the difference between an enemy and a friend, and this though I myself love nature in one sense, love its colors, its warmth, its music and its light. But I believe, when I say I love nature, that I personify and create. When it is sunny and we are happy we feel at one with nature and embrace it. But when it is gray we may resist it, and often do. I would not put myself in the hands of nature, and neither would you. Nature will go on its own way regardless of our cry, unless, of course, we force it to do otherwise.

Natural *laws* are nothing to be obeyed or respected. Quite the reverse. In natural science results are not right or wrong. They are just results. What is observed, what is done, behavior—here I do not say "what is chosen," "decided," or "said," for such anthropomorphic terms cannot be used in natural science except in a fanciful way[3]—is never unlawful or against scientific law. Results are the sovereign. If they are inconsistent with scientific law, the law is changed to eliminate the inconsistency, or elaborated to explain the inconsistency (and thus make it no inconsistency at all) by adding additional variables that had not been thought of before or included in the rule. If the very perception of a result is tied to a concept that has no existing place in scientific thought, the result may be put aside and ignored, or not perceived; but it may precipitate a change that is not in form an elaboration, rather a move toward apparent simplicity. The newly stated rule or the more elaborate rule (or collection of proliferated subrules) then becomes the scientific law, which remains until new results come in which falsify the statement. Natural laws are not even addressed to that which they are said—again fancifully—to govern, and the joy of the practicing scientist is pitting himself against them.

CONSIDER AGAIN the search for law through description, as that technique is practiced upon nature.

In examining how the American criminal justice system really works, the student today looks at that vast bulk of its workings which take place before and after the criminal trial. Indeed, when one views the criminal justice system as a system, a trial and conviction of substantive crime is largely a jurisdictional event: it does not determine what actually happens to anyone. If there is a trial, what the trial is about—what facts and substantive law are involved in it—is determined by an administrative process through which some particular criminal charge is chosen. Whether there is a trial at all—that is, whether the mode by which jurisdiction over a defendant's life is obtained is trial rather than conviction by guilty plea—is determined by an administrative process in which prosecutor and defense attorney participate and a large number of factors, including the cost and time of a trial, are taken into account. After conviction, sentencing is entirely administrative, with prosecutors, probation officers, and judges acting as administrative officials. If sentence is not suspended, further decisions are made administratively by probation officers, prison officials, and parole boards, with judges engaged in some judicial review of all these various decisions and, if necessary, in their ultimate enforcement. Where is the *law* in all this? How does one go about finding it and stating it? By what technique, what methods?

Suppose you examine the records carefully, putting one sentencing case with another, and discover that in a particular district all judges take into account whether a young girl smokes cigarettes in deciding whether to grant or revoke probation. You might induce a rule that young girls on probation may not smoke. This rule can be restated as a practical rule that at least some young girls who smoke may or will be jailed for smoking. Is this the law?

The same problem arises in the perennial attempt to define what administrative law is. The question with which scholars and compilers of casebooks constantly wrestle is how far administrative law is to be treated as a study of doctrine, and how far it is to be treated as a study of the way administrative agencies go about making policy and decisions. As the description of an administrative system increases in detail and sophistication, more and more prominence is given to the daily interaction between the agency and organized parts of its regulatory field—consumer groups, industry, professional societies, and the like—and to the frequent bargaining with congressional oversight committees, figures in Congress who influence agency budgets, higher officials within government departments who set priorities, the Office of Management and Budget, and special task forces on the president's staff. A practitioner seeking to guide a client and predict how an agency will behave will want to know these things. The legal scholar seeking to know what is really going on must likewise have a good sense of these things. But suppose it is discovered that the Environmental Protection Agency issues a rule taking into account the larger budgetary hopes of the agency after discussions with White House staff and members of Congress in which industry and other group representatives have been deeply involved. Can we say it is the law that, pursuant to the governing environmental statute, there is to be lower air quality if the next budget of the Environmental Protection Agency would be improved thereby? Do we not lose anything that we can identify as law or teach as law as we penetrate deeper and deeper into system and process? The line between law and policy fades, and then the line between policy and politics fades too.

Laughter, Seriousness, and Authority

We search for law, for the legitimate. The legitimate is authoritative. It can order us, order our minds and our actions. This word "order" has at least two connotations which, in our inherited language, are joined together for a very good reason. What cannot speak to us cannot order us. If it does not order us we will not obey. It is not that we will disobey. It is just that obedience and disobedience do not enter into the situation at all. We may adapt, go along just so long as we have to, in the same way that a walker coming to a river is led by the river along its winding bank, the way the river is going and not the way the walker wants to go. The river gives no order to the walker to change his course, and the walker does not think the river has any authority over him. The river just is, at least for the time being, until a ford is reached. The difference can perhaps be brought home to lawyers by recalling the first of the choices they face, which is met with every day in the practice of law. There are two attitudes toward a command, and the choice between them is always open to lawyers and their clients. One possibility is to take the command into account in good faith when making decisions. The other is not to take the command into account except insofar as we are forced to or it is convenient and good strategy to do so.[4] The one partakes of faith. The other is to pursue our various ends to gain whatever advantage we can until a superior force comes after us and makes us stop.[5] The one is active, the other passive: we can take the initiative with respect to the purpose and sense of the command, or we can shift the burden of initiative to those seeking to affect our behavior, and use the advantages of delay and congestion that two of the givens of existence, namely, the passage of time and the limits of space, always hold out to us. We externalize the command, or we can internalize it, with large practical consequences for the everyday conduct of affairs, as everybody well knows.[6] An organization which is alive and whose members are full of morale is infused with the one attitude and goes forward rapidly toward its goals. An organization that is dead or dying and whose members are disengaged and estranged is marked by the other attitude. I suggest that when we search for the law, what we find is the law—or it is not—depending upon which attitude it evokes in us: faith, activity, and life—or their fearful opposites.

Consider our reactions to computers and other complex machines that enter our lives. The touch-tone dialing system uses music (or at least tones in sequence) to convey information to its vast and complex control center. We are often presented such a place in television advertisements. It is a room filled with whirring wheels and blinking lights, and we are shown, as in a painting by Magritte, the backs of the heads of human beings who face, as we do, the banks of machinery. At a telephone in a dimly lit college dormitory a student with a panpipe plays a little tune which gains him entry to the system and a free call to a friend three thousand miles away. The student has the key to the system. He knows its secret. What is the common attitude toward the student and what he has managed to do? What is your attitude, really? Is there not an element of delight in it, just a *little* desire to applaud? Does it immediately seem to you that he is a thief?

When we do not pay our credit card bills exactly on time, a computer begins to speak to us. Messages are printed out on subsequent bills, beginning with gentle reminders and then becoming more ominous as time goes on, with words like "please," "appreciate," and "thank you" progressively deleted, until finally sharp threats are made in a personal letter addressed to us in a separate envelope—just before we send our check. What is the common attitude toward a fulminating computer creditor? What is yours? Do you pay attention as you would to the pleas or commands of a person? Do you warm to the politeness and concern expressed in the early messages, quiver at the sternness and threats programmed into the last? Do you feel badly that the computer had to print out a special personal letter to you? Are you moved, or do you look to your convenience, affected only by the thought that at some point the computer may put a black mark on your credit rating for tardy payment?

Or consider the phenomenon of cheating on computer administered examinations. A large part of a recent graduating class at a prominent graduate professional school took advantage of a defect in the programming of a nutrition test. For each student, the computer was to select 40 out of 350 questions, flashing them on the screen one by one, and the student was to respond by punching in the answer. At the end of the test the computer flashed the student's grade and then stored the grade in its memory. The system had a feature that allowed the student to skip a question, as he might on a written test, and come back to it later. The computer was to flash the question again at a later time. Unfortunately the computer was programmed to forget the questions skipped and postponed by the student, and, moreover, not to count them in tallying the percentage answered correctly. Any clever student, who could draw the proper inferences from reports of the computer's behavior casually dropped by students who had taken the test, was in a position to go in, start skipping questions until he came to one he knew he could answer, answer that, skip all the rest, and then ask for his grade, which would be a perfect score.

When the error was discovered—there had been an astonishingly large number of high grades—the school administration did not simply reprogram the computer and give the test again. It invoked the honor code and accused the students of doing something wrong, of cheating. Many students responded that there was nothing wrong with using ingenuity to beat a computer. The school, they said, was simply punishing them for its own sloppy computer programming. And to the administrators' horror, some parents called up to defend their children, saying they had all had a good laugh about it.

Laughter. What was done was considered to be no more than beating a machine, the dean lamented. None of this is really hard to understand. You need only ask whether your own sense of honesty, when you encounter mistakes or inconsistencies in pricing, feels a bit more unmoored in a large supermarket than in a small corner store. In all these instances, there is a loss of the sense of obligation. In all of them, individuals are dealing, or sense that they are dealing, with a mindless system.

In some cases the designer of the system can be conceived as standing behind it. But it is a striking feature of machines in the modern world— particularly those to which intelligence is attributed—that they stand independent of their creators. From the time of Mary Shelley and Frankenstein the very attribution of intelligence to machines, whether or not it is correct, has resulted in this independence. Moreover, when the system is not given the attributes of intelligence and a designer can be conceived standing behind it, the designer is often not a person who cares about those the system is affecting. There is an observable difference in the attitude even of the young toward a system of training, obstacles, and tests set up for them by a coach, and their attitude toward the other systems and processes in which they are enmeshed. In the case of the long-distance telephone, the telephone company behind the system is profit-maximizing, or is thought to be.[7] In the case of the school that creates a testing machine there is some ambiguity, and this, I should suppose, is what produces the difficulty in deciding whether beating that system is wrong. But what we truly see as a system, whose existence can be set out for us exhaustively through the technique of description alone, can make no claim at all upon our behavior.

A system can demand no trust from you. You cannot trust a system. A system will not look out for you or be concerned about the consequences of its operations for you. So long as it is just a system, it cannot. Outcomes, results, effects, for a system, just are. You cannot let down your defenses, put yourself into its hands, go along with it, any more than you can let down your defenses and go along with a chemical reaction or invite an unknown gas to join you behind your scuba diving mask. It will come in if you let it and do what it must do, and it may possibly not come in if you do not let it. A system does not pity you, and you do not pity a system. You observe it, and wait. A system will not respond if you cry out to it. It cannot hear you. Nor can it cry out to you. It cannot speak. You do not seek to persuade a system to do anything: you punch it, punch into it, put something into it. Obeying would be as foolish as the opposite, getting angry and kicking the machine. No feeling is in place when facing a system, a process, a machine, save the one feeling of coolness—which is absence of warmth, of life, of being inside. No emotion is appropriate in your relation with it—nothing of that from which man's motion comes.

And if a system consists of words—instead of musical tones, wires, prices, or radar signals—the situation is not different. Words themselves cannot speak.

4
METHOD
The Creation of Authority

LAWYERS PRACTICING law's method are not scientists, except insofar as they share with scientists a desire to know what is really going on and, like scientists, are not sure of what they have to demonstrate until they have demonstrated it. The analogy between law and science breaks down, and if we are to have an analogy at all we must turn elsewhere for it.[1]

Now, one may well ask, Why this search for an analogy? Why not say simply what the thing is rather than what it is like and how it compares with other things? We could try to say directly what legal analysis is. But any direct approach would slip rapidly into a demonstration. Legal analysis is *this*, we would say, and run through a course of professional training. Even then we would be only halfway to understanding, because legal analysis would not have been placed in our minds. It would in fact be left at the mercy of the analogies that do lurk there, for nothing in our minds is unplaced, rightly or wrongly.

IN THE 1930s Max Radin observed that mathematics was the ideal toward which those who asserted that law was a hard science were pushing. They desired to deal with legal relations in symbolic form and to set up a system which, in Radin's words, was "untainted with emotions and reaches its result as a process of cold and inexorable calculation or deduction." But this desire was at base only a desire. Mathematics had a grip on their minds. It was an urge to imitate, to emulate, to become like, that produced the tradition of legal thinking represented by Wesley Hohfeld's legal equations.

Such governing desires, at the root of so much, are often axiomatic, neither justified nor even particularly self-conscious. They are not the object of thought but serve rather as starting points for active work and lifelong commitments. Compare our own experience of the computer, the tool that has astounded, the genie that has produced such a great and sudden flow of freedom and power. It has a grip on our minds now. Lying behind contemporary efforts to computerize legal analysis is the proposition that it is highly desirable that law and legal decision making be computer-like. This desire is founded as much in the conceptual as in the normative. There is from the beginning of the effort the thought that law *is* "like a computer."

Analogy and metaphor are a powerful force in our thought about what we do, and perhaps are necessary to it. The nineteenth-century historian and philosopher Taine, for example, used analogy in seeking to say what the writing of history was. It was geometry, physiology, zoology, he said. Reaching out to something other than the thing itself to explain what the thing is does not mean that the first thing is subservient. Other things look outside themselves too to decide what they are. Taine in our own day would find some philosophers of science reversing the flow of metaphor and saying that science is like history. And placing is more than part of our thinking about method; it is, in law, part of our method—how we go about understanding what we see and hear. Indeed, *thinking about* law, and *doing* law,[2] are not far apart.

THE COUSIN DISCIPLINES OF LAW

If we build on what lawyers actually do and say while they practice their profession—in contrast to what they say when they characterize their profession—the natural turn is to those activities that also have texts as their subject matter and the close reading of texts as their method. We should not say that law is produced only by the analysis of texts or that legal analysis consists only of the examination of texts. But law begins with the analysis of texts. The study and discussion of texts is the method of choice in legal analysis. And in this, law is cousin to cultural history, or literary criticism, or certain kinds of philosophy.

THE STUDY AND discussion of texts occupies the minds and talk of historians, critics, and philosophers. Over and over again their method is to take a passage of Aristotle or Wittgenstein, Marx, Marvell or Faulkner, and ask, What does this mean? How does it fit, within this writer's work and the work of others? Does it hang together, with internal

coherence and consistency? Do inconsistencies have a purpose and a justification that we can see? What was *his* method in producing his text? This
is precisely what lawyers (and judges) do with the opinions of judges or the
writings of prominent commentators.

Moreover, particular texts become authoritative in the study of literature or philosophy, as in the study of law. Throughout the land students
study and scholars discuss the same series of philosophers, the same series
of poets. A listing of doctoral dissertations in English or philosophy and
the Index of Legal Periodicals contain the most striking similarities: "The
Law of Federal Jurisdiction after *Erie* v. *Tompkins,*" on the one hand, and,
on the other, "Modern Poetry after the *Cantos* of Ezra Pound"; "Pastoral
Themes in *Paradise Lost,*" on the one hand, and "Corporate Free Speech
in *First National Bank* v. *Bellotti,*" on the other; "The Nietzschean View of
Rationality," on the one hand, "The Conception of Due Process in the
Opinions of Mr. Justice Douglas," on the other.

Now many a student and many a Philistine has thought to himself, "So
what?" So what that Kant meant this but Hegel meant that, so what that
Pope subtly changed the pastoral tradition or that Henry James explored
the psychology of despair in just that way? Above all, so what that an
obscure seventeenth-century poet combined puritanism and paganism?
Why talk about these works and these men? Why not leave it to them to
speak to us themselves if they can, and let us talk about real things, about
the things they are talking about—the lure of the pastoral, the psychology
of despair, or the meaning of rationality? I have been the yawning student
and the Philistine from time to time, and have thought that what this or
that philosophical writer, early, middle, or late, thought and meant was
largely a distraction from proper current work on the things themselves,
that is, on what they were working on. I have thought the deferential talk,
so very like the deferential talk about the opinions of judges, to be a form
of gossip among the intelligentsia, or like the hero worship found in teen
movie magazines or the periodicals that cater to the adult fixation on
celebrities.

I have been wrong even to allow such a thought to lie around in my
head. For this discussion of what particular individuals actually thought or
meant is just one *form* of discussion among many, one using particular
texts as the ground and substance of discussion. Everyone needs material
to work with, a subject matter; and except for those who take the grandest
themes, the subject matter is, in a way, contingent. The novelist talks
about the most mundane things—the births and deaths of ordinary, particular people, their courtships and marriages, departures and returns, the
very material of television soap operas. One can imagine a novelist wishing he had something better to work with as he contemplates starting a

novel. One can imagine Mozart wishing he had better librettos, but those he had were his texts. So, too, are the opinions of judges lawyers' texts, or the texts with which legal analysts begin.

B UT DOES THE lawyer have to admit this similarity with the critic, the novelist, the philosopher? He may be tempted to leap up and say, "Ah, my situation is different, because I deal with texts produced by judges, and what judges say is ipso facto important. The texts they produce come stamped with authority, like the pronouncements of bishops. The texts of Hegel and Kant, Marx, Milton, Pound, or Eliot are discussed either by convention, rather as classical texts became the sole subject of discussion in nineteenth-century formal education, or the texts of the Chinese ancients became the subject matter of the education and talk of Chinese mandarins; or those texts *earn* their authority and place in the accepted canon of subject matter discussion."[3]

But the law is in fact not so different. There are many judges. Each of them does not speak the law. It is not just that they say different things and so cannot each speak the law. There is no assumption whatever in legal method that, when each of them speaks, what each says is simply "the law." They do have the power to dispose of the case for the litigants because of a convention to that effect, but the litigants need not think that the judge is right and neither need anyone else. Why does the judge write an opinion if not to justify his decision and his statements? And why would anyone read the opinion if it made no difference whether one was persuaded by it or not? The authority of a legal text is in this sense not automatic. Its authority must be earned too.

Since there are so many voices, it may be wondered whether the use of statistical techniques might not be indicated, to relieve lawyers of the task of close reading and authors of the task of securing and maintaining attention. Unfortunately, no: law is not a gas, and judges are not molecules even though, like molecules in a gas, they vibrate in different directions at the same time. Nor, as we have already noted, is there any present understanding that one can determine the law by discovering what a majority of judges say it is; lawyers of an earlier day flirted with such a notion, but they never accepted it. There is majority rule with respect to judges on a multi-member court: the decision of the court is the decision of a majority of the court. But even there a distinction is drawn between the disposition of the case for the litigants and the disposition of legal questions. A five-to-four decision has less "precedential weight"—the phrase is common: the metaphor of weight is widely used by lawyers—than a unanimous decision, though both are equally conclusive on the litigants. A decision without opinion, like a decision of a unanimous committee that cannot come to any agreement on reasons for its unanimity, will have little weight. A decision accompanied by opinions that cannot be understood, or that are internally inconsistent, will have little weight. Certainly when lawyers deal with texts written not by a committee or collegial body but by individuals, it is quite evident that law is not determined by counting and that something else is involved. Polling is no more the way to law than to scientific truth: scientists would be horrified at the thought that a valid scientific statement, or legitimate science, was what a majority of scientists said. For that matter, even in political democracy majority rule is in part merely a deadlock-breaking device, a mechanism to allow a unit to produce some outcome, whatever it may be, and not different in this respect from looking for a flight of birds overhead or personal combat between knightly champions.[4]

THE PROBLEM OF TIME AND THE PRACTICE OF SAVING

Thus legal texts do not come prestamped with authority and are not radically and qualitatively different from the texts the philosopher, the literary critic, or the cultural historian examines. Legal texts too must earn their way into the canon, unless they are there by chance or convention. How is this brought about? What is involved? What does the analyst do, what is the analyst looking for, when he searches for the authoritative, the legitimate, the law?

FIRST OF ALL, the legal analyst seeks a connection to the past. If the words "transcendence," "transcend," and "transcendental" are not too off-putting because of their use as technical and even jargon terms, we may say the analyst is seeking to transcend time, for that *is* what he is seeking to do. The analyst is in the present, and all the texts he examines are in the past. For him, as for the literary critic, the historian, and the philosopher, the texts generally extend far back from the contemporary past.[5] Very little of the material a lawyer must work with in any field of law does not go back at least a generation, if only because contemporary courts do not have time to cover a field. The reader, the searcher, is present and young; the speaker, the authority, is past and old; and this immediately requires the reconstruction of meaning. Did the words he used mean what the words mean today?[6] Are there assumptions he was making that we would not make today, assumptions critical to an understanding of what he meant and did not mean? Were there distinctions valid to him then, such as those based on race or social class, which are not valid or even perhaps, as in the case of social class, comprehensible to us today? To what extent was the speaker in some sense younger than we are today, less sophisticated, less wise? Are we more aware of the operations and unpredictability of complex systems than he, or, if not more aware of mystery, at least more nakedly aware because we lack any trust in Providence?

All this is seeking a connection between the present and the text by shearing away the time-bound. No doubt in the study of ancient literature, ancient ways of thinking, or ancient history, there is also the fascination of the merely curious and novel. They expand our present world, as if we were adding rooms to the present house we live in, with doors that can be entered only through imagination. But what seems so new and different in them could not be perceived or understood at all if it were not connected to the present.[7]

T HEN THE ANALYST sets out to understand the text.
To do this he must place it—in the period and among all the things said and texts produced by the speaker or speakers of the period. When we go about understanding a contemporary, we do the same thing. In either case, if the text in question is inconsistent with what the speaker has said before or after, or internally inconsistent in itself, we do not know whether he really means it (or do not know what he means) until we have done further work. If he is beside us we can speak to him and do the work with his help. If he is not beside us, as he generally is not—law courts, poets, philosophers, letter writers, and legislatures are rarely directly accessible—we must do the work by ourselves. We go about saving what he says.

Thus a man may remark, "The company of women is a bore." How curious! The day before, he was seen ebullient in a discussion group consisting only of women and himself. The day after, he and his daughters announce they are looking forward to a month-long trip across the country. What could this man have meant? Can what he said be saved?

Sometimes after a period of work analysts throw up their hands and criticize. They say, "I have done all I can, and still I do not know what you mean. You are being aberrational. You were sick, drunk, careless, mad. You said something, but didn't mean it, or mean anything else for that matter." And the analyst does this on quite personal grounds. *I* don't understand, he says. But though the grounds are personal and the confession is always of a personal failure to understand, the criticism is expressed in such a way as to appeal to other analysts and to persuade them that the speaker is not just poorly understood by the one who is criticizing him but is not understandable.

Generally, however, the analyst assumes the sanity and sobriety of the speaker and does not jump to the conclusion that the speaker is mistaken or out of tune with himself. To save what he says, it is categorized. This in it is deemed important, that is not. This reference to a green door refers to a door, not to greenness, nor to a green door only. The greenness doesn't matter. This last will and testament of this merchant is a form of commercial finance. As such it fits. One can understand what the merchant was saying. As a means of providing for a family, it makes no sense. This stanza of poetry, about figures in Greek mythology, is a statement about the poet's inner life. As such, it fits his work and the emerging poetry of the time. As a fragment of an epic, it makes little sense. The categorizing goes on and on. The analyst decides what is important in the situation presented to him and what is not important, and then begins to fit together what is important and to find consistency, to understand, perhaps at another level or in a larger context. He looks for hints, for image and nuance. But the hints he looks for are those that would make the statement fit the presumed category. As he saves, he constructs, and always with categories and distinctions that have meaning for his own contemporaries, those whom, after all, *he* is talking to. He constructs an edifice, an understandable whole.

And as the text he is examining becomes understandable, it shrinks to become a part of something larger, a life, a person, a period, a culture, a class, Poetry, a philosophy.

The analyst may engage in saving even where he is forced to reinsert the time-bound because, in order to make anything like the point the speaker is making, those categories the speaker is using and those distinctions upon which the speaker is relying insist upon being used, as it were, even though they have no significance for the analyst and his contemporaries. If what the speaker is saying then seems arbitrary, the analyst may entertain the possibility that it was not understandable even to the speaker and his time: if the speaker had been fully self-aware, he himself would have concluded that his thought was structured and that he was proceeding from axioms that could be understood only in light of their origins. That, the analyst knows, would not of itself act to separate speaker and analyst utterly. The analyst also proceeds from axioms that are understandable only historically and knows that general truth about himself. Thus the saving and the understanding: the analyst may step back from the speaker and the text for a moment and, instead of shearing off the time-bound, treat it as intrinsic *and perhaps part of the analyst's own struc-ture.* The analyst becomes aware of things slowly growing and things in disguise, of transforming redefinitions and fictionalizations, so that what he was just about to exclude as time-bound and foreign or as aberrational and criticizable, is instead illuminating, evidence of common structure and change in structure, and now, pulled thus into the light, perhaps itself productive of further change in structure.

W HAT literary critics, historians, philosophers do not do as they prac-tice their craft is also familiar to the lawyer.

The lawyer does not simply look for venality, duplicity, temper, class bias, ambition, or illness when he approaches the materials he is trying to understand. He does not look for these in the first instance. He may have to deal with such matters ultimately, but to confine himself to them or to begin with them would be to ignore the text—just as if you focused your attention on the movement of the eyes and the fingers of one speaking to you and paid no attention to what he was saying. The initial focus is on the text, on what the speaker means, what he wants to say.

Though there may be messages hidden in the text such as "I want love," or "I hate you," or "I am afraid," the legal analyst would no more concentrate on them (in the manner of a therapist who was looking for them particularly because he had undertaken to *help* the speaker) than would the ordinary literary critic or biographical or cultural historian. He may have to circle around to such messages ultimately. Tone is undeniably important, in a piece of music, a legal opinion, a poem, or a life—William James cried out in his last letter to his dying father, "Life is but a day, and expresses mainly but a single note"—but much, much more is being said that tone in itself, or any hidden message found, does not explain or help us understand.

And of course the legal analyst does not seek simply to reproduce what he finds in his material, to *describe* it, any more than the critic working on the novel or the novelist working on his own material. Legal texts are material, not the law. The novelist does not *reproduce* life: he shows us only the important scenes and those points in the unimportant, the rou-tine and the dull parts of life, at which turns were or might have been made.

The legal analyst, like these others, builds edifices. Like these others who build but not in brick and stone, he caps them with names. What *he* constructs is the law of torts, or the law of California, or international law, or Western law, or the law of This Court.[8]

The Giving of Names

There is a manner of speaking passed down from teacher to law student, from judge to teacher, from judge to judge, and from practitioner to judge, just as there is a manner of speaking among students of divinity, writers of philosophical papers, and accountants. We would do well to listen to it, for however conventional or metaphorical a manner of speaking may be, it is indicative.

The forms of speech adopted in writing and analyzing Supreme Court opinions, for example, are far more important than is ordinarily allowed. They are absorbed half consciously during the formation of lawyers' habits, but deeply. They do not hang like loose casual clothes over the live and sinewy body of thought. They form the thought; they are part of the thought itself, and should be noticed and heard. Listen to this passage by a careful and sophisticated commentator who is both practicing lawyer and academic, examining, or searching for, the constitutional law of alienage (the treatment by government of noncitizens):

> [I]t took almost twenty-five years before the Court was prepared to take the additional step of equating alienage cases and race cases, applying to both an extremely strict standard of review.
>
> In almost every conceivable way 1971 was an unlikely time for the Court to take that additional step. The Court had two new members who had not participated in the equal protection revolution of the 1960s, and it was showing signs of diminished interest in the marvels of suspect classification analysis. There seemed to be no significant political pressure to give aliens increased Constitutional protection. And the Court was already having difficulty fixing on an appropriate standard of review in cases involving discrimination on the basis of gender and legitimacy. Yet, without any dissent, the Court upheld the aliens' constitutional claims in *Graham* and brought aliens under the protection of the strict scrutiny doctrine. In subsequent cases the Court has not wavered in its commitment to the view that alienage classifications are inherently suspect. . . .

The legal analyst seems to be describing in the way the historian describes, and, in a way, he is: he is describing what he sees. But what he sees is "the Court" taking this step and that step, although the steps are taken a generation apart and the individuals on the Court are not the same. He has worked with the materials to arrive at a picture of temporal development in an entity, the Court or the Law of Alienage.

At the beginning, and from the beginning, he has used description as part of his method. He has tried to look at everything (seeing the whole is another matter), and to assemble the material upon which he is to work, with as little preconception as possible, suspending his critical and constructive faculties. In the same way a historian or a literary critic reads widely, reads everything, as he assembles his material. But almost from the beginning the legal analyst is engaged in selecting, arranging, and classifying. He does so on the basis of present, current categories and expectations. He must, for these are the only ones alive in his mind.

His mind is not closed and fixed. The conceptions and categories, the notions of what is important and what is not, which can be said to be *in* his mind, are themselves not closed. They are open, little mysteries each. Any half-aware lawyer or judge knows that although he regularly uses terms such as "property," "contract," "equality," or "business judgment," he would be hard put to it to say what those terms mean to him without looking outside himself. They are terms he has inherited and learned from others around him past and present. They are terms used in communication with others. If he presses himself, asking "What do *I* mean by this?" "Why do *I* make this distinction?" "What is this distinction *I* am making?" one of his responses will be to ask where the distinction or the conception or the sense of importance came from that is guiding his thought, just as, on the highest plane of generality, a person asking "Who am I?" goes on to ask "Where did I come from?" Nonetheless, in the end it is he who arranges and categorizes.

THUS HE TALKS to his material, open to what is said to him, but in the end deciding what is said to him as he searches for consistency. Faced with a set of texts, horizontally arranged according to subject matter, he asks what order can be drawn from them. The author of this text emphasized *this* and *that,* or said he was relying upon *this* and *that,* in coming to his conclusion. But was *this* as important as *that*? Was *this* important at all? What the text says here is contradicted by what the same text says there. What this text says here is contradicted by what that other text says there. Are the two parts of the same text or the two different texts talking about the same thing? Do the words used mean the same thing? Is *this* what this precedent is about, or is it about something else, so that I can distinguish it?

The same occurs when texts are arranged sequentially. The legal analyst becomes much like an intellectual historian, looking for the transformation and development of ideas, the idea of equality or the idea of disclosure, the idea of a corporate director's duty or of a reliance interest in contract law, changing so slowly and subtly that they seem beyond the control of any individual or group of individuals, however aware they may be, perhaps even not changing at all, only dipping, disguising themselves and appearing in different forms.

The same goes on in the analysis of a single case. The text has different paragraphs, different sallies as to this and that, that must be put together to be understood. The case may include concurring opinions and dissents to which the main opinion often directs itself. What a case means is often a matter of argument for the very men and women who wrote on behalf of the court. In the late 1970s the public was presented with speeches by four Supreme Court justices disagreeing about the meaning of the opinions in a case, in which they had just participated, on the extent of press access to criminal trials. The form of discussion—public speeches—was extraordinary, but the phenomena of disagreement and discussion were not, as any look inside the case reports will show.

Lawyers' signals, as they are called, introducing citations to other legal texts, to precedent, commentary, treatise, administrative regulation, statute, and so forth, convey the special flavor of this continuous search for unity. Lawyers say, "*See.*" They point. They say, "*Look at that*"—as if they were pointing to a building or a painting. Or they say "*Cf.,*" which means compare. Sometimes they say, "*But see,*" or "*Contra,*" pointing to something that might detract from the authority of their statement of law by detracting from its comprehensiveness. On the other hand, the text that follows the *contra* or the *but see* might also be dismissed, excluded, forgotten, not listened to, not heard. And who knows which it should be, in the law? In science of course we know that nothing can be dismissed unless it is presumed away. A scientific theory is tentative precisely in proportion to the number of *but sees* and *contras* that are to be found in the listing of the support for it. But not so with law. What is *contra* may be in the end ignored as a mistake or not meant, as wrong *because* it is inconsistent. But we never know in advance. The legal analyst must *decide* whether an opinion (or a statement within an opinion) is an aberration, whether it is to be excluded as a mistake, just as the literary critic must decide whether a poet, a poem, or a line within a poem is an aberration and without significance.

THE LEGAL ANALYST must make such a decision even with respect to the newest opinion of the highest court on a matter. The analyst tries to fit its propositions with other propositions that the utterer seems to have no intention of abandoning or denying, and to fit its terminology with the use of the same terminology in other contexts. If they cannot be fitted together, the analyst wonders whether the utterer really means what he seems to be saying, whether indeed the utterer really means anything at all by his utterance; this is the same as to wonder whether the text has anything to say, which is, in turn, to wonder whether it has weight or authority. (The analyst wonders before he decides, for terminology can change its meaning.) In *Vermont Yankee Nuclear Power Corp.* v. *Natural Resources Defense Council, Inc.*, for example, the Supreme Court addressed the procedural requirements for administrative decision making, gradually developed over many years by federal courts of appeal to help resolve the dilemmas courts faced in usurping the administrative function when they made substantive judgments about the arbitrariness of administrative decisions. The Court unanimously forbade the requirement of such procedures as unauthorized by Congress. Yet in footnotes and summary paragraphs seeming almost to be written by another hand, the opinion simultaneously directed lower courts to continue unabated their limited substantive review of administrative decisions. Procedural review and a limited substantive evaluation were conceptually interlocked before the decision. They remained interlocked no less afterward because the opinion showed no way to sever them. It could not be assumed that the opinion really meant one thing rather than the other. The text seemed internally inconsistent, and commentators were quick to point out this and other incompatibilities with the ordering notions of adminstrative law. Lower courts proceeded as best they could, changing somewhat the language of their justifications but otherwise not greatly affected by the decision. In reaching their judgment and making their response both commentators and lower courts used the techniques of literary and historical analysis to decide what the law was. They did, indeed, what they might have done if they were reading a letter from a friend, or listening and trying to understand a person speaking to them.

Vermont Yankee is an example from ordinary law. It was not constitutional in the grand sense, stirring large populations and taking its place in standard histories. Neither was it an overturning of precedent in any explicit way (the decisions being overturned, though longstanding, were of courts inferior in the hierarchy). But lawyers read the newest decisions on matters of constitutional or political moment in much the same way. No lawyer assumes that a single decision overturns or rejects widespread understandings, until that decision can be placed. There is a sense in which it is impossible to reject previous understandings, for a decision that did absolutely and categorically reject previous understandings would be found, inevitably, to be inconsistent. One of the conventions of legal writing, the attempt to stick as close as possible to a particular context though all the while using and creating general ideas and rules in discussing it, reflects this realistic stance. The convention eases the work that must go on so continuously, just as do conventions of polite discourse, and keeps courts from sounding too much like the candid friend who says one thing one day and another thing the next and thus directly confronts his companion with his development, ambivalence, and difficulty.

DOING AND SAYING

Throughout the practice of legal method there remains the difference we considered in Chapter 3 between a system or process we can describe, on the one hand, and what we grant to be the law, on the other. One still hears quite often the misconception that what legal analysis consists of is an attempt to predict what judges will do in the future, not what they will say but what they will do. This view is associated with Holmes's powerful and unhappy metaphor of the bad man: law is what the bad man, who never asks himself what he should do but wants to know only what bad thing will happen to him if he does this or that, would think it is.

The metaphor of the bad man appeals to the juvenile and the fearful side of ourselves, and Holmes's contribution is really better characterized as a bad boy's view of law. In retrospect it was perhaps to be expected. Holmes was a man of his era, many think its paragon, and the era was one in which the educated were for the first time viewing nature as heartless and hostile, and, simultaneously though paradoxically, wanting to view man as part of nature. They made men's competition into a law of nature rather than of man. And in competition, of course, one is always looking over one's shoulder. But as a description of what law and legal analysis are, it never fit the facts of legal practice and was incoherent to boot. The scientist qua scientist leaves himself out of his picture of man. Scientific jurisprudence left the judge out of its picture of law.

What was the judge to do in going about finding the law? Was he to be a bad boy too, or at least put himself imaginatively into the shoes of a bad boy, and look over his shoulder? If not, if the judge were to predict what he himself would do, but on the assumption that he himself was not to be a bad boy, then what he would do would be to seek to discover what the law was. This is exactly what ancient and modern practice assumes those not judges will do also. There is, to be sure, some uncertainty within the adversarial setting of litigation in court, but virtually none when the actors are lawyers writing letters of opinion, corporate officials mandated by the definition of their roles to act in good faith, or individuals deciding what they should do in the various capacities of their daily life.

Of course any analyst pays attention to what a speaker *did* after speaking, but only as an aid in determining what the speaker meant. What a judge did is evidence only, not the object of investigation. He may not have done what he wanted to do, or meant to do, or would have done if he had thought more about it and searched his mind more fully.

∽⁓∿⁓

Legal analysis consists of working with texts, as others work with texts. There is much else in addition in the practice of law and much else in the deciding of a wrenching case. But this is what the legally trained do when asked to find the law and say what the law is, whether they are judges, or among those who are, in fact, the source of statements of law in that greater part of human affairs that does not and never can reach a court.[9]

Are they foolish to engage in this kind of activity? Is it a front, a cover? Is it beside the point, superfluous or superstructural? The question is always with us and may be asked now, though we will be pursuing it to the end of our discussion. The shape of the answer that will emerge should be evident. It is an answer of the not-if kind. Not foolish, not superfluous, if law is to have authority. Not if law is to hold us, evoke our willing acceptance rather than our resistance. Not if law is to be a source to be looked to in discovering what we ought to do. Perhaps we do not or ought not to want that; but if we do not, then we cannot complain about disintegration, disappearance of authority, of respect, and of self-respect, or loss of meaning in the modern state.

5
AUTHENTICITY
Connecting the Speaker and the Spoken

T HESE TECHNIQUES AND METHODS, all this activity of lawyers and all this manner of speaking by lawyers, assume that the materials with which legal analysts work are authentic. Authenticity is a necessity, a methodological requirement, a condition of using the method or technique at all. The first step in legal method is to see whether the assumption of authenticity can be made, and alertness to whether an assumption of authenticity made at the beginning was a correct one continues as the work proceeds.

Historians, philosophers, critics of literature and art are not very different in what they demand of their material. The literary critic wants to know, at the beginning of his work, whether an author is pulling his leg or not, whether, for instance, words before him in verse form are the words of one trying to write poetry or only pretending to do so. If the critic concludes the latter he may reclassify the text, as parody perhaps or something else parasitic, even mere hackwork. Whatever his classification, the distinction he makes is between literature worth his while and other texts, and in making that distinction he is not so much exercising his critical faculties (although they help in telling whether a piece of literature is serious or not) as he is determining whether the presuppositions for the exercise of his critical faculties are present.[1]

In the same way, one of the first of the things a practicing historian does is to determine whether a treaty which comes to hand, or a letter, a contemporary chronicle, a bill of lading for a ship, or a set of financial accounts, is what it appears to be or is misleading or a forgery. If a forgery, it still may tell the historian something. It may, like the Donation of Constantine to the Pope, which centuries later was discovered to have been a forgery, have had important contemporary impact on those who thought it was authentic, and this the historian will take into account. But the document will not be a text he can use to draw direct conclusions about economic, political, or social history.

So, too, the art critic or historian always wants to look at the original, and the philosopher wants to know whether the text he reads is one result-ing from an attempt by his predecessor to write philosophy or whether, again, it is only the appearance of an attempt to write philosophy. Each wants to work with realities, not appearances.

AUTHENTICITY AND AUTHENTICATION

A statement, document, or text is authentic when it can be taken se-riously. If a statement is to be taken seriously the author of it must mean what he says. He must be speaking in what we call good faith and not thinking only of the reaction to what he says. He must not deliberately mean two incompatible things, be deliberately ambiguous with the inten-tion of choosing later, after the reaction, the meaning best for his interests and treating that as if he had meant it all along.

And to be taken seriously one must not be imitating, unless of course one is making a joke. One can ask that a joke be taken seriously. Often indeed the substance of that open imitation we call a joke is a pointing to another imitation that is deceptive in trying to appear authentic. Joking derision—or mockery—is in fact evoked by a deceptive imitation, and the deceptive imitation is itself referred to by the same word. It is a *mockery*, the joke about it mocks it. Laughter, passing contempt are the responses if there is response at all.

Why must texts be authentic, written in good faith, not deceptive, not imitative? To avoid the mocking smile, of course; but there is more.

Philosophers who examine philosophers' texts are interested in philoso-phy, what philosophy is to be for them, their own philosophy. Novelists seek to bring to life the lives they write about, and literary critics seek as critics to bring the novelist's work to life, to bring it to life *now*, to help the reader who is reading it now. Legal analysts are also seeking a *present* law, a law for themselves: if one is seeking what one ought to do, given all the circumstances and complexity of the world, if one is looking for what is truly authoritative, what can be internalized and pursued with good faith, obeyed rather than resisted, one is seeking in part to discover what one oneself believes in this world where one lives with others, for others, and by others. In the world one uses an inherited language, speaking and spoken to in an understandable way. The texts of others one analyzes are a clue to one's own mind, both the structure and the substance of it: a clue to what one believes and wants, to what is inside one rather than outside.

And when, in looking at a text, one concludes that the speaker did not believe what he said, then one might wonder whether one believes it oneself. Certainly if one has no reason to believe the speaker believed what he said, one is not, from reading that text, any closer to knowing what one does believe.

We may also understand the demand for authenticity in a more purely methodological way.

The legal analyst, whether lawyer or judge, in erecting the edifice that, after he is finished, he presents as the law of this or that, or as the opinion of a court—who is structuring precedents, or sentences, and deciding which have more weight than others and which are aberrations and mistakes—will put aside first those texts and expressions in which the speaker was not attempting at all to say what the law was but was rather saying what he wanted his listeners to think the law was. The analyst will put them aside for the same reason people generally put aside such statements in ordinary discourse. If a speaker who says a thing was not even trying to speak as an integrated person, then what he was saying at that time is useless in building up an image of him as integrated and thus understandable. As a building block such a statement simply will not do. It will turn out to mean something entirely different from what it appears to mean if it means anything at all; it will dissolve away, and leave whatever was erected on it without support (as in the familiar dream sequences echoed in the best animated cartoons, in which the thing on which one rides, horse, dog, or airplane, dissolves and becomes something else or nothing at all, leaving one without support, in danger, falling). The listener must move away from what the speaker was saying at such a time, to other statements that he makes at other times which do reveal what he really thinks, and then come back to the statement in question to understand *why* he said it.

People who deal with the chronically manipulative and mendacious, we may note, must put aside virtually all their statements, or put them all aside until one or another is shown to be *not* manipulative or *not* a lie. Conceiving of such individuals as integrated persons is difficult and may eventually be too difficult. Our tendency is to type their personalities scientifically and give them clinical names, and they are then often institutionalized, which is to say, expelled. They are not heard to speak. They have no authority over us once so typed and read out of the world of persons to whom we pay attention.

The chronically manipulative and mendacious may thus be treated as things, to be manipulated themselves. For disclosure, absence of deception, almost defines what it means to be *inside* rather than *outside* an entity. It is a doctrine as old as the *Iliad* and as contemporary as the securities laws that individuals *within* an organization—a partnership, a corporation, a public agency, a family—are to be loyal and candid, make full disclosure, not mislead others within the organization.[2] (Those outside do not have the same claim not to be manipulated or deceived.) For only with authenticity of statement is cohesion possible: in constructing any organized entity, whether it be a corporation, the law, Romantic Poetry, or the character of Sir Thomas More, authenticity must not only be demanded. It is required, necessary.[3]

"AUTHENTICATION" is the pursuit of authenticity in a discipline that demands it.

A person making statements that are not authentic could be so clever that he would never be found out. Conceivably a speaker's manipulation might produce an appearance of honesty so convincing that the hollowness of what he says is never penetrated, and the fact he really does not think or believe what he is saying, and thinks and believes either nothing or something different, would be forever unknown. But this is unlikely. All the techniques of analysis we have touched upon are designed to ferret out emptiness and lack of connection between the speaker and the spoken. The success of cross-examination as a technique in one kind of legal process, the court trial, suggests that fabrications and lies are in fact quite difficult to maintain. The complexity and interconnections of the actual world do seem to outstrip the cleverest imagination.

And the complexities of the work of the artist who is imitated and copied by others are hardly less. Indeed, as the discussion of proposals to disseminate works of art through perfect copies, rather than through display in museums, has brought out, the supposition that there can be an absolutely perfect imitation, accepted as such, is highly suspect.

The very slightest difference between the imitation and the original—in art or in law—might make all the difference, and if there are differences someone must make a decision about what differences are immaterial. If there are said to be no differences at all, the viewer must take the imitator's word for the perfection of the imitation, and as the viewer goes about reacting to the piece he may be in a state of continuous anxiety about whether the imitator is correct or truthful.[4] If this is the situation where imitation is open, it is compounded when the imitation is undisclosed. If the imitator does not reveal that what he puts forth is an imitation and not his own, then he is a deceiver at least in some things, and his assurance (on being found out) that the imitation is perfect becomes the more difficult to take.

How many undisclosed imitations, forgeries and copies, remain undetected in art of course we do not know. There have been famous ones that fooled museum curators for years. Paintings from the Master's school long have been thought to be by the Master. But they *have* eventually yielded. Authentication in art no less than in law has been encouraged by its successes to develop ever more sophisticated techniques, not defeated by revelations that it has, for a time, failed. There is the strongest drive behind it.

But, of course, though a statement of law is like a statement of a painter or sculptor and approached with methods that are much the same—indeed lawyers engaged in placing a text are heard to ask "What are the *contours* of this decision?" (their phraseology rooted in aesthetics as much as in images of territorial sovereignty)—a statement of law is not the same as a work of art. Law is law, and not some other discipline. Why is the drive to authenticate so particularly strong in law?

There are reasons that can be understood in terms that do not need to be borrowed. Invert the truth of the matter, that authority must be earned, and suppose that a decision or precedent did come prestamped with authority. One is to follow the decision (as the saying goes), one is to be led by it, obey it.

How does one imagine oneself going about *following* a decision? What are called "the rules laid down by a decision" are verbal formulations of the reasons relied upon by a decision maker in making the decision.[5] Those reasons are values, importances; any decision maker acting in a particular role necessarily gives relative weights to them in making a particular decision. One *follows* the decision by focusing upon the values appropriate for that role and discovering the weights used by the decision maker.

But how can one discover the values or the weights attributed to them if the language in which the decision is explained is deceptive or strategic and not truly meant? The language and its subject matter have been separated, the spoken and the speaker have been separated.

So too are the spoken and the speaker separated where the speaker is different from the decision maker and does not know the decision maker's mind, or the spoken is the mere outcome of a process that has no mind and there is, in a very real sense, no speaker. Thus if, playing with the notion that words can come prestamped with authority, we decided to erect a computer as god, rather as the Hebrews erected their golden calf, and we agreed absolutely that what the computer said would be our law and that we would follow it, we would find that it could not act as law because we could not understand it. All the computer could tell us is that the outcome of the system, an outcome represented by words typed out on pieces of paper, was what it turned out to be. Instead of words typed out, the outcome could have been a puff or smoke, or a light flashing.

This was perhaps the primary difference between the Hebrew god and the golden calf. Jehovah spoke, the god of the golden calf only acted. It produced famine or fortune but always only in reaction to what the human beings facing it did; and when human beings said a thing to it, what they said was of a formal nature, an action. Of course the words of such a god, like a flash of light or smoke, communicate to the person who senses them, but they communicate in the same way that the person must communicate with the system, as an input. The system would work very well for calculation, that is, for manipulation; but it does not do if the question is, "What am I to do?" because it cannot answer the question in an understandable way. For readers with an ear tuned to quotation from scripture, the word is not with it, it is not the word.

Could people obey willingly and act under guidance of the authoritative and the legitimate if they believed that the authority they heard did not care about them, their hopes and fears, their wants and hurts? Search yourself. You would not really follow the lead of another who was not responsible. But there is no way you could suppose another responsible if his statements, by which alone you knew him, are manipulative, treating you as a thing, or if those statements are only actions, outcomes of a system or process that has no center, no heart. The phenomenon of authority, existing in the world as it does, carries with it its imperatives. If people believed that what was guiding them was cold, distant, and not only uncaring but incapable of caring, irresponsible with regard to the consequences it brings about or not capable of responsibility for consequences, people could not allow themselves to be guided by it, accept its guidance, really follow it. This is a simple point, one of those each of us draws with some certainty from personal experience. Only to the extent that another is responsible, only to that degree can we risk putting ourselves into his hands, siding with him, entering into his purposes, giving ourselves up. Only if he is responsible will he take care, look out for us and not abandon us, as time flies on and consequences unfold which neither he nor we can predict.

D ECEPTIVE SPEECH, speech which is not the speaker's own, speech which has no speaker, cannot be taken seriously. It is no access to mind. No speaking person can be drawn from it. The mind behind it, if there is one, remains veiled. The speech is cold, dead, inanimate, as much a thing as it implies the listener is to whom it is addressed. Thus the drive, in law, in art, in literature, in history and philosophy, to strip it away and cast it aside, or to turn it over to other disciplines and other workers for whose methods and purposes it is a proper material. Deception, unreality, deadness, coldness, lack of concern by speaker and listener alike: all these are connected. Recall Carroll's Mock Turtle. The Mock Turtle evoked no pity. He seemed very sad. But even his sadness was not real, and not believed. "What is his sorrow?" Alice asked. The Gryphon replied, "It's all his fancy that: he hasn't got no sorrow, you know. Come on!" Nor could Alice and the Gryphon look to the Mock Turtle's past to understand him. There was a long silence when they sat down to listen to his history. Then he began speaking. "'Once,' said the Mock Turtle at last, with a deep sigh, 'I was a real Turtle.'" The only history he could tell was the history of a real Turtle.

DETACHMENT

Let us return to the Supreme Court as it is and might be.

Our guiding inquiry is into the consequences of what we may call the bureaucratization of the Supreme Court, the change already perceived within it that appears to have been quietly progressing over time. If the Court were truly to become a bureaucracy as that form of organization is known in the modern world, would the texts produced by such a bureaucratic Court be treated properly or necessarily like the opinions produced by the opinion-writing division of an administrative agency, such as the Interstate Commerce Commission? If so, what would that mean for law and legal analysis? This, as we have seen, becomes a question of what a lawyer would do with such texts, and this in turn is related to the question of what other professionals, and individuals generally, do with texts of a similar kind.

BUREAUCRATIC WRITING is not just writing that appears under the name of one who did not write it. In its fully developed form it is writing that is written by many hands. The more elaborate the formal process a document goes through as its words and sentences are put together and the more hands involved in the process, the more the document becomes a thing that takes off on its own. A document that is *hammered out*—circulated again and again, with proposals for inclusion or exclusion to be negotiated between various parties, with responsibility for different sections turned over to different individuals—becomes detached, the outcome of a system; indeed, it becomes a system itself. Contracts, treaties, legislation, and administrative rules are often of this kind. Analysts shift to speaking of the intent of the document rather than the intent of the authors of it, but a thing that takes off on its own is still a thing.

Books written by a single hand also tend to take on a mimic life of their own in the course of being written. The author will find that he cannot change this or do that without starting over and changing the whole, which he does not have time or energy to do, and which, if he did, he suspects he would just have to do again, and then again, without end. To finish he must give up some control. Buildings too take on what seems to be a life of their own while being designed and built, and so do gardens that you dig yourself. When the thing is finished, you stand back and ask, "What have I wrought?" and you look; you do not know without looking.

To the extent this occurs, the book or the design does not express what the author wants to say or do. And as the work detaches itself from the author—Keats's *Endymion,* in Keats's own view, presented an advanced case of this—one finds oneself working with it and understanding it more in light of its origin, *how* it came to be that way, seeing it perhaps in retrospect as part of a process of further development leading to true and accurate expression: one does not search so much for *what* it expresses.

But in these cases of the single hand, the author is at least trying. The escape of the thing from him is a matter of degree. In looking at a building, for instance, one tends to identify, separate, and exclude from one's reaction to it the various unfortunate but historically necessary parts of its design, and in literature there are a variety of techniques for discovering the extent to which the production had gotten out of hand (as we say). One can often *see* the structure of a book creaking, the author sticking in footnotes here and there in an effort to twist it and control it.

O F   C O U R S E the performance of a work of art is the product of many hands, and it is not a mindless unexpressive thing. But a performer is presenting a work. He is not copying, to be sure, or merely transmitting as a loudspeaker might. He is adding. But in adding he is interpreting what it means to him, and the audience of a play or a piece of music sees the work through him and through any other individuals who may be involved. At the end of the chain of lenses or behind the multiple lenses spread before the audience (the sets, the lighting, the singing, the acting, the costumes, the pacing) there is a text, which is not simply the outcome of a process. The same chain can be seen in the connections between the reader, the literary critic, and the novel or the poem; and novelists and poets may lengthen the chain within the work itself, introducing narrators, characters characterizing other characters, perhaps even fictional readers, performers, and artists again. Behind it all there is still an authentic voice. That is what galvanizes the commitment and esprit characteristic of the theatrical and musical worlds. And that is what sets hack work apart. Nothing is really being said by a hack.

It is frequently said that the viewer or reader can look at a work of art without also seeing the artist, because the work is a creation independent of the artist. It is not limited by the artist's own limitations, and what he says it means may be the worst guide to what it does mean. But in saying that a work of art is a statement in itself, one is not saying that it was never said. The work is not a Rorschach blot, or the jumbled words emerging from the lips of an oracle under the influence of fumes, or the laid-out entrails of a sheep, or the pattern of birds flying overhead, in which the viewer sees a reflection only of himself because there was nothing meant to be expressed in it in the first place. It is a creation, but it was created by a designing hand. When one "approaches it on its own terms," as one hears people say they are doing, one does not treat it merely as the outcome of a process.

To approach a work on its own terms means that we do not need to know anything about the author other than what we learn through the work. Ancient art is art; primitive art by the anonymous craftsman is art. In fact, no lawyer knows much of anything about the private life of the judge whose opinion he seeks to understand. What lawyers do know they tend to ignore or dismiss. The striking fact, for instance, that the central figures of early twentieth-century American law—Holmes, Brandeis, and Cardozo—were men who never had children is rarely mentioned or addressed, and this is for what we should call a methodological reason: to understand what is being said we do not need to know facts such as these. Sometimes independent knowledge about the author is helpful, particularly if parts of the expressive idiom are time-bound and the work threatens to become progressively more like a Rorschach shape. More often, however, knowledge of the author is worse than useless, because it can slip into a search for causes and a reduction of the work to its antecedents, eliminating the act of creation and the work itself.

To say that a work of art stands independent of its author is also to say something not quite so explicitly methodological. It is that an author (or a man) can transcend his own limitations. The universal which the artist sometimes reaches and embodies in a work that stands physically apart from him may be brother or sister to the authoritative we discuss here. We transcend our limitations also when we discover that we need not follow our first instincts. The authoritative we sometimes reach does not even then limit us, bind us, or enslave us, any more than a work of art does; nor does it cause us to "lose our*selves*" in it. We *need* not follow or obey our better view embodied in what speaks legitimately and authoritatively to us. That we ought to do something does not mean that we will, any more than the fact we do something means we must do it and will continue to do it. The consequences of not following what we find to be authoritative may be very severe, not just in immediate sanctions but in ultimate aloneness. But it is still *we* that must obey, internalize what we perceive, go one way rather than another, and what *makes* us do one rather than another has not been discovered. Perhaps nothing does, and that is where *we* live—in the present, in the making. After all, what *makes* energy energetic?[6]

The proposition that an author can transcend his limitations does imply a difference between the weak, querulous, nasty, and ungenerous man himself and a universal that can speak through him; and we do slip naturally into references to inspiration, the muse, or genius standing outside him and whispering into his ear. There is a voice in either case, the artist's, or the muse whispering. But we should note that the contrast implied between the two is the product of our own definitions, and that any delimitation of *self* as including only what is not universal—any speaking of self as what is left over after the universal has been decanted—is entirely arbitrary: a forgivable form of false modesty perhaps, a twitting of ourselves out of embarrassment at what we are, or may be.

W HEN THERE IS virtually complete detachment of words, sentences, and paragraphs for an integrating mind, the techniques of stripping and saving designed to penetrate through awkward and inadequate expression simply fail, for they have nothing to work on.[7]

In the law, courts in such a situation commonly say, and express their saying of it in one or another doctrine, that there has not been any decision at all, or at least not one judicially reviewable or cognizable. There are then various responses to this perception, with various consequences. Sometimes the absence of a legally cognizable decision means that the decision is vacated. (That, of course, is superficially nonsense, but it is the way we talk. The challenged *action* that occurred, which is action rather than a decision though dressed in the form of a decision, is reversed and declared to be without legal effect, so that no legal consequences, at least insofar as the capacity and power of courts extend, may be built on it and flow from it.) This is frequently the response in public administrative law and can be found also in corporate law.

Sometimes, on the other hand, the perception of text as outcome, a thing, floating, unattached to any responsible agent, means just the opposite. Not being the sort of stuff legal analysis can operate upon there is to be no analysis of the decision or review of it (the reader will understand if I do not always put "decision" in quotation marks). Instead of being vacated and ignored, it is accepted and allowed to stand without any court taking jurisdiction over it—an intrusion of nature into the world of men. Its consequences are then most uncertain; at the least those facing the text are thrown into a dilemma. This happens in corporate law and very often in constitutional law, where the products of those decision-making systems known as business corporations and legislatures are brought into question.

And if the decisions of the Supreme Court were perceived in the same way? What would the response be? Suppose that, after conferring, the justices assigned the preparation of the opinion not to one of their number, who would seek to express their deliberation, but to their staff, which would act as an opinion-writing office for the Court. One of the nine or more available staffs on the current organizational chart of the Court begins the process. The wording of the text is negotiated among the staffs. No mind that believes all of what is being said puts the sentences and parts together. The document is reviewed by the justices individually or in conference, with varying degrees of attention but full awareness of how many hands have gone into the production and what costs in time and energy would be entailed in starting over or making major changes—costs not just of their time with other cases waiting, but the time of others too, who also have duties to perform and limited time to perform them in. Suppose, in short, the justices begin to act according to a very familiar pattern, that of the board controlling but dependent upon an organized executive, like the usual board of directors in a business corporation or an international organization with a secretariat.

Or suppose the justices do not really confer at all but meet instead (as now seems true in agencies and legislatures) to cast votes, votes determined in advance with heavy reliance upon the advice of a substantial and organized staff, so that in the writing of an opinion there are no deliberations to express, or, rather, to be approximated by one who did not himself participate in them. Any staff author of one or another part of the draft being put together writes like a lawyer stating a case on behalf of a client. He does not write like a lawyer composing a statutorily required opinion letter on his view of the law—or like a judge. A judge after all would view a lawyers's brief as no more than a useful aid to the analysis which must go on in his own mind; a judge would produce a statement quite different from a statement whose end is predetermined or determined by someone else.

Or suppose that not only the opinion but the decision is delegated to the staffs (as is the situation with some petitions for certiorari already in the Supreme Court), so that the determining votes cast are not the votes of the persons responsible for the decision but the votes of persons reporting to those responsible. This may seem extreme but, in any examination of the operation of bureaucratic decision-making systems, the line between "informing," "advising on," and "explaining" a decision, on the one hand, and making the decision itself, on the other, becomes difficult to draw. Looking *back* from a given decision to the process of making it, one is hard put to say just where the die was cast or whether any one more than another contributed to the outcome, particularly if there are feed-back loops so that tentative outcomes are reprocessed or trigger the begin-ning of the system again. And to a contributor looking *forward* to a decision that is not yet final, it is difficult to know what the results of his contribution will be, given the other contending forces. The outcome itself, both to one looking back and one looking forward, is like a billiard ball, set in motion in a particular direction with a particular speed by the simultaneous impact of a number of smaller billiard balls coming at it from various angles and with various speeds. And there is *no one* in the present looking, not to the future nor back into the past, but acting now, *actually*.

Then, one might say in response to these supposings, there is no legally cognizable decision by the Court, nothing with the force of law. I erect "one" to say it. What would the Supreme Court say? What would it say if it looked at itself as it looks at other decision-making systems—or with the troubles and the dilemmas with which it approaches the outputs of other decision-making systems? Would it say, "Ah, *whatever trouble we have in giving force to legislatures' statements or to corporations' statements, we manage to do it and can do it for our own as well. Besides, there are similar difficulties with the Court throughout most of its history. 'This Court' is an institution; there have been nine of us on it always, not one oracle.*" Would the Court say this, looking back at itself? It could. But while it was bravely saying things of this sort, its practice and its method would be alerting us to what it actually saw. By its practice we would know it, and the justices and their staffs would know themselves. It is doubtful that they would pay the same attention to their own opinions argued to them as precedents. It is doubt-ful that they could. Dilemmas and difficulties are matters of degree. What is a dilemma when facing the private sphere (the business corporation's statement) or the political sphere (the text that emerges from the legisla-tive process) may be crippling here. The Supreme Court might continue producing legal texts, but legal analysts including the justices themselves might cease to pay attention to them or might respond to them at arm's length, manipulating them rather than being in any way affected by them. The authority of the texts would dim and they would lose their hold on those who read them. The Court might be lost to us, and to itself, and we would face a legal system without a central authority.

DELEGATION

Examining what the loss of a Supreme Court would mean will be our way of learning more about legal method and of exploring further the relation between method and institutional structure in the chapters that follow. But before we pursue the questions that would be raised by such a loss we should turn to consider delegation itself, for delegation need not be to many hands. We have been speaking of bureaucracy. In the bureaucratic or industrial production of legal texts the text is written by no one. But the writing of a text might be delegated to some one person.

We would do well to consider this separately and at this point because it introduces a phenomenon related to authenticity, the phenomenon of office, at which we shall be looking further in later chapters. And though delegation to one person is often the first step in bureaucratization, it may have another outcome. We must not suppose that the imitation and the real are, in law, always worlds apart. The imitation can become real: office can be transferred.

W HENEVER AN AUTHOR delegates any writing of a text that is to be put forth under his name as if he had written it, there is immediate pretense and unreality, in that "as if." If the purported author keeps a hand in, saying, "Here, use this," or "Insert that," or "Take that out," the resulting text approaches the text produced by bureaucratic process. It is by no *one;* it becomes a patchwork. This is the difficulty of editing— whether the purported author edits the text written by the true author or the true author's text is edited by others who are called editors—and this is the reason why, in literature, there is constant interest in the original holograph of a work.

To be sure, quoting goes on all the time in writing, and adopting another's change or insertion or indeed entire draft could be viewed as a form of quoting. We have all had the experience of exclaiming, "You have said what I think better than I ever could." That is one reason for the constant turn to Shakespeare. But in analyzing what is said, when we probe and *work with it,* we cannot go very far before we find ourselves analyzing the meaning of Shakespeare rather than the meaning of the person who quoted him—unless, of course, the quoter successfully disguises his quotation, plagiarizing as it were; and that success is generally short-lived against the techniques of authentication. Only the true merger of two active minds can produce a text that is not a patchwork of plagiarized quotes and thus vulnerable to dissolution in analysis.

Unfortunately lawyers are not helped by the law of agency at all. Judges and commissioners, like authors, do authorize the signature of their names to texts, or parts of texts, written by others. It might be thought that since a contract written and signed by an authorized agent is the contract of the principal and is enforced against the principal, the same would be true here; but not so. A book written by an agent is not the author's book. It is a ghostwritten book. And a judicial opinion is not held against a judge in the way an agent's contract is held against a principal any more than a ghostwriter's words are held against an author for purposes of literary analysis. An opinion is held against a judge only through the doctrine of precedent, and quite the opposite occurs in working with precedent: instead of holding what is not his against him, any disavowal he might want to make is done for him without his asking. Every effort is made to discount that which is not meant and to save only that which is evidence of an integrating mind over time.[8]

B UT THE PROBLEM of delegation is not just the problem of patchwork. The entirety of writing can be delegated and there may be no editing, but so long as the name and office, the author's identity if you will, are not delegated together with the writing, there is deception still. The speaker is separated from the spoken. To move for a moment away from writing, if Kandinsky permitted or authorized another to imitate him, it would make the resulting painting no less a forgery, and the law of agency is, again, no aid. Kandinsky's authorization for purposes of the law of agency would affect only questions of property and claims for damages or participation in profits. Property is not the concern, for the problem posed by this kind of deception—independent of the problem of patchwork—is not so much that someone says the work is his when it is not as that the writer says the work is another's when it is not. The writer is a mock judge. There is no reality to what he does, no history to it. It is not serious, and somewhere within him there is a smile as he writes, if he has any sense of humor.

The lack of authenticity is suggested in style. One would suppose the writing would be stiff, and it is, like the faces and gestures of children imitating grown-ups, or some Hellenistic sculpture, or an imitation smile. "Here," says the judge or chief clerk, "here is what you do. Imitate this." And over time the imitation of imitations produces the mechanical quality that marks all inauthentic work, work that is not meant and therefore has no meaning. The staff member pens, "I think," or "This court concludes." He lies. He does not mean what he says with regard to who he is or for whom he speaks. It is nothing so small as taint from little obvious deceptions that spoils the whole. A liar in one thing is not necessarily a liar in all things. No; it is rather that if the utterer of a statement does not mean what he says with regard to who he is, one may doubt whether he means what he says in the substance of his statement, because, not being who he says he is, and knowing it, he will not easily think and speak as a judge—

or a king, or a parent, or whoever it is that he is not. Anyone, lawyer, professor of law, law student, may, like an actor, imitate a judge, but he will not be a judge, or know what it is like really to be a judge unless he has been one, and that will have been in the past. He will know himself to be an imitation judge when he speaks and there will thus be a constant difficulty in meaning what he says. There is always the danger of breaking into laughter in the midst of his playing or pretense; amusement is at once a signal (to oneself and others), a betrayal, and a protection, as one plays with a role rather than really entering into it.

Indeed it is this that opens law up to invasion. This imitativeness within, the consequence of writing without responsibility, works against the possibility of any intuitively clear and confident sense on the part of lawyers and judges themselves of what it is they distinctively do. Without a sense of what makes it distinctive, the discipline of law is open more and more to invasion by the self-conceptions of other fields and endeavors. This becomes the more widespread (and for that reason alone the harder to counteract) as judges high and low progressively reduce their own engagement with the making and expression of law, and leave the writing of legal texts and the myriad decisions associated with it to others who are not real decision makers struggling with real decisions. Those others are likely to proceed upon the basis of theories adopted or learned in school. It is neater and quicker to do this; but more important, there is authority for proceeding in this way—the authority of their former teachers or of the other disciplines from which the theories are taken. Clerks and assistants do not have their own authority and cannot proceed independently as the judge himself can. What they write, therefore, is no longer as good evidence of what doing law really is, from which a theory might be drawn, or, in the absence of theory, to which teachers in or out of school might point in seeking to transmit a sense of distinctive identity. Without such real evidence of what law and the doing of law is, the sense of what it is can be expected to fade.[9]

T HUS THE PROBLEM of delegation is not simply one of deceptive packaging, which is immaterial and can be forgotten (as the dust jacket of a book is forgotten) because it is the writing that is important, not its packaging. Supreme Court opinions which are not the product of the justices but rather the product of their staffs are not to be taken as the poems of Chatterton, which he presented as written by Rowley (as Macpherson did with Ossian), and which Shelley, Keats, and Wordsworth found excellent nonetheless. Chatterton spoke for himself.

But, it may be said, justices do not speak for themselves even when they themselves think and write. They speak for the Court. Great authorities, it may be said, rarely speak for themselves. Moses came down from Mount Sinai with tablets purporting to have been written by the finger of God, and Joseph Smith presented a translation of a Book of Mormon supposedly written by the last of a lost Hebrew race in America. The only difference seems to be that the justices sign their own names when speaking for another and Moses and Smith did not. In all three instances the putative author and the true author are separate, yet the texts have had authority. Knowing, or believing, or assuming that Jehovah himself did not cut the tablets does not seem to affect the authority of what is written on them.

But here is the mystery of office. A putative author is put forward to gain attention. In fact, when the beautiful and the curious or extraordinary are not involved, who a person says he is, and whether to pay attention to what he says, are the same question. (This is the advantage religious texts take from their beauty.) That is why Rowley was put forward by Chatterton and Ossian by Macpherson, and is indeed a reason for writing in imitative styles generally, journalistic or philosophical. Moses and Smith put forward their putative authors to gain attention. Attention must be paid to a statement in the first place, before any question of obedience, or examination of its quality, can arise.

But attention must also be maintained. Whether a person *is* indeed who he says he is, and whether to *continue* paying attention, are the same question—again, if the beautiful or curious are not involved. And it is not at all clear that Moses and Smith lied, or that the speaker and the spoken were separated. Prophets think themselves inspired: their authenticity and their sincerity come through.

And none of this—maintenance of attention or sincerity to come through or concluding they did not lie—would be possible if the putative authors existed in the world as individuals. Office assumes they do not. If the putative authors *did* exist in the world as individuals, anyone listening would want to know what those individuals said; and if they did exist, what the writer said, writing for another and to imitate another, would not be his own.

However, individuals can in a sense—insofar, that is, as they have authority—cease to exist as individuals and, like the kings and queens of England, become themselves personifications of offices filled in fact by others; and it is this that makes the delegation of writing different from the writing of texts by no one. As time goes on, responsibility for speaking can shift and a new authentic voice emerge. The clerk can become the king's judge, speaking for another, but for another who does not speak otherwise. The minister to the king can become, over time, the head of government.

When the whole of a task is assigned and this becomes known to all, listener and speaker alike, we can no longer talk of deception. Delegation with office is akin to an individual stepping into office for the first time—or becoming a parent, a custodian, a trustee, a coach, a director. The speech and action undertaken begin imitatively, but the imitation is imitation without deception, and with responsibility it can grow into speech and action that are not imitation but embodiment. In this the imitation is somewhat like the open imitation in the theater, extended beyond the theater's short hours. Great actors, like great characters of fiction, grip us when we experience them and make us think from time to time that All the world's a stage, though we know it is not because we know the world includes the darkness where we sit beyond the bright certainties of the play.

Indeed even an impostor, with a fault in the pedigree of his entitlement to office, can gradually cease to be an impostor as he fulfills the office in a genuine way. The defect in pedigree can be forgotten (as it does not appear that defects in the pedigree of titles to property can be forgotten), in the same way it is forgotten that Moses, Joseph Smith, William the Conqueror, or the Founding Fathers had no one to give them office. Such a shift of office to clerks is not likely to happen at a court where clerks only spend a few years. But it could, and if it did, the actual author under the prior arrangement would then become serious, and the listener would begin to pay attention.

It is not necessary that authority be based upon pedigree, that is, upon whether one or another historical fact was true—blood connection, the number of votes, the fulfillment or not of a rule in a game—and certainly pedigree is not sufficient: as we have seen, texts do not come prestamped with authority. If we look for the defects in pedigree which are critical and the lineages which are sufficient, they are to be found in what may be called the pedigree of what is said, not in the pedigree of office but in the pedigree of the statements made by an individual in office, his entitlement to office being a different matter. The pedigree of a statement must be something more of a metaphor than the pedigree of office, but, if the use of the term is allowed, the difference between the two kinds of pedigree can be seen to reflect the difference we have spoken of before between something said and meant, and something that is done.

A fault in the pedigree of something said and meant tends to deprive the statement of its meaning. A fault in the pedigree of a thing done or of the outcome of a game or system does not mean that the thing did not happen. That it happened affected causally much that came after, and therefore we have a large number of doctrines of repose, estoppels, and statutes of limitations, which stop us from trying to remake the past. They reflect to some degree the fact that what happened in fact may in fact be part of our own structure, like it or not.[10] The situation is different when we encounter, in the present, a voice coming to us from which we are seeking to construct a person speaking to us in the present. Then a fault in pedigree means that what we hear is not material we can use to construct the person (this being the root of the term "material" in its sense of "relevant," the reference being a methodological one). And so, in seeking what is meant, we put aside this thing that is said.

If a listener does not put aside a thing that is said, he pays attention to it. If he puts aside other things that are also being said by other voices, he continues to pay attention, and as he continues to pay attention, what is said will begin to affect him, in the way we indicate when we use the word authority. Whether a listener continues to pay attention to a speaker, and whether a speaker has authority for him, are the same question. But delegating writing without office does not produce a new authentic voice, nor attention, nor authority. One cannot pay very much attention to a forgery or an imitation. It is not real and does not have depth, the boundless depth that is the mystery of the real thing. It falls apart, like the forged treaty before the historian's critical eye or the forged letter before the lawyer's cross-examination. If one did begin to pay attention one would soon stop. And actually one would not pay attention in the first place if the deception were known from the beginning—any more than one would pay serious attention to an opinion that one knows is only the outcome of a process, the speech of no one.[11]

Listener or reader is disenchanted, is he not, when the spell a thing has cast on his attention is broken and he pulls back and turns away? The realization that what he is looking at so hard and listening to so carefully is not what it presents itself as being—but is mimicry, mock-up, imitation, forgery, plagiarism—raises in him, however inarticulately, the knowledge that speaker and spoken are not connected and that he cannot see for himself. He ceases to pay the attention that must accompany assent and action: he ceases to take into himself what is being said to him, does not absorb it and is not absorbed by it. The voice becomes a thing, not a voice. He is no longer spellbound, as it were, but instead removed, thinking of other things—thinking of and looking for the *process* of fabrication, what might have been *done* to produce the trompe l'oeil, if not thinking of other things entirely—or listening to other voices.

So, writing, picture, voice loses its persuasive force. It cannot be trusted. When one is presented with something one is to take seriously one is asked to do a great deal: to pay much attention to it and spend much time on it, rather than on the many other things there are to spend time on, and to take it into oneself, perhaps change oneself as a result. Knowing that he is deceived man does not then treat the disclosed illusion as authentic. He is disenchanted. He treats it differently and moves to protect himself from vulnerability, that the joke be not on him, or worse: the authoritarian is in the air.

To speak of enchantment and disenchantment is to speak of magic. Magic might be thought to put one in the grip of illusion itself, bound by a spell, enthralled and hardly better off than a subject in an authoritarian world. But there is a difference between magic on the stage and magic in life. We sit inactive in the theater. The theater ends and we then know the illusion there for what it is. Knowledge of illusion and reality is not given us when magic in life ends. In life we act. We press and we test to know, but so long as we are enchanted we are not living in illusion. A disillusioned man, who stops, has lost his illusions. But why are they illusions? They are illusions because he has lost them. Before, when he is active, we cannot think illusion is all he has and all he has to lose, any more than we can think what draws us on is illusion so long as we continue to believe in it and it continues to draw us on. Enchantment makes life real. Human life is action and initiative. There must be sources of action and initiative. There must be delight and embracing and all that goes with the enchanting. To be enchanted is to live most fully and without reservation. Enchantment is a state of reality and a fusion of reality. Only when we are not enchanted is what we see and hear illusion. Then voices become things and things empty appearances deceiving us.

It is the actual, the memory of it, the sense of it, the hope of it, that enchants and draws out our action from us. This is the reason for law's drive for the actual in all the ways in which law reveals that drive, with a method designed to continuously unmask the inauthentic and turn law's practitioners away from the mock to that which can be taken seriously. Literature, philosophy, art, and history, law's cousin disciplines, have reasons special to themselves for their drive for the actual. This is law's reason.

PART II

AUTHORITY
and
INSTITUTIONAL ARRANGEMENT

Illusion, self-delusion, personification, maintenance of true attention, mockeries and tricks in legal thought and method: let us pause and consider to what point we have come in our journey through the forest of law. Our guiding question will stay still a moment.

That which speaks law's command, we find, does not pop out from behind a tree like an eighteenth-century footpad and say something short and crisp about which there can be no question, such as, "Hand over your purse." Many things are said by that which speaks the law, over a long period of time. And not only are those subject to law's command hearing not one thing spoken to them but many things over time—as listening to a friend you hear not one thing but many things over time—but the law, or that which speaks the law, is not there before you, as the footpad is who pops out from behind a tree.

Oh yes, there may be a judge or administrative official speaking particular sentences, and you might discourse with them and ascertain the meaning they put upon their words as you might discourse with a footpad; but in deciding what the law's command is, one hears and attends to far more than their particular sentences, for the method by which one ascertains what the command of the law is, or what the law is, has one looking to all the authoritative material pertinent to the question. One consults or is spoken to by "all the authorities," as the phrase goes.

And, yes, like the footpad, some individual judge or administrative official may be able to tell you what to do in some particular instance and force you to do it; but there is no necessary connection between what they order you to do and what the law would have you do. It is certain that once you are safely out of their clutches you will pay no attention to what they would want you to do in similar circumstances if you do not think that is what the law would have you do; and if you come up against another judge or administrative official, popping out from behind another tree, you can most certainly argue that the speaker who popped out from behind the previous tree should be ignored.

But does this that you know, that the sovereign does not speak in any crisp and circumscribed way and does not stand before you as an individual stands before you, mean that no one speaks the law and the words of the law are the outcome of a system that is as impersonal as we now think nature is? No. There is a person speaking, and to this we shall come. The person, however, is one that we conceive—when we have the will to do so. The person's mind is one that we help construct—as long as we can continue to pay serious attention to what is being said.

The question with us is not whether there is a person speaking but whether that person is mock or real and whether we can ever know that such a person is or is not real. But luckily this is not such a new question or a question peculiar to law. Who is the individual, your friend, who speaks to you over time? What does he believe, and how do you know what he believes? Is that person, whom you conceive your individual friend to be, real? Does it make a difference whether your friend is real? In answering these questions one equips oneself to answer the questions posed by law and legal analysis. As a matter of fact, if one thinks about it, the footpad who pops out from behind a tree to issue a crisp and circumscribed command is hardly a person at all, hardly even what we would call an individual. He is a force, to be dealt with as a force of nature.

CHAPTERS 6 through 10 turn from method to the institutional arrangements serving method and the ends for which method is practiced.

In Chapters 6, 7, and 8 the implications of bureaucratization are taken to their limit and the effect upon lawyers and law of actually eliminating the Supreme Court as a source of law is considered. Hierarchy is a phenomenon for which lawyers, maintaining ancient forms of deference, now bear special responsibility. What place is there for hierarchy of the kind displayed by legal institutions, in a free society which seeks the equal dignity of individuals? Beyond the question of hierarchy is the more general question, How hard should one work in any setting to keep a functioning center for the statement of law?

The two chapters following, Chapters 9 and 10, place beside courts as they exist today the other grand institutions of law that American lawyers face, legislatures and electorates. Administrative agencies have been with us from the beginning.

6
HIERARCHY
Law without a Supreme Court

Our guiding question—What would happen if the Supreme Court became a bureaucracy within?—has led us through a consideration of what lawyers say and do, and the presuppositions of their method and speech, to institutional questions beyond. Suppose the production of Supreme Court opinions did become industrialized, as it were, and the fact was generally acknowledged? Suppose that gradually, imperceptibly, a threshold was passed, and we ended with a Supreme Court that was not taken seriously as an author of texts from which law could be drawn, a Court indeed that did not take its own product seriously? No mere anomaly would be presented. If, in the pyramid of those making statements of law, it is the supreme point that fades, then questions about the very purpose of hierarchy and center in institutional arrangement are presented.

These may be viewed as questions principally of institutional design and maintenance. They bear, for instance, on the quite practical issues of how hard and long we should struggle, in an economy of time and effort, to maintain current legal institutions in pyramidal form with a functioning center, or with what seriousness and conviction man should work to establish a supreme institution of supranational or worldwide jurisdiction.

For our purposes, however, examining what the loss of the Supreme Court would mean to the practice of law in the United States will be a way of learning more about legal method and the relation between method and institutional structure. In particular, it will be a way of examining the place of hierarchy in legal thinking and the creation of authority.

We will start in this chapter with the simpler points, before moving on in the next to the more difficult.

SUPREMACY AND LAW

If Supreme Court texts could not be taken seriously, there would be a change. The change would not be in legal method. There is every reason to think that would remain as constant, at base, as scientific method. The change would rather be in the material upon which legal analysis was focused. Conceivably there might still be a flow of material from the Court, private memoranda, letters, speeches, and interviews of the kind a sophisticated lawyer reads in the trade journals every morning before he sets out to advise clients subject to the jurisdiction of an administrative agency. But let us suppose there is no attempt to make such material support an authoritative statement of law. To simplify, and throw into relief the question of the place of hierarchy in legal thinking, let us suppose there were no Supreme Court at all. That would leave the growing body of sometimes authentic texts we have today—without those from the Supreme Court—and legal method.

G IVEN THIS—the way we go about finding law, and these texts—we could still have law. "The law is, by definition, what the Supreme Court says it is." We hear that today. Convention, definition, points to the Supreme Court. But just who the "Supreme Court" is, and how it speaks, and whether, when it says a particular thing, it can be understood, are questions for which one must find answers by looking to legal practice and method. When we do look at practice and method we see that we save a supreme court's utterances from incoherence over time. We must, for different individuals speak them in different years. Saving the utterances of different individuals, who are scattered over space rather than time, is not intrinsically different.

Among those who use similar techniques, indeed, only lawyers and theologians tend to pay special attention to texts produced by hierarchical authorities. The method of social, intellectual, or cultural historians, for instance, does not depend upon a structure of authority—or, we might say, upon the authoritarian seeking to become authoritative. To be sure, the method of choice in cultural and intellectual history has been to examine the works of great men or the "authorities" of an Age. Mere habit this is in part, passed down from the period when the texts studied were classical texts and only those of great men survived, just as political history which focuses upon the doings of great men is in part an inheritance from chroniclers attached to princely courts. Insofar as it is not inherited convention, the study of great men above the mass is in large measure the study of exemplars.

This is not to say that Plato, Aristotle, Kant, and Hegel did not influence men and women right down to the masses. This is not to say that no heroes and giants stand outside the ordinary mind as causes of it, to be examined with the fascination causes evoke, and to be returned to again and again and listened to in their own words as revelatory not just of steady truth to which they speak as universal beings but of clues to our own minds as they are today. It is to say only that the symbiotic relationship between any individual and his culture should be kept in view and is in fact kept in view. In cultural and intellectual history there has been, running with the study of the authorities of an Age, a rather explicit assumption that there is a common mind independent of great men's contributions and that, with perhaps a very few exceptions, those individuals whose names survive express more than they create changes in that mind.

Lawyers thus need not be devastated, certainly not among their peers, if the formal hierarchy that produces legal texts flattens out, and the task of integration falls more heavily upon them than it would if the Supreme Court were also engaged in it.

IN FACT, common law analysis as pursued in the United States, which, unlike Commonwealth countries, never looked to the Judicial Committee of the House of Lords at Westminster as a final arbiter, has never included a convention that pointed to the statements of a single institution as the final source of law. This was one reason (apart from the force of the hope or assumption that law and legal method might be like the law and method of mechanics and the hard sciences at the turn of the century) for the formation of the American Law Institute and the writing of the great American treatises in tort, contract, property, agency, trusts, and criminal law. Both institute and treatise indicate the absence of central authority as much as a desire for it.

Beyond standard common law analysis in the United States, there is the method of the comparativist, which has always been a form of intellectual history. The comparativist presumes similarities between different jurisdictions in the very act of searching for them, reaching for the substance beneath the confusing difference of forms, and separating the common and basic from the inevitable arbitrariness of detail and application. And in international law there is no authoritarian central organ. That has never meant that there was no such law. We certainly do not act as if there were no such law, though lawyers, deprived of their method of choice, have voiced complaints couched in the form of challenges to the authority of international law, characteristically phrased as doubts to its existence.

Finally, in lawyers' everyday dealing with multistate organizations—multinational corporations, national corporations in federal systems—it is a commonplace that the "law of choice of law" determining what jurisdiction's law to look to in a particular situation is inadequate or deliberately ambiguous. For example, in resolving an issue raised about a corporation, there is a shifting reliance upon the law of the state of incorporation (whose secretary issued the corporate charter), the law of the state where the seat or headquarters of the corporation is found, the law of the state where a body of shareholders substantial in number or in capital interests is located, and the law of the state where assets, operations, or employees other than the principal executives are located. The absence of an adequate law of choice of law (or "conflicts," as such law is also called) does not stop lawyers.

The language of those involved in conflicts discussions today, even the language of the supreme courts of the various states that may be involved, amply reveals that lawyers and judges live and work not just or even principally in a geographical jurisdiction but in a jurisdiction of ideas. Labor and capital, property and contract, shareholder and partner, taxation and public health, environment and crime, are not words that can be reduced to counters or symbols within a closed system, whose definition or meaning is determined by their use within that system under the sanction of a central, integrating mechanism.[1] Lawyers from different and separate jurisdictions understand one another—whether those jurisdictions are defined geographically, or by subject matter. Just as lawyers from different fields of law can argue with one another, lawyers for multinational organizations can argue with lawyers from particular national jurisdictions without an overriding sense of futility. Lawyers from different multinational organizations can discuss matters with one another. Partners from different offices of the emerging multinational law firms can discuss issues with one another. However much this discussion is of a manipulative and strategic kind, devoted to capitalizing upon the very absence of an integrating legal mechanism, it does contain enough of a search for what organizations ought in good faith to do, to give some indication of what life for lawyers in the United States might be like if the Supreme Court ceased to function. A professional life in the law, and not just an appearance of one, would still be possible.

Efficiency in Close Reading

But, for all this, the practice of saying what the law is would suffer if the Supreme Court were simply not there.

WHY WOULD THE PRACTICE of legal method suffer, rather than just see a change in the materials upon which it operates? What might immediately occur to us is that without a Supreme Court there would be no way of finally settling particular disputes or more general issues, or of avoiding contradictory commands, permissions, or prohibitions. This, strange to say, is not a concern of great force. Lawyers and lawyers' clients live with a massive amount of contradiction already. Whether there is today any central pronouncement upon an issue or final resolution of a particular conflict is determined by the Court's discretionary selection of cases to hear—and the Supreme Court often bides its time; by the caseload of the Court—and the Court can reach but a fraction of the conflict and must remand most cases to lawyers' own determination of what the law is; and most of all by the litigating resources available to the parties who are in a procedural position to argue the merits of the matter.

Much conflict over particulars therefore is settled now by the workings of the passage of time and by discussion outside the judicial forum. If things are not settled to anyone's satisfaction, they may at least be settled, for the short run. For the long run there can be adjustment to the situation. Money finds new streams to flow in, if it is money that is the issue. Corporate systems allocating benefits and burdens adjust to the loss of particular damage actions. And even after disposal of a legal issue in or out of court, new schemes may be legislatively enacted. In fact, lawyers regularly watch settlements to which they have attached a judicial seal, dearly bought, coming unraveled not just legislatively but in the unruly world: in child custody cases, for example, the child may be lured away or kidnapped by the defeated parent.

Moreover, we must remember that despite the strong desire that there be final and definitive statements of opinion, they happen no more in law than in one's dealings with one's friends, family, or colleagues. We blurt out what we do not mean. We are tired, rushed, words do not work for us on a particular day, we are distracted by the events of a week. We are not perfect. Neither are courts in the authorship of what they say.

No doubt we are uncomfortable with having to retract, limit, or creep away from what we have pronounced at a particular point in time, and we try to stand by it or conceal withdrawal from it to maintain credibility in the eyes of others. But others do the same and know they do the same, just as they know we do it, and mutual credibility is maintained by tolerance of good faith efforts to reach the impossible ideal of absolute consistency and perfect articulation. Others even delete (sometimes automatically) statements of ours that are not in character, from that full record of our statements to which they are continually referring in their minds. We *do* limit, recharacterize, withdraw from and silently abandon positions taken at some particular previous point, because consistency is more important than the appearance of consistency, which is hollow, fragile, and always collapses. And so do others, even others speaking from high and central places.

T HE LOSS OF THE Supreme Court therefore would not mean the loss of a finality and certainty we now enjoy.

But we are impatient with friends who will not even try to make a definitive statement of what they think or to sum up and integrate their perceptions in any way, but instead hem and haw, postpone and qualify, hint and wink, and leave it entirely up to us to do the work. Methodologically, we find it difficult to handle the material they offer us. And this common experience points to a loss we would suffer in the loss of the Supreme Court, about which we would be absolutely concerned.

The presence of the Supreme Court means, at the least, that there are presumptively fewer documents for the legal analyst to examine. Its *being there* serves the function of any presumption in thought or action. It is a place to start. And perhaps, if one is satisfied, one need not go much beyond the texts that it produces. That is at least conceivably possible.

We are told that our minds—or brains—cannot maintain in contemplation more than a limited number of different things at once, and most of us are not disposed to dispute the accusation on the basis of our own experience. There is of course a question of what this means. Much can be done with categorizing, patterning, and grouping, and with the mystery of the symbol. The line between what is one thing and what is (or are) many things is always most difficult to discern. Still there seems to be an advantage rooted in the nature of things in institutionally limiting the production of the evidence with which we work to discover the law, if our capacities are in fact limited along these lines in one or another way. The great attraction of work in ancient as opposed to modern history is this very limitation of material, this *given* core of what has survived. It is the place to start. It is not too much. Perhaps one need not go beyond it.

This is also part of the attraction of social or cultural history of a certain kind: convenience, efficiency, being able to get on with the job at all, may attract historians to the study and discussion of the authorities and great men of an Age, quite as much as habit or the presumption that the authorities of an Age are either exemplars or causes. It is not clear much is lost in this unself-consciously deliberate limitation, for it does not appear that one mind need know all or have had all experience to reach the common mind. How many men and women did Shakespeare, Keats, or Freud actually know before they worked through their material to the universal statements that speak so authoritatively to so many? And how were those chosen with whom a Shakespeare, Keats, or Freud came into contact?

So, the work produced by the twenty or so individuals on the Supreme Court over a generation may be enough, if it is authentic work, however unexceptional their backgrounds may be and however odd the reasons for their appointments, it mattering less which set of texts analysts examine and discuss than that they work with the same or roughly the same set. There may be a quite serious loss in having more, and having therefore to work with more material. It might be reflected in resistance to the work itself.[2]

THE FORCE OF OFFICE

The documents produced by a supreme court are also of a certain kind, an especially useful kind.

If, by presumption or convention, the number of texts to be worked with is limited for convenience, efficiency, and commonality of material, the limitation is more palatable if the texts thus enclosed within the circle have some special value. Specialness in a text is most certainly relevant if there is actually a question whether there is to be a limitation—through choice of particular institutional arrangements, such as a supreme court, and their continuing maintenance—of the material upon which legal analysis is to be done.

L ET US AGAIN note first what might occur to us first, that the texts produced by the Supreme Court of the United States are all texts with which a comparatively large number of individuals agree.

As constituted in the United States, the federal Supreme Court is a large court, and, except where the federal courts of appeal sit *en banc,* its size sets it apart from other courts. A court that sits in panels of three, and in which a decision upon a statement requires the agreement of only two individuals, may in fact be qualitatively different from a court that sits in a panel of nine and which requires the agreement of five to a statement. Persuading four others is a task rarely undertaken by others in the legal system seeking to state what the law is.

The five may only appear to agree; that is, they may agree for strategic reasons. Compromise on one issue or statement may be traded for compromise on another, so that, when the two are put together, there is a composite statement in which no one believes, and which therefore must be treated with special care as evidence. Pressure to negotiate and trade, to engage in acceding and accepting rather than agreeing, may increase as the number of judges on a court increases. Nonetheless, where there is genuine agreement as the result of true discussion and persuasion on the merits, the resulting statement is rather special, again, not conclusive, for these are only five men and women among many others, but special.

Having noted this aspect of institutional arrangement, however, let us set it aside for further consideration in Chapter 9. It is not clear just what degree of advantage is gained by moving from the agreement of two to the agreement of five, given the increased difficulties of common discourse. Whatever the advantage of size, that advantage is not one arising from position at the peak of a hierarchy. It is an advantage contingent upon the way the Supreme Court happens to be constituted, and it need not necessarily be lost if the Supreme Court were lost.

T HERE IS ANOTHER special quality of Supreme Court texts that does arise from the fact of hierarchy itself.

The opinions of the Supreme Court seek to integrate and save the law, to state definitively what the law is. Some other judges do so also, and we do not know how they would behave if they were not subordinate in a hierarchical system and did not pay special attention to the opinions of a supreme court. But no other court works with quite the sense of responsibility for the whole as a supreme court.

Strip them of the presumption of authority, and the statements of Supreme Court justices seem no more than the statements of nine individuals among hundreds or thousands of men and women making statements on the same subjects, nine whose credentials usually do not mark them out for appointment—utilities lawyers, campaign managers, politicians, personal friends of the president. But office may make the man. The role is a teacher, and an individual may transcend his limitations in making a role his own. The Dalai Lama chosen as a baby by wise men from among those born at the time of the previous Dalai Lama's death, or a pope chosen by cardinals, or an Aga Khan chosen by blood, or Darwin and Peirce and other philosophers and scientists admitted to the practice of philosophy and science through the possession of sufficient independent inherited wealth when neither patron nor university provided support for philosophers and scientists without independent wealth, are not clearly the worse for their mode of selection or clearly better than those selected by means more congenial to today's conventions. The role rather than the man may be the more important factor, and within a rather broad range of candidates, changing the man without also changing the role may affect performance surprisingly little. The anointing of the king, the swearing in of the president, the crowning of the pope, these are all archaic expressions of a social function which is as alive today and as modern as any—the telling of an individual (and we will not attempt to say who is telling) that a particular decision is his or hers to make.

The role is given, not assumed. Though judge, king, or priest individually may have seized office or engineered appointment, once office is handed to him—always by someone else except in the extraordinary and properly shocking case where a king crowns himself—the office exerts its force over him as well as us. He finds himself open to a new set of criticisms, most important, criticisms for inaction: the difference between omission and commission fades and he is, to that extent, less free. No one says to the treatise writer, for example, "It is your function, your duty to write this treatise." The author of so-called secondary legal literature assumes his role, thrusts himself forward upon the attention of the public. If he does not write his treatise, no one criticizes him for it, at least not very strongly. If he comments on only part of a subject, he is applauded for his caution and his circumspection rather more than he is criticized for not going the whole way. The documents produced by an individual operating under the goad of office who has been *told* that the decisions are his and that no one else has been told to do what he is doing, so that he cannot assume that others will do what he fails to do, can be expected to be somewhat different from those produced by other individuals also seeking to state what the law is.

That the statements of those in office are different does not mean that they are always better. Perception and construction being what it is, a book written before the author is ready to write may be worse than no book at all, despite the truism that having to write may make one ready to write. The same is true of legal opinions. One can force oneself to act, but not to see or hear. But the documents produced by those in office may always have more of a thrust to the complete in them. And as the result of at least trying to speak to the whole, their inadequacies, their failures, and their omissions may be illuminating, in a way that what is left out by one who carves out his own subject cannot match.

W E SHOULD HASTEN to reemphasize that the fact the supreme office holder is instructed that the decision of what the law is is his to make, and no one else's, does not mean that when he speaks, whether well or poorly, he *has* stated what the law is. It is not the case that, if a lawyer's or a student's or an unofficial commentator's statement turns out to be different from that of a supreme office holder when the two are laid side by side, the official statement must be chosen and the unofficial rejected because by definition the law *is* what the official says it is.

The tendency to think this is reinforced by the architecture and ritual of the legal world. Law students sit in a mass *below* a teacher who is high on a podium. Traditionally their teacher confronts them in an embarrassing way with the *error* of their statements, by appearing to contrast—lay side by side—what they say with what a citation from authority says. Lawyers engage in repeated public obeisance to judges, and judges employ a variety of techniques to express deference to other judges higher in the hierarchy. All this inculcation and apparent celebration of obedience for obedience's sake, so reminiscent of a military structure, is belied by what lawyers actually do, what we have here called their methodology. But it has its effect. It contributes also, as much as the grip of scientific analogies upon the modern mind, to the related methodological illusion that every single utterance of every judge is the law, and that what lawyers do is to gather all these true statements together, look at them, and induce the rules.

An authoritarian streak may be functional where action is in question, and the body politic must move as one, one way or another, if it is to move at all. A touch of authoritarianism is not so obviously functional where thought is in question, except insofar as it has the effect of making people discuss the same texts, begin together *somewhere,* even if in the course of illuminating them through reference to the texts of authors inferior in the hierarchy one ends up essentially replacing them with the superior texts of the inferior authors.[3] It may be necessary to *do* what the Supreme Court says to do, necessary in light of the alternative, necessary if we are to have order in life, necessary for lawyers in the sense that their role as obedient ministers demands it of them. But there is no such necessity at all in believing what the Supreme Court *says.* There cannot be, that chilling scene in Orwell's *Nineteen Eighty-Four* notwithstanding, where Winston is required to see five fingers when in fact only four are being held up. A whimsical statement of law by a supreme officeholder would not be the law, because it was never conceived that his personal whim should be the law. That was not the function, role, or power given to him. When a minor official says to a citizen, "Sorry, buddy, that's the law," it is clear to all that the word "law" is being used in a special sense. The sentence means, "This is what you have to do right now," not "This is what you must believe the law is, this is what the law is." Hierarchy simply makes it difficult to remember that the same is true when a high official says, "That's the law."

I T SHOULD ALSO BE repeated that what we may call the qualitative specialness of supreme court texts is somewhat untested. The office and duty of stating what the law is might be given to multiple bodies of equal status. Such might have been the situation in the American system of separation of powers if constitutional judicial review of congressional and executive decisions had not emerged. The situation of the state supreme courts in the United States is ambiguous in this regard. Theoretically they are not organized by the Supreme Court, though the constitutionalization of state legal issues has provided something of a substitute for formal hierarchical subjection. As we have seen, they do speak to a national common law and beyond, and in their legal analysis they reach for texts produced by authors beyond their respective borders. But they purport to be speaking only to the law of a particular geographical area, for example, the law of Illinois. The federal courts of appeals present a clearer case. Geographically limited in their jurisdiction, they nonetheless do purport to be speaking to the law of the United States. In their opinions now they spend much time working with opinions of the Supreme Court to construct their statements of that federal law, with due regard for their place in a hierarchical system; we do not know what quality their opinions would have if there were no supreme court. The effect of the responsibility of office and the thrust to completeness might appear even more strongly in them than it does today. Then it would be principally the effect of knowing you are *alone*—if you stumble no one else will pick up the baton, at least not for the time being—that would qualitatively distinguish opinions of a supreme court. We cannot venture how strong this last effect, by itself, may be.

THE WORK OF RECHARACTERIZATION

We have spoken of evident quantitative losses and possible qualitative losses associated with the loss of the peak. There is one further loss of a relatively straightforward kind, which is the loss entailed in the removal of any stage in an appellate hierarchy.

A supreme court, is, in most systems, only the second appellate stage. Two stages are generally thought to be enough beyond the heat and turbulence of the trial court. If anything other than conventional deference is to be paid to the statements of those who speak at the second appellate stage, their statements must be thought better in some sense for some reason. The reason to which we refer here is, oddly, simply the fact that the statements are made at a point higher in the hierarchy.

The virtue in them is a consequence of the nature of legal reasoning, which is syllogistic, definitional, and deductive in form, while in substance it is dialectic and—how shall we say it?—whatever might eventually become the name of working with texts, or listening and making sense of a whole. The formal logic of a legal argument builds and branches out from the initial steps and then the successive steps taken at each stage. Categorizations are made, units of reference are chosen, one thing linking and snapping into another, that other evoking and leading to further sets of relevant considerations. This means that the outcome of the reasoning, like the outcome of a trial, depends enormously upon initial steps and critical turns along the way.[4]

If there is discomfort with one or another of those steps, looking back from well along the way, the problem often cannot be rectified without going back and starting over. And often one cannot do that. One does not have time. One must act, and then, if the statement is to be used in future reasoning or as the basis for future action as to which one still has time, one must try to purify it or strip it and limit its significance in light of the degree of perceived arbitrariness in its genesis.

Where outcomes thus depend upon initial categorizations, definitions, and choices of units of reference, and cannot be rectified unless there is an opportunity to start over, an additional appellate stage is of importance in itself. An additional appellate stage provides just such an opportunity to start over. While there is a great deal of designed procedural obstacle to shifting the issue as an argument moves up the hierarchy, shifting does occur. The case is recharacterized. What it is about changes. An issue argued desultorily earlier, and fed into thinking without much notice, is made critical and set up for intense argument. Matters are excluded or shifted to the periphery of attention. New linkages are made. One or a few issues among many that were argued equally are now selected and focused upon. Roads not taken are taken, or at least tried.

The loss of a stage of argument that attends the slicing off of the peak in a hierarchy is the loss of an opportunity for recharacterization, thus the loss of an opportunity to escape from the consequences of prior decisions made in the process of deciding what to say about the law. There is in us a continuous process of building up and tearing down, a continuous struggle to escape being bound by what we have built. We must build edifices, but the edifices we build are always inadequate. We build them before we might otherwise do if we had all the time in the world, from the few items we have in our minds at any one time, and continuously cast ourselves into this necessity of tearing down and modification. Sometimes we lose the struggle and wake up to the fact that we are bound by what we built out of those things initially in our minds. Fear of these shackles, particularly when we are undertaking to make a statement of law, may be reason enough to regret the loss of a higher court.

But here, I know, we have begun to talk of authority and the making of authoritative statements as a process rather than, or as well as, the creation of substance, of present voice and glittering eye we can hear and look back into in the present where we are. We have also begun to speak of freedom and self-determination in talking about escape from being bound by the edifices we build, cap with names, and breathe life into. How can we want to escape from them when we take life from them too? These things should not be discussed further in a chapter on the simpler aspects of hierarchy. They need chapters of their own.

7

FOCUS

The Function of a Center in a Search for the Authoritative

EQUALITY AND INSTITUTIONAL FORM

WHEN FIRST BUILT the pyramids may have had shining caps, and those seeing a pyramid from near or far might be brought to think of the sun which they could not look at directly, with its rays flowing perfectly from the bright high point out and down to the earth below. But the shining caps are gone, and so is this view of the pyramid. The pyramid has become the very symbol of tyranny.

The pyramid is also the shape of hierarchy. If there is a connection between the authority with which lawyers are concerned, and freedom, it cannot run through hierarchy so conceived. Nor can hierarchy, of which a supreme court, being supreme, makes us think, be a *condition* of authority. The distance and the debasement of the belowness and aboveness that it entails are inconsistent with the candor between speaker and listener presupposed by legal method.

This should be a point of some importance to lawyers, who bow and scrape more than most. Subjection, blind obedience, is not part of being a lawyer. And of course this is a point of importance to those beyond lawyers, who are being asked to obey. Hierarchy is not a necessary attendant to the authority of law. There is no need to turn to the anthropology of primitive cultures, with all the difficulties of transferability and translation, to learn this. We have only to contemplate law in the United States with the Supreme Court absent, silent, or ignored. We could get along.

Yet there would be losses. We have spoken of the losses of presumption and limitation of textual material, of the driving force of office, and of a stage in the appellate process. Asking what would happen if there were no Supreme Court is thus not just a means of asking what the connection is between authority and authoritarianism, or willing obedience and obedience for its own sake. But neither is our question just a means of asking what the connection is between law and hierarchy as such. The Supreme Court is far more than part of the abstraction we call hierarchy, the phenomenon of graduated dignity. If the authority of law suffers from the absence of a Supreme Court, it is important to press forward and disentangle so far as we can just what the deeper losses are. This must help us know what a Supreme Court's various and perhaps separable contributions are, if our interest is in institutional design and maintenance; it must also help us in our exploration of law itself.

The Maintenance of True Attention

Most serious would be the loss of a center. Not in an apocalyptic sense, that the center would not hold and things would fall apart: the center of the legal system would continue to be the law. The center has never been the *institutions* producing over time the numerous texts from which the law is drawn. But—King, Pope, President, Governor, Allah, Jehovah, Buddha, Jove, Wotan: why is there so often only one set up to speak?

WHERE THE SINGLE UNIT above is an individual human being, we might say, "Well, men love power and domination, and the urge to dominate is satisfied in no individual man until this form, of one above all others, this pyramidal form, emerges from the struggle produced by the presence of the urge in each man. (And only then, perhaps, can others enjoy domination too, vicariously, by identifying themselves with the one on top.)" But could not the urge to power, which is so often thus put forward as an axiom or a basic datum to be used in the fashioning of explanations, be itself a product of something else, of dissatisfaction with organization that lacks an apparent center, a given center, a sensed center, a center one does not have to work to perceive? After all, we readily transfer talk of domination and power to the situation each of us faces within ourselves, so that we speak of struggles within and the achievement of self-control, and in the twentieth century the mythic images of our minds and personalities are as hierarchical as they ever were in the centuries before. The urge to power and the workings of competition are not enough to account for the singleness of the speaking entity, even in the simplest situation where the speaking entity is an individual.

WHERE THE SPEAKER is an individual human being and also part of an ongoing human institution, he and his singleness may be the product of organization designed to avoid paralysis in action. King and president do not simply speak and produce texts for discussion, any more than do courts. They also decide upon action, and through their resolution of ambivalence within the institution, the institution is able to act as one. This is true even of priesthoods, which have internal institutional pressures leading to the supremacy of one over all if they together want to *do* anything, tax the populace or build a building or even dress in a uniform way. It is thus difficult to draw conclusions about what may be necessary or conducive to organized thought, from situations on which the imperatives of organized action have had a strong influence.

But speaking and action are often separated, so that coming to grips with the one can be disentangled from coming to grips with the other. The speaker and producer of texts is often separated from the source of orders to act within the confines of what we call a single institution—that seeks to act as one, that is, in an organized way—and the speaker is still generally a single person. Furthermore, where the speaker can be viewed (despite the difficulties of doing so) as *not* part of or within an acting institution, there can still be observed a striking tendency toward singleness of speaker. One oracle, prophet, or holy man is listened to above the rest, rises above them not in a sense of controlling them but in the sense that more attention is paid to the one over the others, and the others take their places in listeners' minds by comparison and contrast with him. Jupiter rules the heavens, and even the Torah is put into a single box at the center of the room. And beyond this, we have extending well into the modern age the mysterious phenomenon of the *statue, idol, icon,* or *image* of the deity. Why erect the idol? Why set up the image? Why are the *words* one hears or reads not enough?

We cannot push the facts too far. There is no dearth of counterexamples. The rule of Jupiter, like that of Saturn before him, was uneasy. The Christian God is divided within the mystery of the trinity. The organization of the Islamic and the Jewish religious worlds, like that of the radical Protestant, is not formally hierarchical however often one prophet, holy man, rabbi, or preacher comes to be the focus of attention. The gods, it may also be maintained, are projections of the result produced in human affairs by the necessities of practical action and are not an independent source of information about the needs or the structure of the human mind. Still, as we look around us, at the facts of what we do, their suggestiveness is not exhausted when we have finished with evolutionary explanations or functional understanding—functional, that is, where the function of a thing is not allowed to include the function of aiding or making possible understanding in itself.

Consider: in the individual human being, inconsistency and madness are not so very far apart. The inconsistent person speaks with two voices, each saying different things. The common reaction is to drive either the individual or ourselves, his hearer, toward consistency, by showing that the different things said are about different things and therefore do not clash, or about different aspects of the same thing, or by showing that the different things said are steps in an evolution toward a new consistency that transcends the differences or reformulates the things said so that, in a sense, they were never said, or are steps toward the abandonment of the premises or schemas that led to the inconsistency (whatever else may take the place of the abandoned schemas or remain after they are abandoned). Simplest of all, we may seek to make the individual abandon one or the other of the statements.

If we fail in all this, we may conclude, in an extreme case, that we have a mad individual on our hands, one who suffers a split personality, is subject to fits of delusion, is schizophrenic. What we do then is radically shift our attitude toward him and begin searching for causes rather than understanding, explaining how the inconsistency came about as a matter of process, and manipulating him toward our ends rather than his.

But what is the difference between these two inconsistent voices we hear coming from the same mouth, and two inconsistent voices we hear coming from two different mouths? What is the difference between what we call schizoid behavior, on the one hand, and what we call disagreement, which we consider quite healthy, on the other? Is not at least part of the difference simply that we perceive the two voices as coming from a single entity rather than multiple entities, that is, that it is the units of reference, which we give to ourselves or which are given to us, that determine whether a given state of affairs is mad, meaningless, and disturbing to us, or challenging, forward-looking, and God's gift to the human taste for novelty?

I SUGGEST THIS on the basis of insights that can be drawn as much from what can be observed in legal thinking as from modern psychological and psychiatric observation and experience. Once a person is viewed as "inside" a corporate entity, requirements of loyalty and coordination are imposed quite different from those imposed on persons still viewed as "outside" the entity. Radically different positions taken by government agencies—the Department of Commerce, the Federal Trade Commission, and the Environmental Protection Agency, for instance—are upsetting to a court so long and only so long as, each time they speak, "the government" or "the United States" is viewed as speaking. Different positions are normal and to be expected when agencies are viewed as entities entrusted by law with the pursuit of different values. There is, I now think, no necessary priority to the drawing of the line around what is within or a part of a legal entity, and what is expected or demanded of those who may fall inside or outside the line that is drawn. The placing or perceiving of a voice as within an entity fosters a demand for consistency and coordination; demand for consistency and coordination fosters the placing or perceiving of a voice as within rather than outside an entity.

Thus wrapping the primary texts of law in a single entity, a Supreme Court, drives us toward consistency. It intensifies the hold, the grip, and the pull of the voices, and draws us into the active, even laborious work of understanding. It is one of the bulwarks we erect against madness. Just as in the case of erecting an image, statue, or idol of a god which, being metal, stone, or paint, does not itself speak—texts, priests, or inner voices communicate what is heard—what we are doing here is putting ourselves in a position to pay attention. We call to ourselves in a way that will make us listen. The poet and the novelist attending to form does the same.

We can still work and hear without erecting the Supreme Court or wrapping the texts upon which we work in a single entity. As we have said, the statements produced by different judges at different times on the federal courts of appeal are similar to the statements produced by different judges at different times on the Supreme Court. The material of legal analysis is similar, and the problems of putting it together and the techniques for doing so do not change, as the legal analyst moves from one set of materials to the other. But without the central entity and what the entity does for us, the results of legal analysis will have less authority: we will pay attention less, work less hard and long, achieve less meaning in what we hear, obey less willingly, pursue the command we think we hear with less imagination and commitment.

THE AFFECTING OF
THOUGHT BY ACTION

The loss to which we have just alluded, which might be expected to be associated with the disappearance of a single, primary, central, focal entity doing work in legal analysis, we may judge to be the most important. We may judge it most important in view of the unfortunate fact of nature, that for human beings there is an ever-present alternative to action, which is passivity in all its degrees, as there is an ever-present alternative to life, which is suicide in its various degrees. Whatever excites and sustains the will and the drive must be most important, in the end. The purely spontaneous springs of action bubble sometimes high, sometimes low, and sometimes not at all—certainly if the fears of hunger, cold, and pain are laid at rest. Even the fear most pertinent to the work of understanding, the fear of meaninglessness, chaos, utter loneliness, and madness, may be insufficient to sustain the level of effort required.

But, if a central unit makes a contribution of this kind, we might then wonder whether a central unit which has become mechanical and without substance might be worse than no central unit at all, might be not just "not there" but instead a persistent impediment, as dead things can be. In light of the danger, it might be thought better as a matter of initial design not to set up a central entity at all. In erecting it we raise the possibility that its form will remain after the life and meaning have gone from it, and the effects of this may prove especially demoralizing, a word which is quite precise, joining as it does the loss of morality and the loss of will.

There is, however, another gain that can be traced from the presence of a central entity whose texts and statements become themselves the primary material for legal analysis. We must remember that the entity itself is doing legal analysis in making statements that become the material for the practice of legal method by others. The gain that is drawn from this is of a somewhat different kind from that we have just discussed. It has to do with the drive to achieve understanding because hope is part of that drive; it may have something to do with the provision to ourselves of means to understanding; but it has most to do with our sense of self-determination.

I T IS A COMMONPLACE that thought and action are difficult to separate, and that what we do can affect the way we think in the same way if not in the same degree as what we think affects what we do.

Fashion—change in thought which is purely habitual—proceeds in this way. We may think ladies wearing enormous pointed shoulder pads look horrendous, but if they do it for a year we may think unexaggerated shoulders puny. A necklace on a man is an effeminate touch one year, but as necklaces spread to the young and from young to old and from football players to fishermen, they become an accoutrement of virility.

Some suppose that morality can proceed in this way. If a society that believes the brutalization of children horrendous begins to allow it and to do it for various reasons, that society may, it is thought, soon find that brutalization of children does not seem so horrendous but rather, as in certain Victorian child-raising practices, natural or morally neutral. If we, now, sense that becoming so hardened would be a misfortune even if those future hardened souls did not know that they were hardened and even if they approved of it (a proposition which I myself find inherently implausible, if only because of the splicing together of generations), then we do well to take into account this reaction-back, of what we do upon the process of deciding what to do, in making particular decisions.

Indeed, this reaction and effect, and the possibility of guiding our moral evolution that it raises, produce the classic dilemma of the cultural or moral relativist, who believes that what is good and what is wrong, what is to be sought and what avoided, is determined entirely by the culture, future, past, or present, in which the decision maker finds himself and by which he is molded: the cultural relativist discovers that he must decide what kind of future culture there is to be, molded as it is in part by the decision he makes in the present.

Now this same connection between thought and action that we can see in fashion and perhaps in morality may be traced in what may be termed more purely intellectual processes (in contrast to habitual processes and the processes of moral judgment). And it is here that there is both an opportunity for a contribution from a central institution and a reason for setting one up and protecting it from disintegration. We are not, we should note, returning to the observation (to which we referred above in discussing the impact of office) that the judgment of a supreme court usually has immediate consequences. Awareness of consequences can sharpen perceptions and supply a sense of urgency to textual work, but this same sharpening of perception is enjoyed by every court and indeed every practicing lawyer on whose judgments of law immediate consequences attend.[1] We are speaking rather of an internal connection between act and thought, and the function of a central institution with respect to that connection.

I F ONE UNDERTAKES to decide whether something is a rock, and one is not allowed direct contact with it—so that one cannot kick it and discover whether one has stubbed one's toe—one takes various factors into account. At the grossest level, one considers its hardness, its heaviness, its glitter, its color, its shape, and so forth (and in packaging each of these factors, so that they can be taken into account as such, one has generally gone through the same process before, in the case of color, for instance, taking into account the various factors that one does take into account in determining color). Rules of inference are associated with the metaphorical weighting that is involved in taking these factors into account. The rules of inference express the weight ordinarily given to a particular factor, given the purpose for which one is making the decision, and are what individuals appeal to in disputes during the making of a decision: "One can infer that a thing is a rock from its brownness often enough for a decision with these purposes and these consequences in these circumstances." Disputes over whether a thing is a rock are disputes over statements of this kind, or over statements of this kind made about the factors taken into account in determining that there is brownness in the first place.

When one is finished, one does not *know* that the thing is a rock. What one *knows* is that one has decided that it is a rock and that disputes have been settled: one knows the rules of inference that have been used, the factors that have been thought relevant and the weights that have been given to those factors (insofar, that is, as one can know such matters with any determinateness, write them down or otherwise record them and draw, from what has been recorded, evidence of what went on in the decision making through appropriate methods of analysis). But nonetheless one assumes that the thing is a rock or not, and that if one could just have direct contact with it, one could test the validity of one's decision.

Deciding a legal question proceeds in very much the same way, but with one important difference:

Suppose the undisputed law provides for employer compensation to the families of those employees who die while acting "within the scope of their employment." A number of factors are taken into account in deciding whether compensation is due—death, employment, and death-causing action "within the scope of employment." As to the last, it has been assumed that, outside slavery, some things an employee does are not done in his role as employee. For instance, kissing his child good-night would not traditionally be action within the scope of his employment. And so a decision must be made, and various factors are taken into account in deciding whether action associated with death is action within the scope of employment.

If a legal analyst looked at prior opinions on the question, he would find such factors as, first, the intent of the employee, whether his object in the action was to advance the employer's purposes; second, the location of the action, whether it was on the employer's premises; third, the time of the action, whether it was during working hours if there were definable working hours; fourth, the mandates and prohibitions of the employer, whether the employer said to do or not to do a particular thing; and so forth through a numbered list the analyst might make. If the legal analyst probed and worked with the material, he might be able to discern and persuade others to agree why a particular factor had come to be relevant and taken into account in deciding scope of employment. If he could not discern why, at least he might be able to discern how, historically, it came to be relevant. And he would draw out also what factors were taken into account in determining the subquestions of just what was the working place of an employer or just what working hours consisted of or just what employers had said or implied by their actions or silences, if those factors themselves were put into dispute.

A case comes along in which an employee of an American firm, working on a construction project in Korea, goes for the weekend to a remote lake in the Korean countryside to get away from it all, decides to build a sand castle on a little island in the middle of the lake, and therefore fills a rowboat with sand and attempts to row out to the island with the gunwales an inch above water. He ships water halfway to the island, the boat sinks, and he drowns. Does the law provide for compensation? What is the law?

An administrative agency applying the law in the first instance awards compensation to the family. In doing so the agency discounts the purpose of the employee, the specific location, and the time of day or week, and, in addition, takes into account various new or apparently new factors, such as the special hazards in the employee's private life arising from the mere fact of employment (for example, the disorienting effects of being required to vacation in a strange and foreign land), and whether the accident was foreseeable in such a way that the employer could take out insurance against it. The majority of one court of appeals disagrees, the majority of another court of appeals agrees that such factors are sufficient and that failing the tests of time, place, and purpose is not sufficient to require a decision that the lethal action is not "within the scope of employment." And a majority of the Supreme Court agrees that the new factors may be taken into account and a decision that action is within the scope of employment may be legally predicated upon them.

If, after the Supreme Court has spoken, the legal analyst looks at the opinions and the dissents and the commentaries on them in the law reviews or in lawyers' briefs in later cases, he will find the questions all still couched in the form *Is the action presented within the scope of employment?* just as he might find arguments over whether something is a rock couched in the form *Is this thing a rock?* Indeed, the questions will both be called "questions of fact," arguments will be couched in terms of the "substantiality" of the supporting "evidence" with various invocations of notions of probability, and dissents will refer angrily to the arbitrariness of a *finding* that the employee was within the scope of his employment without any factual basis whatever for so concluding. These are the fascinating but quite standard terms of discourse about the legality of an administrative decision.

What, however, have the majority and the minorities on the courts, the lawyers on either side, and the commentators commenting on the question as it proceeds from the administrative agency to the courts of appeals to the Supreme Court, what have they all been arguing about? Obviously about whether the action presented is "action within the scope of employment." But they have also been arguing about what action within the scope of employment is. To translate into talk of rocks, they have been arguing not only whether the thing presented is a rock but over what a rock is. And there is only the faintest sense in which it could possibly be said that the definition that emerges is correct or incorrect or that, if one could have direct access to the situation presented, one would know whether it was action within the scope of employment or not. If the Supreme Court's conclusion becomes authoritative, if it is not reversed or eroded by latter decisions of the Court, or ignored or confined to its particular facts by lower courts viewing it in the context of the whole, or resisted by lawyers and their clients (or reversed in short order by the Congress, which would be saying, in effect, that there must be a mistake somewhere), then the definition of "action within the scope of employment," which can be drawn from examining what factors were taken into account or authorized by the Court to be taken into account, *is* what action within the scope of employment *is*. The legal system shakes itself into a new form and responds internally to the conclusions of its own processes.

T HIS FEATURE IS what gives life in the law such a very different feeling from life in any of the organized sciences. At its uncomfortable edge the feeling is akin to that of the man living within the ultimately authoritarian system imagined by Orwell in *Nineteen Eighty-Four* where if the official, beyond whom there was no recourse, said that the four fingers he was holding up were five fingers, those four fingers were five fingers. Where the meanings of words seem most immediately important, where immediate consequences flow from the meanings of words, just there one's individual control over their meaning seems weakest, seems indeed to have been taken away. The words slip and slide away from one, and one is left without the very means of thought and argument, most helpless when most vulnerable. If officials with power over one were to speak in a foreign tongue, or argued among themselves in terms that had meaning only within a symbolic system into which they alone had been initiated, so that one was in the position of a fourteenth-century English peasant listening to law French, or a Greek listening to the arguments of priests looking at the entrails of a sacrificed animal, it might be better. The combination that we have, of a system of authority together with the use of ordinary language, means that one's mind is not one's own.

But the truth is that one's mind is not one's own. Words slip and slide over the surface of reality in any event, and we are always turning away from them to music and dance, gesture, dress, and coiffure. This feature of law, that the definition of a word is openly being determined *at the same time* that a decision whether to use the word is being made, and that there is a method in use for the retrieval of that meaning after the decision has been made, may be seen as one of the strengths of law. As the characterizing of things changes the categories by which they are characterized, the language is being worked upon in an open and at least semi-conscious way. It is in fact this way of working upon language—lay, ordinary language— that sets law apart from other disciplines.

And a formal central point in a legal system facilitates this focus of language and makes possible an even more pointed discourse. Much more is involved in a central point than just the limitation on the number of texts to which one looks, or looks presumptively, that is effected when the Supreme Court is present, created, or preserved. More certainly is involved than just a saving of time and energy—a good that would have to be measured by the good of the other uses to which we would put that saved time. It is no mere dictionary we elect to read. A dictionary cannot hear or speak and is today, in any event, a bureaucratic product unlike the work of Dr. Johnson or James A. H. Murray. A supreme court acts functionally as a focal point for work on language. It is working too, along with everyone else. The introduction and maintenance of a central point is a contribution to such focus. Its loss is a loss of such focus.

How is this focus a good? It enhances the possibility of speaking a common language—commonality of language being in part the product of the constant practice of legal method in daily life. The greater commonality of language that can result may aid our understanding of each other and the world. That at least is what is generally advanced as the reason for work toward a common language.

But work on language has another purpose, in law particularly. We seek some escape from language and control over it. Though we may not often think of ourselves as bound by our language, or attempting through law to achieve some means of control over it, that may be what we are doing: The importance of a central legal institution may be measured by what it adds to the sense of freedom or self-determination we may have.

FOCUS, FREEDOM, AND UNDERSTANDING

We suggested earlier that the part a focal entity plays in sustaining the will and the drive to achieve understanding is the most important. Its provision of a means to freedom and its contribution to freedom helps us, we said, to accept the danger of a dead center that attends the establishment of any center at all. Freedom, as we have approached it, is subordinate.

But freedom can never be kept just a makeweight in our thought. We know any institution that treads close to it treads close to what is immensely important in its own right. We should therefore pursue this aspect of a central point in a new chapter—and not just to flesh out a sense of the relative importance of the gains and losses attributable to a central institution but because the hope of the achievement of freedom, and the will to understand and live, may yet be intertwined.

Is freedom itself really a good? We sometimes have our doubts. How can we answer this? We can ask, Is existence a good? Is living in actuality rather than illusion a good? Is our individuality a good? As we proceed let us at least wonder about the connections between these questions, and whether an answer "yes" to one of them would lead us to answer "yes" to another, including the question of the good of freedom.

W E W I L L C L O S E this chapter on a cautionary note.
   Would understanding of things and of one another be advanced if all variety of language were placed by commonality, between individuals or, more broadly, through a merger of French, and Chinese, and English, and more? Or would understanding be retarded? I do not know. I propose we pursue a connection between commonality and freedom or self-determination as a separate matter of inquiry.

To be sure, all around us connections are made between understanding and freedom. They are found in the promises of Christianity—ye shall know the truth and the truth shall make ye free; in psychoanalysis—understanding and cure are merged; in Jeffersonian democracy—only through public education is the tyranny of the mob transformed into self-governance by the people. If freedom is associated with understanding, and freedom is also associated with commonality of language, one would think that understanding and commonality would be associated, as siblings or cousins are by blood.

But the metaphor may not hold, and logic of a syllogistic kind is never an arbiter on questions of this kind. It does not seem that understanding would be advanced by merging music, art, and gesture into that which is written and spoken, if such a merger were conceivable or possible; the avoidance of all need to translate across individuals, across time, or across ways of expressing, might give us more control but not more understanding. Such doubts lead me to advance as a separate matter a connection between focus in language, facilitated by an institutional structure with a center, and freedom. It is only with great reluctance that I raise and leave the question whether understanding itself would be advanced by commonality of language. Perhaps we will find our answer in exploring somewhat further, as we go along, what we truly mean by understanding. Understanding of a static or frozen kind most certainly would not advance freedom in this rushing world, and too often understanding is understood in this static sense. Understanding is not captured by any closed system or reducible to a demonstration that one has made agreeably appropriate moves within it. What understanding may be in an open system we have yet to approach. We can always speak more confidently about what we know is not so than about what we know is true.

8

TIME

The Achievement of Freedom

C AN THE IMPORTANCE of a hierarchical institutional arrangement be measured even in part by what it adds to our sense of freedom and self-determination? Can this be one of its functions in human society? The very suggestion, that the linguistic aspect of legal hierarchy advances freedom, seems an indulgence in deliberate paradox. But it is not, any more than speaking in the same breath of freedom and authority is itself paradoxical. Why this should be so—why the focus that a single center brings may possibly be associated with freedom—will be our subject in this chapter.

THE SELF-GOVERNANCE MADE POSSIBLE BY TIME

We noted in the last chapter the peculiar helplessness an individual must feel when the meaning of an ordinary word appears to be determined by the way another individual uses it. Such bondage is not lessened by exaltation of the other individual, though, plucked out and set above, he would not be so easily seen when one looked around, and one might more easily think one's situation was like that of all one's fellows and therefore a natural condition.

We have also noted that this is not the situation in legal analysis. The law, the meaning of the words in which the law is cast, is not what "the Supreme Court says it is," except as that phrase is a shorthand reference to the whole set of methods used to decide what one should take into account in making one's own decision on a matter, beginning with the examination of focal texts. We have sought to show why this is so, and how we are saved from the abject foolishness of paying attention to a mechanical voice that is saying nothing or to a voice of the particular moment that cannot be heard to mean what it says and is no more the voice of the Supreme Court than a particular statement of the day is the voice of the friend we have known over the years.

If the presence of a focal point in the legal system did debase us so, as a forelock-tugging serf or slave is debased, then we might well think to eliminate it and work toward that end. Taking a long and evolutionary view, we might consider its elimination part of a mopping-up operation that has been going on in the West ever since the king was beheaded. We might even experiment with intermediate positions, maintaining a supreme authority for purposes of determining action but forbidding it the writing of opinions, so that we would not know, or be tempted to invest with magic significance, the factors taken into account by the supreme authority in deciding as it did, or what *it* thought the law was. We would look instead to the texts produced by numerous authorities horizontally arranged below.

But this debasing and smallness, all that is summed up in the gesture of lowering the eyes, or in the picturing of hierarchical authority as a pyramid before the height of which men's eyes will usually be lowered as they go about the business of living, is not, I think, what we have to fear. Though I fear to say it, if there were no formal central point in the legal system I think we would move to draw one in. For we are all helpless before our language, which comes to us, together with its structure, organizing concepts, and categories, in organized form; and organization is necessary to change it and replace it.

SUCH ORGANIZATION as there is within the confines of the individual will not suffice. The word floats between individuals. Nor will the device of individuals meeting and agreeing or voting do. We are too many. We could never all agree on just what the issue or agenda was, on just what it was we were all discussing or agreeing to. Besides, it is most difficult to believe that all of us could agree to change in any effective way. To look at the living population at any point in time is to see not a group of lives who face the givenness of language on an equal footing, but rather a group who are related to one another somewhat like the strands in the splice of a rope, from the young who are learning to the old who cannot change, and all between are individuals of whom only a small fraction were equipped with language at any one time in the past. In a decision to change achieved by voting, language and all that goes with it would still be given by some to others. Perhaps the bulk of the population would be in a position of receiving rather than giving.

Further, what we would put in place of the language and categories we "have" is, if not inconceivable, bordering on the inconceivable. The ingredients of utopias are mostly familiar; those that are not familiar are vague. The innate conservatism of legislatures with ostensible sovereignty and freedom is far more striking than their capacity to break the bonds of the past, and this should not be surprising, since legislators speak the same language and think in the same terms as lawyers, judges, and citizens.

I⊤ IS, ⊤HEN, legal method or something like legal method, aided by the presence of a central point, that puts us in some control of language however slight, frees us a bit, to at least the possibility of greater self-determination, jointly achieved rather than individually, but achieved.

Of course it may be said that, with regard to self-determination, control of the meaning of language and the modification and change of the categories and concepts embedded in language are quite beside the point. And we may admit that there is a sense, a faint sense, in which the legal decision maker and the scientific decision maker are alike.

The scientist's words are approximations to a world that exists apart; his decisions that a thing is so are theoretically correct or incorrect, even though, because of the lack of direct access, their correctness cannot be tested by comparison of the conclusion with the actual facts. The legal decision maker, we said, is in a different position, despite his use of the language of fact. But it is certainly possible, and often true, that changes in the definition of a legal thing are only semantic. The terms have been rearranged, but the essence persists.

An individual put on trial for the crime of arson after a fire was kindled while he was lighting a candle in a barn, who had read ancient authority as saying that one must have had an intent to set an unlawful fire before one can be found to be an arsonist, might discover that courts were finding arson without even hearing any evidence about what the defendant was seeking to do when he caused the fire, and were declaring that if the defendant knew that striking a match would be dangerous in the circumstances, that would be fully sufficient to establish intent. The individual might protest that he is not an arsonist and did not have intent because he did not seek to set an unlawful fire, that the fire was an accident which occurred while he was lighting the candle. His protestations would fall on deaf ears. He would be heard as if he were speaking a different language or using words idiosyncratically. "You are mistaken," he would be told, "about what intent *is*. The legal meaning of intent for purposes of a conviction of arson is recklessness, or, if you insist on using the word intent in your way, the definition of arson does not require a finding of intent, at least not any more: it requires only a finding of recklessness." And for a fact, intent in the definition of arson may no longer mean purpose, or arson may *no longer* require intent. That is something the defendant or any other individual, including a judge, would find in the records of decision making and the opinions.

But at the same time we might well discover that convictions for arson are no longer treated as they were treated before: the "arsonist" under the newer formulation is seen for what he "is," nothing more than a lighter of matches in risky situations.

Or, to take another example, the responsibilities of directors of business corporations become empty and fictional under Delaware corporate law, but they simultaneously bloom under different rubrics in federal securities law.

Indeed, as we open up and peer into the records in field after field of legal decision making (which is both stated and conceived as a taking into account of factors, making them relevant, giving them degrees of importance), we can immediately perceive that, in a dynamic world, a world of time and decay and feedback and conflict, where decisions are being *made* again and again, what is significant beyond the particular, concrete decision that rapidly recedes into the past is not so much what factors were taken into account and what weights were given to them, as what made the decision maker choose to take those factors into account rather than others, and choose to give them the weight he did. That is what is solid and persistent. That is the law, that is what governs us. And that stands below or outside its product, including its semantic product, as the reality of the scientist, *which neither he nor man before him creates*, stands below or outside what he does. Does it not?

But does anything make us choose? The fact *that* we choose does not demonstrate that we were *made* to choose the one course rather than another, to treat one thing as relevant and another not. That is a theory upon which scientific work is done, but it is not the theory of the law and it ignores, or treats as an epiphenomenon, our experience that things are otherwise. What would *make* us, inexorably, choose to take a factor into account would not have any authority over us in any event. We could fight it and try to master or outmaneuver it, just as the scientist tries to master nature. We do not disappear, or, to say the same thing, there is no shift to what is outside us, when analysis is shifted to a greater level of generality over time or a greater level of particularity in the instant.

When analysis concentrates upon the factors that were taken into account and the weights that were given to factors, the chooser or decider resides at the yet unanalyzed point where factors are put together. The putting of them together seems not at all determined, except as it must be understandable to the rest of us who will be called upon by the decision, and thus the rest of us will confine the possible puttings together to something like a range of alternatives so that we ourselves, jointly, determine the outcome. But we can shift our analysis to the next level, which can be described in parallel fashion (albeit with a bit of tongue twisting) as analysis of the factors that were taken into account in choosing the factors, the weights given to those, and the factors taken into account in choosing the weights, and the weights given to *those* factors. We might thus, after the manner of statistics, eliminate the mysterious, particular, present, in-time point of putting the factors together at the previous level, wash out those points, so to speak.

But we would find that *we* were still there at the second level, choosing and deciding upon factors and weights, even if perhaps more semi-consciously and thus apparently more automatically. Analysis could then shift to a third and similar level, and to level after level ad infinitum; but it would not eliminate the presence of a chooser and a decider, of *us,* or be removed outside the chooser and decider, unless we choose outsideness or the elimination of a chooser and decider as a premise of thinking and analysis, which is what the cast of mind called scientific does. Useful in science, that would not be useful here, for it would not produce power and understanding, but rather disintegration and failure of the will.

What we are actually brought to as we move to deeper levels of analysis, or to levels of greater and greater generality, as if we were following a system of roots, is that which has been chosen jointly. The reason preliminary legal analysis does not generally move past one or two levels of choosing, and into increasingly elaborate metaphorical descriptions of choice as "taking factors into account," is that at the deeper levels we in fact agree or at least agree not to disagree. (I say agree *or* agree not to disagree because we cannot disagree on everything at once and expect to move forward in any direction.) The appropriateness of the factors, the weights, the desires, the values, is not challenged. The level at which we stop is the level where challenge is no longer heard.

The satisfying wholenesses to which we move have a character different from the matter, energy, waves, corpuscles, fields, quarks, and baryons to which physical scientists have reduced, or elevated, the immediacies of present experience. We agree partly because we have substance. We do believe, and our belief makes us who we are, gives us our content, gives us a sense of being rather than of nothingness.

We also disagree, which makes each of us wonder whether we actually believe what we believe, and introduces skepticism. Some find skepticism corrosive and grounds for despair. To the lawyer and those using any of the family of methods of which the lawyer's is one, disagreement and the question whether one actually believes what one believes can be galvaniz-ing. It pushes one on. A search in the texts is, after all, a search for what one believes oneself, now, in the present. Skepticism and the presence of disagreement animate the design and building of legal institutions, that are not merely to resolve particular disputes and prevent violence (the grossest form of disintegration and cause of the most obvious form of death), but are actually to change what one half believes into what one actually believes, embraces, and says, Yes, that is me, that is who I am, that is my identity, I now have an identity, I have substance, I am at one with myself.

And freedom, as Hegel pointed out at length and others have dis-covered over and over again on their own, is not a state of emptiness.[1]

THE AUTHORITY OF THE DEFINING VALUE

Exploring what economists may have in mind in speaking of freedom, Frank Knight defines the sense of freedom as acceptance of the restraints one faces. It is possible, for instance, not to feel one's freedom threatened by being unable to have a fur coat in a store window, because one accepts the restraint that a limited budget and the requirement of purchase places upon one. But Knight's definition trips over itself in speaking of accep-tance of restraint. What one truly accepts is no restraint. The problem is that one does not truly and fully accept what one believes, one's goals, objects, and values; and what is half-accepted and half-believed is half-restraining. One's goals and values, what one seeks, are what one is. In any attempt to define an individual, it is by his goals and values that he is personified and characterized. But those goals and values conflict. Thus as events unfold we find ourselves unfulfilled and ask, "Did we really want this?" We find that we defeat ourselves, and we therefore become wary of ourselves and to this extent step outside ourselves, critical of the very goals that give meaning to our lives.

Some of this conflict is sought to be resolved legislatively, a phe-nomenon we will touch upon in the next chapter. But as we have just noted, legislators reflect more than they affect the values with which they work. Insofar as the acceptability of what we accept and the freedom that goes with it is a matter of changing the defining value or goal itself, we need to proceed in an additional way. It is this additional way that a legal system with a center, a central speaking entity, provides. This is a way to freedom in fact, freedom through advancement of the acceptability of who we are and what we seek, by working toward the integration that may be possible only with change in the very meaning and definition of the values themselves. Instead of freedom, we can say self-determination, that is, determination by a self which one accepts as truly oneself, and is not resisting as something still outside oneself.

NEED IT BE SAID that we do not have to obey even ourselves? The great defect in so much systematic analysis outside law is that it begins with men's wants, whereas there is a question for men what their wants really are. We obey ourselves willingly if what we want, or think we want, has authority for us. We do so willingly and with good heart if we think it right. If, on the other hand, we are in doubt about this, or secretly know that it is not right, we often resist ourselves, defeat ourselves, or act slowly and reluctantly, waiting to be overtaken by events or rescued by consequences and reactions.

An individual may begin by using his behavior, viewed from the outside, as evidence of what he wants and what he is. Asking what he wants, and looking at his behavior and its consequences over time, he may be tempted to conclude that what he really wants is there to be seen in the consequences of his behavior.

But if he becomes fully aware of his behavior and its effects, he is put in a position to make a choice. He may say, "Yes, that is me, I will accept that, I will not seek to change that"; or he may say, "No, I do not accept that, I will struggle against it, I will try to stay aware of it and to change my behavior and its consequences."

In the latter course he may or may not be successful. It may take action and change by others with him to be successful. But there is at least a possibility he may be successful. Grace and redemption, psychiatric insight, strength of character—however it may be called—this possibility is what perpetuates the memory of the great counselors East and West whose precept was Know Thyself. Insofar as art is didactic, this is the teaching of the nineteenth-century novel, the ancient tragic play. Whatever he *is*, *he* can yet criticize. *He* is not at one with what he *is*—unless, of course, *he* accepts it.

If he accepts it, as he may for a time, even a very long time, he becomes one of those people who are at peace. He has a special reality for others, and seems to look out far more than in. If he does not accept it, he struggles, however quietly, and loses to that degree reality in the eyes of others as well as a sense of his own reality. But in either case what he is is not *necessarily* what he is. There is always a person, the referent of the pronoun in discourse, behind the person that is defined by his present wants. Disintegrated, *he* does not willingly accept what he sees and hears himself say and do (though he is forced to acknowledge it because it *is* his speech and action). Even during those periods in which he accepts himself and thus fuses what he does with what he wants and what has meaning and coherence for him, there are still two, the one that wants, and the one that can criticize what is wanted and ask the question whether that is what *he* really wants.

THE AUTHORITY OF THE
STRUCTURE OF THOUGHT

There is a second way in which freedom is advanced by enhancing the organization of joint work on our language. Our goals govern and we may wish, separating ourselves somewhat from them, to govern those goals. But we are also limited and determined in our choices by a structure of thinking embedded in the language which makes thinking together possible. A structure of thought is distinguishable from the goals of thought. A structure is not so animating, so pulling and glowing and unquestionably identified with us. It is the framework for thought, and I do not suppose most of us feel as identified with our skeletons as with the more living parts of our body. Indeed, the skeleton is what remains after we are gone.

Often there is no disagreement about the structure of thinking. If there is a difference in the degree of conscious awareness of structure and object, I should think we were less conscious of structure. But sometimes there is disagreement, expressed variously as disagreement over what the structure of thought is or what the structure of thought ought to be, and often choices must be made on matters affecting structure. Here, particularly, a means of working on the language through a center is helpful.

THE CORPORATION, for instance, is part of our thinking, an organizer of thought, a standard unit of reference. Statements that a business corporation is reducible to and is nothing more than a shorthand term to refer to a group of individual people called shareholders trying to do business together are the wishful thinking of those who regret that the structure of our thinking is as complex and ambiguous as it is: such statements do not reflect the law that is alive in either the texts or the minds of social actors. If one did not know at all what a corporation was and settled down to listen over some period of time to those making such statements, one would draw the meaning of the term "corporation" from the whole of what they said, and the listener would find, in the whole of what they said, innumerable pointers away from the simple reduction or identification of the business corporation with shareholders.

Nonetheless, business corporations are associated with shareholders in a special way, and shareholders stand in contrast to bondholders or to employees. Anyone who said in the 1980s that shareholders are no more connected to the corporation than employees or bondholders also would be engaged in wishful thinking.

It is possible, however, to affect this connection, to weaken it, or strengthen it, and thus reach the structure of our thinking, by taking that object into account, as a factor, in making particular decisions. For example, there is a perennial question whether taxation of the income of a corporation is to be followed by taxation of income received by a shareholder from the corporation. The question can arise as an administrative matter before the Internal Revenue Service, or as a judicial matter in interpreting the Revenue Code, or within the legislature. Is corporate income to be "attributed" to shareholders when it is received by the corporation, as if shareholders were partners? Or are shareholders to be viewed as separate entities with respect to the income they receive, as banks receiving interest on the money they have put into the corporation are entities separate from it, or suppliers are separate in receiving income from the corporation paying them for supplies of assets other than money? In responding to the question, the difficulties of treating matters such as corporate tax preferences (deductions, exclusions from income, credits against tax owed) or multinational transactions subject to more than one tax code might in the end be determinative. Analysis would certainly proceed through detailed consideration of all the distributional effects of any proposed change or interpretation of tax law. But the problems that each effect posed would be as much structural as distributional. And if attribution of corporate income to shareholders were allowed, it would certainly strengthen the connection between the corporation and the shareholder.

Taxing shareholders *as if* they were partners would not mean that they *were* partners, but in the context of all that is said and done about the corporation, the separateness of the corporation, and the presence of a unit of reference different from the shareholders connected to it, would be diminished. Denying attribution and maintaining so-called double taxation (a widely used and revealingly ambiguous term) would be a move in the opposite direction. Recognizing, under the First Amendment of the federal constitution, the speech of business corporations on political and public issues as speech which is not by or on behalf of shareholders is another such move in the opposite direction, a move, that is, with the opposite effect, as is the recognition of what is called "successor liability" of corporations associated with the originally liable corporation through connections that do not involve share transfer, common ownership, or contract with respect to the liability.

THERE MAY BE strong pressure from some legal analysts, particularly those who call themselves pragmatists or functionalists, not to take into account any such effect as the one we have just described. They may urge that it not be addressed or given weight negative or positive. Such functionalists simply abstract out the function of working on the conceptual system—indeed, often in denying the existence of a conceptual system they are all the more slaves to it. Such pragmatists are not pragmatic about the conceptual consequences of what they do. No doubt both pragmatists and functionalists want to think themselves freer than they are.

What they do is to treat each problem as if it were discrete—and this is much taught to students in law schools even today—and seek to settle it on its own terms. The meaning of "corporation," they say, is entirely the function of the specific purpose for which one is using the term. There is no spillover into other specific situations where one uses the term, unless one is careless.

But the organizing terms of sentences and statements simply do not stay empty of meaning. Many lawyers are conscious, for example, of how the notion of conspiracy that developed in criminal antitrust has been carried over into other areas of the criminal law. The thrust of the legal method involved in working with texts is organization and integration, and however carefully the context of use of a term is examined and however sensitive the analyst is to the special meaning the utterer may have in mind in using it, the premise upon which analysis proceeds, that integration is possible, is not abandoned. Nor would it be true to the utterer's mind to treat a term as totally conclusory; it was not a cipher for him when he used it, and when he was young he looked back to see how it was used while building up for himself a sense of its meaning and when he might use it.

What we meet here is not just the phenomenon of the legal fiction. It is possible that a language system is self-adjusting and there are really no such things as fictions in it. And the term "fiction" implies too readily that there is an authoritative and unchanging definition of what a term really means, against which a particular usage can be compared to determine whether it is fictional or not. But there is no such authoritative definition. The definition of a term is continuously being built up and evolving.

How often it is that resistance to perception of conceptual problems is associated with the absence of the historical sense and the sense of the interconnectedness of things over time! Those who consider themselves most free to approach a problem afresh and solve it "on its own terms" or "on its own facts" can always be shown to have any number of hidden axioms in their thinking, which they accept unthinkingly and unquestioningly, as givens. They often also profess to be relativists, and like all relativists they trip upon the fact that present decisions, on the basis of what is and what is given in the present, change what is and what is to be and what is given in the future. It is the historical sense, the awareness of change and process, including change in the animating values and the basic structure of thinking, that makes passive acceptance of what is, subjection to what is, detachment from what is, a nearly impossible stance. A sense of the crumbling of the present and of development over time does not put life outside us and make us pawns, the acted upon rather than the actors. It need not result in a loss of the sense of the present itself, the loss of loves that are real loves and values that animate the will of the believer because they have present substance he can embrace. The world is the way it is because of the cumulative effects of decisions made by individuals in the past; and so are men's minds the way they are.

So, to return to the corporation, the question arises whether, under the federal constitutional guarantee of jury trial, shareholders may have a jury trial when they bring what in American law is called a "derivative suit" (that is, a suit on a corporate claim) for negligence against the current managers of the corporation. The constitutional guarantee of jury trial applies to issues that would have been "legal" rather than "equitable" when that distinction was alive in the law. The decision made is made in light of its "consequences," which are surrogates for the values relevant to the decider and to the identity of the decider. The texts are searched for help. The issue is sharpened. When a shareholder brings an action on behalf of the corporation against its managers, is he appearing as a beneficiary suing his own trustees ("in equity") or does he appear as the representative, not of himself but of an entity quite separate from himself, which has interests not reducible to his and which would bring, or would have brought, its suit in a court "of law"? A decision in favor of jury trial, entailing a statement that the claim is the corporation's against some who have made themselves outsiders in harming it and is not a claim of the shareholder against persons acting as trustees for *him,* is a move that weakens the connection between shareholders and corporations. In fact the Supreme Court made such a move in 1970, deciding that the claim was the entity's and the suit was "at law," since it was for the tort of negligence. Instance after instance of moves of this kind may eventually have the effect of severing the connection, although there would remain much done and much said that could be understood only on the assumption of such a connection—contrary evidence of what we think, evidence of prior conflict.

A DECISION MADE truly taking into account its consequences would take into account its conceptual consequences.

But it should be evident that decisions made without taking into account their effect upon the underlying structure of thought may have the same effect as decisions that are more self-conscious. The way one thinks is determined with or without the intervention of the self. In fact, one can decide to take a step one knows will have an effect opposite from that which one would like upon the underlying structure of thought. And to this degree we are indeed in the hands of history, and must rely upon continuous textual analysis of a historical kind to identify those parts of a structure that just grew, mindlessly, and distinguish them from those parts that are of human making or that were weeded, tended, clipped, and, if not wholly of human making, at least bear the shape and pattern of human cultivation.

And for any part of structure, of course, there is still the question of acceptance. What is of human making is not necessarily of our making. Generation splicing can take us only so far. We may not like what our forebears wrought, even if they intended and desired it (adolescents do not like it *if* it was intended for them). But we can wonder whether what was intended for us is not more in some sense us, more us certainly than our genetic predispositions, which we fight and change and do not really consider to be us unless, as with any other objets trouvés, we like them and decide to keep them. Generally the objet trouvé is less satisfying than the work of art.[2]

THE JOKES PLAYED BY TIME

How then does a supreme court increase the possibility that structure can be self-determined and the objects of striving more acceptable to us who seek them, and thus increase our freedom? It does so through organization. As it makes its contribution it raises the danger of authoritarianism. But turn the pyramid of hierarchy on its side, or float up and look down on it from above. Put aside lowness, remoteness, inferiority, and obedience for obedience's sake, that are suggested by a pyramid standing on a plain. They are not necessary. On its side the pyramid is a sketch of focus. Viewed from above, its high point is a center.

The formation, maintenance, or change of values and structures proceeds by incremental steps. This is reflected in the organization of legal thinking into cases (though surely the maintenance of that peculiar form of organization is also a function of the desire, consonant with the desire for authority, and opposed to authoritarianism, to have eyes for the speaker to look into, and thus make caring easier and responsibility more unavoidable). The legal case is an amalgam of general statement of law and particular decision, but, as we have seen, even a general statement of law, so long as it is uttered by an entity that has made statements before and will make statements after, is, no matter how general and how assertive, still only an incremental step.

It is necessary to move by incremental steps. It would be necessary even if one were the only individual in the world. All particulars are incremental. The present, full in itself, is yet an increment. This, the situation that would be faced by an individual if he were the only individual in the world, is compounded by the fact that there are many individuals. The situation faced by thinking man every day is thus rather like the situation faced by acting man in a revolution. To be free at all of what has been, individuals must act together, lest individual decisions be cancelled out by one another or so slow in having an effect that they are swallowed up by time, and the outcome of action is what no one sought, no one predicted, and no one really wants.

Delay transforms the intended effect into an unintended effect, and makes what one thinks to be the consequence of what one has chosen to do and in light of which one has chosen to do it into something quite different. When a central agency is set up to decide what factors to take into account in making a particular decision, and to provide a focal set of decisions and records of decisions for inquiries into what the structure of thinking is and what the substance of our actual values are, the problem of delay is at least reduced. To speak pictorially, the addition is not of a grain of sand but of a great boulder onto what may become a levee.

Not separate from this is the fact that the issue is sharpened and individuals can thus talk to one another about the same thing, speak *to* one another, to greater degree. Dialogue in law is commonly conceived of as between two adversaries arguing before a court. But in the production of meaningful statements of law the dialogue is between the speaking entity and those arguing to it, the court on the one side and those represented before it on the other; and between those two sides there is no adversariness.

The sharpening of an issue is itself an organizing event. The issue can be sharpened because so few are talking. There is one running conversation, between, in some sense, the same people, rather than a number of conversations among different people. It is possible therefore to stay in more control of what is said, to reach it and recall it for comparison, to hold off saying what matters about one thing until one has finished talking about the other. "This was said here. That was said there. What do we do now?"—and what was said *there* is not being unsaid while consideration of what to do now goes forward. Indeed, the proper metaphor might be writing rather than conversing. It is possible for an author to make his use of words more consistent in a book and to shade his words more effectively than in his daily conversation, though he be the same person speaking, because the book is organized.[3]

THE PROTECTIONS AFFORDED BY TIME

All very well, it may be said: So the actions of individuals do not have enough of an effect upon the structure of thought or the formation of value to produce an intended effect. So organization enhances the possibility that the action of individuals will have such intended effects. Why is this not the creation of power rather than freedom? Is not a centrally orga-nized, focused system of legal decision making simply one where, because of convention and the presumption of authority, the decisions of a few—litigators and justices—will have an effect? There is connection only to their own freedom, not the freedom of all.

B UT JUST AS their minds are not their own, neither is this freedom. It is only possible, really, to think of making this effect (of what one does and says upon the structure of one's thought) a factor to be taken into account in deciding what to do and say, if the "one" in the thought is an entity stretching over much time. The effect is realized when those using a term or concept look back to see how it has been used—what the concept *is*, as we say—in their continuous effort to make sense of what they say and do. The court, as one thing in time, can look back upon what it has said and done to discover the meanings of the terms it uses, and thus this freedom is its own in the sense that the freedom of one individual is not the freedom of another—not that other's own. But an individual, *including a justice and a litigator,* must look back at what other individuals have said and done.

Individuals now can only seek freedom, from what is now given, for the minds of individuals later, and individuals later will be seeking to free the minds of those who come after them. If the freedom is in the form of greater acceptability of what they are—what moves them and what they seek for its own sake—that freedom will be felt by individuals then living. If freedom is in escape from the structure of the minds of those that came before, then it lies in the difference between being bound and limited by structures in part designed and intended by persons with human purposes with which one can perhaps identify, and being bound and limited by structures that have evolved on their own.

Some might say they prefer to be in the hands of fate. Insofar as they do prefer fate they despair. Since they do not know what would have evolved without the designing hand, they have no way to compare the acceptability of what they have and no reason to think they would like the alternative better. They simply do not like the intentions of those that came before them, they do not like themselves, they are split off, separated from what might be their substance, and alone.

THAT THOSE WORKING at the central point of a centralized institutional arrangement must act as representatives and trustees does not put any special strain upon their goodness, or deliver other individuals into the hands of the inevitably weak and corruptible any more than usual. A vast number of decisions taken by private or public decision makers are for the sake of and will affect people who are not here now. When lawyers sit down and seriously consider procedures to improve participation in the making of decisions by those who are affected by them and who might be able to trace for the decision maker the subtly resulting and unintended fall-out effects of a proposal, it is discovered how infrequently such persons can be directly heard, not to mention bargained with. A building, a road, a program of insurance or medical care, a new curriculum, a new automobile, all take time to create. They are experienced by individuals who have moved into a town and did not reside there at the time the decision was made; by consumers who were not then in the market; by employees who were not then employed; by those once young who did not need insurance when they were young and the decision was made. If those individuals are represented and heard at all, they must be represented by others speaking on their behalf. It is not just unwieldiness that prevents the participation of all those affected in the decisions affecting them. Typically they do not exist, for they dwell in the future. If they do exist, it is through those entities, defined by their substantive purpose, with which individuals today identify themselves and seek to realize one or another valued end.

THERE IS, MOREOVER, a check in the method lawyers use. The authority of what is said, as opposed to what is done, such as hitting with a club, rests heavily upon the presupposition that what has been said and is being looked to for guidance has been said honestly and with belief, and is not the product of manipulators with private ends and hidden purposes. There is a connection that lawyers know well, part of the structure of our thinking now, between trusteeship and disclosure, between inclusion or membership within an entity or organization (as opposed to being treated as an outsider) and the experience of openness. Each suggests and presses toward the other, as two sides of one thing lead to each other, and it is the presence of openness that is continuously tested by legal method as it searches for an understandable, consistent, and authentic statement of law.

There is protection also in the incremental quality of a court's work, even that of a central court.

Again, this is not a matter of *self*-restraint, entirely or even in large part. A new justice added to the Court who wrote idiosyncratically and without the use of legal method might be ignored to that degree. We need only push in our imagination the degree of idiosyncracy to see the connection between authority and being understood. A very idiosyncratic justice would simply be filtered out in the hearing of the whole that had been said over time, filtered out as static or coughs or the explosions of those who say odd things when they are "not themselves" are filtered out as we go about deciding what they are really saying or really want us to do and be.

Similarly, if a sitting court came out with a decision that stated, "We will no longer reason from the nation-state in international law," or "Human dignity is no concern of ours since it cannot be found in the words of the text of the Constitution," and that decision was not one to which any previous steps had led, three hundred thousand American lawyers would not immediately move to wipe the nation-state from their minds or cease being concerned in any professional way with human dignity. They couldn't. They would be at risk. The statement would take its place among all those statements being looked to. It would aid in sharpening issues to be discussed. It would be tested. It would have its effect, but what effect it had would depend upon later decisions made. When one's foot slips on a slope, one can choose to go the way one has slipped, or to pull back. One may or may not be successful, but so long as one has not fallen, the outcome is not predetermined. The step taken through the medium of a central agency may be large enough to have an effect, and its effect may be felt quickly enough so that it will not be canceled out by chance events following; but it is still small enough to be tentative and tested.

Indeed, it may be that all operations upon the mechanism of the mind and its animating substance must be taken in small steps, out of the corner of the eye so to speak. One's attention, one's imagination, ingenuity, resourcefulness, all one's affirmative qualities are governed and evoked by what one seeks. One definite thing may be transformed into another definite thing by imperceptible degrees, but if it is blurred too much along the way we may cease the striving that is necessary to achieve any value of any description, just as if the structure or mechanism of our thought were dismantled too much at once, we might be expected to stop thinking. It is us, after all, who are being worked on, not some object outside ourselves whose activity we can shut down while we work on it.

Finally, though we may disagree with our representatives in particulars and believe that what they seek is not what we seek—so that, insofar as we as individuals experience over our lifetimes the effects of what they do and say with the intention of affecting the structure and content of thought and action, we are subject to their power, as those coming after us are subject to ours—we all seek meaning, over and above any particular. It is not too different to say that we want to like ourselves and cannot so long as we are at odds with ourselves. The army officer barking orders during the day comes home at night. The farmer loves the land he exploits. The employee is a consumer. As individuals we are never one of these particulars alone. We are many of them together, and how they can be realized together, thus giving us a character and an identity we can like and call our own, is of greater importance to us than whether any one of them is realized in its current form. That is what legal analysis is for, seeking to put our identities together as we individually cannot, and to change them if they cannot fit. We look to the law to take on a human face that we can recognize. It is not the only mirror there is, but it is one of them.

The Rational and the Legal

What is called reason and what has historically been defined as rationality do not sum up and exhaust the law, and we can now, I think, perceive why.

There is a dark side to the great exemplars of rationalism in our recent intellectual history, not often seen, but there to be seen, precisely because their greatness makes them candid. John Dewey defined deliberation as consisting in "selecting some foreseen consequence to serve as a stimulus to present action." But the selected consequences that are foreseen and utilized

> mark out a little island in an infinite sea. This limitation would be fatal were the proper function of ends anything else than to liberate and guide present action out of its perplexities and confusions. But this service constitutes the sole meaning of aims and purposes. Hence their slight extent in comparison with ignored and unforeseen consequences is of no import in itself.

There is no hope in this. It is a vision of drift and meaninglessness. Human ends and purposes are tricks, like the incentives designed by the time and motion engineer in a factory to keep the hands going. Keeping going is the only true end. The journey is from perplexity to perplexity. So too with Frank Knight: In discussing whether the presuppositions of any social planning were plausible, he hinted darkly, "Such inquiries should not be pushed too far, *even in one's private thinking,* to say nothing of a public oral address."

The darkness tells. The rationalism and the radical individualism of our immediate past were intimately associated. The polishing of the methods of calculation necessitated replacing the individual with an integer and rejection of entities beyond the individual, and, with them, the integration and cohesion over time effected through and by those entities. The tools of calculation are not used by those entities; such tools are not appropriate to the task of putting together human experience.

Legal analysis never rejected entities beyond the individual and never substituted the methods of the rationalist and the individualist for its own distinctive method. It did not lose sight of its task.

Nonetheless, though individualism never reached the heart of law, law has been affected by it and may be indebted to it. Individualism may have done its work in the classical way, eliminating its opposite, which is paternalism, treating adults like children, or, worse, as recipients only, not considering them sources and participants as even children can be. It may have been individualism that turned the pyramid on its side and made it a sketch of focus, a glass to see through, a trumpet horn to hear and speak through. Individualism we may eventually acknowledge as having done much to make the voice of law audible and the prospect of justice visible, despite its alien reach for law's heart.

INDIVIDUALITY REMAINS. This is the other reason law and rationality, rationality even of a kind conceived by men before and after the sway of rationalism, are not the same. Dogmatic individualism and rationalism are historical phenomena, historically defined. Individuality is always with us—and legal thinking is always struggling with what seems a conflict at its very root, in that law itself seems hostile to individuality; but we who state and obey the law are individuals, each unique.

That we are each unique is not peculiar to us. Our uniqueness seems to be equaled in the uniqueness of snowflakes. But the fact is presumably not troubling to a snowflake. What it does to us is bring us back again and again from our generalizations and categorizations, indeed, from objectivity itself. Of course we are troubled when this happens.

Yet in our lives we are not nearly so troubled as in our thinking, and we know why. What recognition of individuality brings us back *from* is our categorizations, but what it brings us back *to* is not the equivalent of a snowflake but ourselves: and, in the West, to a movement forward that emerges from this very fact of uniqueness.

The world is not necessarily different for each of us, but we are each different, and the world is as we see it. It cannot be otherwise. One would not say to another, "The world is as you see it and not as I see it." One just would not, one could not truly. The world is as one sees it.

We also know, however, that we are alike, and not just as our fingerprints are alike though they are each of them unique in their billions and their trillions over the ages. We are more alike than these. We have a further avenue of knowledge of each other, beyond the observation of mute objects that produces categorizations haunted by the constant threat of their disappearance to reveal each unique thing as it really is. In life we discover an alikeness of spirit, that we are alike in what we seek.

This likeness, that points forward and pulls us on, does not raise the ordinary tension between the particular and the general, so defeating and such a source of our frequent sense that we must live in a degree of necessary illusion. The world of our hopes is a world into which over time we mean actually to transform the world as it is. The world as it is may indeed be a world fractured by each unique vantage point, but it is one whose fractures do not matter so much because it is not all there is. The disintegrated world's differences are as if they were already half in the past. We are each in a position to look back at them in mind from the point of consummation.

It is this activity, this purposefulness, that saves us from knowledge that is wholly relative to each. Our knowledge is not the knowledge of observers only, who oscillate between seeing likeness and difference. What we think about and know is not just the world as it is. In fact, the world as it is moves and changes each instant for each of us. What we know, to a great degree, is the world as it will be when it becomes what we want it to be.

Complete relativity of knowledge is aloneness, madness, each of us living in a different world. We do not take complete relativity seriously. We cannot, we do not. We do not believe in it. We only play with the idea.

We may wonder of course whether we have to delude ourselves in order to think of ourselves as only playing with the notion that we live in separate worlds.

We do not so delude ourselves; we may at least believe that we do not, for we certainly do not have to deny ourselves as individuals, eliminate ourselves as we are, to escape relativity. The world that becomes, as a result of our joint activity toward common purposes, cannot exist without us, us as we are, each unique. It becomes by reason of the connections between us, our mutual reaching, and not by virtue of a trick, eliminating us—that trick, the means of our seeing the category of the thing or a generalization, which is forgetting through a true act of willful self-deception that each thing and each perception of it is unique.

We are thus not substitutable, fungible, replaceable, and so in ourselves worth nothing and as ourselves hardly there at all, like a slave, or a farm or factory hand toiling in sight of a reserve army of the unemployed. It takes a trick to think even that we are fungible over time, like cells in a body, though we are indeed all of us replaced through death. Individuals in the future are not a reserve army waiting to take our places. Because we must act to create, and because what we create is not, like a postulated body into which and out of which cells move over time, static in time, but is itself being created by us in a particular and often remembered history, there is no substitution for us. We are never replaced by another just like us either now or coming after us later, and we can never be simply ignored.

And so there is no *necessary* hostility between legal thinking and individuality, as there is between legal thinking and individualism. There is only a difficulty, and a difficulty, moreover, in which lawyers can be helped. Uniqueness (like death) remains a point of which we must take account in legal thinking and thinking about law. In fact, almost by itself, in the way it operates upon our life, our uniqueness prevents law from ever being objective and cold and from ever being static. To acknowledge our individuality while still speaking to each other and reasoning in general terms, we are very nearly forced to move toward great ends. Change is necessarily part of law that is not illusion.

You hear the view that law in some way stays the same unless it is changed by the legislative game, else it is not law. This is wholly without foundation, as is its variant, that law changes only in response to change in the brute world of facts and circumstances. Law moves forward, else it is not law. It could not be known otherwise, for it would dissolve into the fractured world. Law has an inner dynamic, born of its very realism, its axiomatic concern with the actual. In Christian and Jewish theology this movement forward is called eschatology. In law it is usually called working toward justice.

Would it have been better if the Tower of Babel had been finished? Would it have been heaven then that we reached, or would heaven have flown on? As it was, we are told every individual's language was made different, and we were stopped from building a solid structure then and there. We know we were given individuality, time, change, and death. We do not know whether, in that, we were also given the possibility of meaning and understanding.

9
ILLUSION
The Mysterious Example of the Legislature

WE HAVE BEEN following the losses that may be expected to attend the loss of the one voice set up to be singled out from among the many speaking, in order to perceive the gains from setting up a single voice. In using the United States Supreme Court as an example of such a single voice, we have done no more than to take seriously what we say and lawyers say in referring to that entity. *The* Court, we say. *This* Court holds today, *this* Court decided fifty years ago, say lawyers writing in the Court's name.

We should now attend to two basic objections that can be made. It may be objected that the loss of the focal voice in question, the voice of the Supreme Court, would not actually be the loss of a single voice at all. We have postponed consideration of this objection in order to make us listen to ourselves. If we want to understand ourselves we must listen to what we say. But now we must turn to the objection, and state it: The Supreme Court is an institution, is it not? Even without its budding bureaucracy and elaborate procedures, it consists of nine individuals, not one. When we look at it, do we sense it as a point of light? Is it not transparent? We see its processes within, as if we were looking into a living cell, or through the door of a washing machine. In fact, other than the Pharoah, the Roman or the Holy Roman Emperor, the Czar and a few kings of the sort that were beheaded, has there ever been a single human voice at the center of a secular legal system of any size and complexity? Even Pharoah, Czar, and Emperor were for the most part figureheads who mouthed what was produced elsewhere for them to say. Is it not true that, even at its best, the Supreme Court never did produce statements that were anything more than the outcome of a process? An authentic focal voice is a dream.

Then there is an objection companion to this, that we do quite well with processes in any event. At its worst, the institution of the Supreme Court could not be any more obviously a process than the institution of the legislature. The legislature's statements are the mere outcomes of a process, yet they surely have authority, some would say the most authority.

THE SINGLE VOICE OF
SEVERAL INDIVIDUALS

Let us address the first objection before the second, for the second is the more serious. The first objection may occur to any of us. The response to it is that it arises from a misperception of the question, though a misperception to which any of us can fall prey.

WHETHER THERE IS an authentic single voice is not the same as the question whether there is a single individual speaking. What is important is not the representation of a speaker, which could be an idol or a statue, but the voice itself; not a speaker given to the listener but a speaker personified by the listener. In question is the presupposition of mind necessary for the very doing of legal analysis and therefore for the making of statements of law, for the very production, the existence of law. The fact that the Supreme Court consists of nine individuals rather than one does not make the presupposition of mind impossible.

We have noted indeed that the nineness of the Court may give its statements an edge over the statements of other courts, at least as presumptive or focal statements. Placing a continuing task of public importance in the hands of more than one individual and instructing them to act jointly has always been a standard protection against tyranny. Several speaking jointly may be more consistent than one speaking alone; individuals can be expected to have spells and lapses, and individuals doing difficult tasks with awful consequences need especially to be supported. Furthermore, an individual who discusses what he believes may know himself better, may speak more of what he actually believes, than an individual who does not discuss.

BUT TO ANSWER that the question is the voice and that a multi-member institution can have a single voice, we must assume that there *is* discussion and that statements made jointly *are* in fact joint and express the actual belief of all whose names are affixed to them. Answering thus assumes particularly that the statement is not merely the product of negotiation and compromise, or so much the product of negotiation and compromise that, when the parts so produced are filtered out by techniques of analysis, there will be very little left (these techniques being literary, or, what may be more congenial to the late twentieth-century ear, psychiatric, designed to isolate what is out of place, dead, and product of conflict, from what the individual actually means to say).

Now negotiation and compromise may have a special meaning in the context of preparing a joint statement.

It is negotiation and compromise in its ordinary modern sense that must be assumed not to be involved or to be so much involved that the statement will be filtered away. This is, of course, whatever can be analogized to the trading on quantity, price, time of payment, time of delivery, and so forth in the exchange of oil or grain in a bazaar, or to the dividing up of food and water between nations when each nation would really rather have both all the food and all the water and others to have none.

The exchange of qualifications, on the other hand—"I will qualify this though I believe it to be unqualifiably true, if you will qualify that even though you believe that to be unqualifiably true"; the dropping of connections between ideas which one individual sees but the other does not; beginning one stage of analysis with an approach favored by one individual and beginning the next stage with an approach favored by another individual: these may well be so different as not to be analogous. The jointly produced product of the three or the nine on a multi-member court is after all a thing written. In producing a thing written, even an author who is a single individual will put in a sentence here, take out a sentence there, in short *work* on it. It is no spontaneous outpouring. The author is in different moods as he works, and is of course at different ages. A piece may take years to write; the beginning may have been written at the end when the author was much older than he was when he wrote the conclusion. It may be that different individuals in different moods and of different ages can work on a piece of writing and come out with something that they can adhere to as a whole almost as much and on the same order as a single person adheres to the piece he writes and works on over time—rather as if an individual had managed to make simultaneous the various identities that he assumes and moves through over time. The consequence of a sentence or word being discussed is not, it should be emphasized again, what is being bargained about, though the consequences of sentences and words are most certainly jointly thought about; for the contemplated consequence may not become a consequence in fact unless the presupposition of mind is fulfilled. The chain of causation, that is, runs through legal method.[1]

ALL THIS ASSUMES also that the statement issued in the name of the Supreme Court is not of that familiar kind that can be called a statement by estoppel. It is one of the maddening—in the literal sense—but yet quite understandable features of judicial determinations to act or not, that an individual can be stopped (or "estopped") from denying the truth of a statement (usually a past statement of his own) if others' past reliance on its truth would place them at a disadvantage in a competitive or adversarial world (including the world of a lawsuit) were the statement now to be treated as untrue. A statement can be treated as true for purposes of coming to a result in a case, even though the individual making the statement would deny it if he could and even though the statement is assumed to be in fact not true. The same can happen in any large organization. A statement is circulated for comment, with invitations to individuals to participate in redrafting. If such statements are circulated frequently enough, individuals do not have time to participate in each, and the consequence is that they do nothing about one or another of them. It is then issued in their name and, since they had the opportunity to object to it but did not, they are estopped from denying it. Such statements may be no more evidence of a joint mind than are the details of a will, passed before the eyes of a dying man whose gaze is fixed on heaven, actual evidence of testamentary intent.

BUT THESE ASSUMPTIONS with respect to discussion, bargaining, and estoppel can be made about a body of nine individuals. That they can readily be made about a nine member court, or a board of directors, a committee, a small faculty, or the fellowship of a college, and cannot readily be made about a large university or an electorate, is one reason why it is so much easier to conceive the committee or fellowship as one thing, an entity, than to conceive of the university or the electorate as one thing. The electorate may be a unit of reference, but it is very difficult to keep it from dissolving into its parts or processes.

The fact that a body of individuals may proceed by majority rule is not necessarily fatal either. Majorities are notoriously shifting, and they often shift around beneath general agreement in the large. If one says that general agreements are nothing until they are applied, and it is the concrete application that is real, one is only partly correct. Viewed over time the applications, over which individuals disagree, may be like the shifting details in a pattern that remains much the same. The disagreements may be static in the communication. And they may be unfinished business: when dissenting opinions are written, the majority opinion is often read by lawyers and given weight in light of the dissent, and all the tales told in law school and elsewhere of famous dissents becoming "the law" at a later time direct the legal analyst away from the case at hand and toward the larger fabric of which it is a part. The disagreement between majority and minority is reflection of the dialectic of the law. The law is neither the majority nor the dissent but rather that edifice to which both appeal. The references in opinions to the fact that a decision was five to four are not idle observations.

THE SPEECH OF A SYSTEM

Turn to the second objection to what we have said about the value of a focal voice in the creation of authority, which is an objection also to what we have said more generally about the fading of authority with perception of process or mechanism. The second objection is the example of the legislature. How can the statements of the legislature have authority? If they do have authority—and we most certainly talk as if they do—does not much to the contrary of what we have said follow a fortiori for statements of courts and other texts from which the law is drawn through the method of legal analysis?

But the legislature is different, and the problem it poses is different.

NEITHER THE LEGISLATURE nor the problem it poses would have seemed so very different two centuries ago. The Massachusetts legislature is still called the General Court. In the formative era of what is now called legislative supremacy reference was often made to the "High Court of Parliament"; and in England today the House of Lords, through its Judicial Committee, is still the supreme judicial body. The notion of standing to argue a matter, which is now absorbed into the determinations of American and British courts that, as courts, they have a part to play in the resolution of a problem, was apparently developed in late nineteenth-century practice in the House of Commons.

Today there is a difference. Apart from what flows conceptually from a difference in size, which can vary, a distinction between courts and legislatures has been pressed in two ways. One is doctrinal, a concept of separation of powers, the legislative and the judicial, which in the United States has not developed organically as a reflection of differences actually perceived and felt but has been strenuously imposed. The premise of separation is part of the structure of legal thinking, which always seeks to bend reality to itself. It has therefore fostered a search for differences: distinctions produce differences quite as much as differences produce distinctions whenever the human mind must take active steps to grasp and understand what lies before it. But being structural, the doctrine of separation of powers has been subject to the changes that can occur to the axioms of legal thinking. It was closely linked to property as the basis of legal identity and to the protection of property as the focus of judicial interest, and with the loosening of the grasp of concepts of property upon the legal mind the doctrine of separation of powers has progressively lost the force it had even within the memory of lawyers still living. It is not that which holds courts and legislatures apart.

THE OTHER AND principal source of the sense of strong difference between courts and legislatures has been the transference, to the study of individuals acting as legislators, of methods and observations derived from the study of individuals' behavior in commodity trading markets. This, like efforts to view the norm of free speech in market terms, shares some common roots with the doctrine of separation of powers, for each assumed actors whose purposes were beside the point, "selfish" or "individual" or "private," in short not to be entered into, and whose statements were things they did rather than things they meant.

Legislators were not individuals each, by role assigned, seeking the good of the whole and discussing and arguing among themselves. The good of the whole or the public interest, even offered as multifaceted and the composite of all the various and discrete values and desires that individual men could bring each other to sympathize with, was eliminated as a term of meaningful discourse or, to say the same, was transformed into a rhetorical cover for a private end.[2] The genus "legislator" became not an individual making statements of law but a petty strategist. The process of legislating became a process of bargaining and negotiation in which secrecy, surprise, proper timing, and bluff played the same part as in a commercial deal. The art of politics became the art of manipulation. The grander ends of politics, which had clung to it into the twentieth century, were stripped away when Machiavelli's *Prince* was translated into the language of social science. The mark of a politician, not just of a political hack to be contrasted with a statesman but the very essence of a politician, was not caring.

Public life became a game, and imported into thinking about public life were all the images and stances associated with playing fields and battlefields virtually from prehistory, including particularly the stance that nothing really mattered because nothing was real—on the playing field because the real world lay outside the boundary and one would quit ultimately and go back to it; on the battlefield because one's opponents were objects to be eliminated from the earth, reduced to nothingness, and concommitantly one had invited death for oneself and thus proven that the objects of desire, for which life was necessary, had lost their hold. Undeniably there is the possibility of self-sacrifice, of dying so that others may attain an object one desires oneself, and thus dying, in a very real sense, for the object; we are speaking here of the images and stances associated with the battlefield, the soldier's humor and the soldier's credo that may in fact be necessary psychologically for direct participation in war. Above all, the politician in the legislature must not care, not for anything other than power or survival. Political science took the military and game analogies actually one step further, for the player postulated could not even consider himself part of a team and treat at least some others as mates. He was instead part of a coalition, and his allies today might be his enemies tomorrow.

W HAT WE HAVE just described takes us into the literature of rational social choice and the debates that can be followed there. It is not to be dismissed. Nothing should be dismissed that begins as a real effort to grasp and understand social action and to aid in human self-determination. Sophisticated practitioners of the elaborate techniques of public policy analysis do not make their hypotheses into norms, and they often come to deal with some of the same mysteries that ordinary lawyers face in legal analysis. Except for the very stout-minded, there would be discomfort at the outright postulation of a political man without ends—other than survival, power, or expansion—a man focused solely on means, like military man, Darwinian man, or the profit-maximizing man of microeconomic theory, who does not know the substantive world of desire and thus has about him an air of unreality and the smell of death.

It would be said instead that political actors of course have ends other than or in addition to survival, power, and winning. Survival, power, winning, expansion, and stature are often sought for the purpose of achieving these ends, at least until increase in power leads to a taste for power and power becomes an end in itself and the sole touchstone for decision. The problem is that these various other ends conflict. There is no way for individuals to choose among the various ends they espouse. Therefore they let a game make the choice, much as ancient judicial systems in our own lineage made decisions through trial by battle. The game, or, if one prefers, the system or the process, is not simply rule by majority, with a voting up or down. It is far more elaborate, with committee structures, parliamentary procedures, much trading on a wide number of disparate issues over time, and, in the American system, at least tripartite negotiations between the president with veto power and the two Houses. Nor is the outcome a simple choice between two sides. A statute is a most elaborate product, with many sections, many sentences, many clauses, subclauses, and words. No one of the participants could possibly have intended it. It is not their creation to intend. When they voted on it or a part of it, they may well have not intended it, their vote being only part of a strategy designed to stymie the process. Therefore the statute can be understood only historically or mechanically, in light of how it came to be the way it is, just like the weather.

B UT THIS RESTATEMENT of the analytic situation offers no protection against what we might call a sociopathic image of man, man without meaningful purpose. Stating the situation in this way serves rather to illustrate how easily the modern image of the legislator or politician has arisen and insinuated itself into the common mind.

Since the outcome is not to be understood in light of the purposes of the minds that created it, inasmuch as their minds did not create it—the outcome being the creation of a process—it readily seems to make no difference what those purposes, objects, desires, or values are. In the workings of the equations from which the outcome pops, only the moves that are made count, not the motives behind the moves. One does not need to know why a move was made, only that it was made. The Bfhusti tribesman wanting roast pig, the bowerbird wanting tinsel for its nest, the legislator wanting to preserve the Alaskan wilderness—they are all the same. The relevance of their object is exhausted in their action. It is useless to dwell on what they wanted. All that remains and all that is relevant is what they did.

From this it is a very short step to seeing the actor himself as without meaningful or understandable purpose. If the product of a group of Bfhusti, the product of a group of bowerbirds, and the product of a group of legislators are to be understood in the same way and by using the same method, then legislators may as well *be* Bfhusti or bowerbirds. Their objects can be replaced by abstract symbols. Their objects can be illusions, there only for the purpose of producing an action since it seems necessary to have at least the illusion of an object in order to act. After all, one of the first rules of logic is to eliminate what is not necessary. Thus can methodology, dictating what is and what is not necessary and relevant, produce a view of man.

There is a story passed on by Zygmunt Bauman about Karl Popper participating in a discussion of a matter of interest to him, the methodology of science, with a group of people of varying backgrounds, including one anthropologist:

> At the end of long and heated argument, to which the anthropologist listened in silence, he was asked to express his view. Much to the dismay of everybody present, the anthropologist replied that he paid little attention to the actual content of the dispute. The content was, he thought, the least interesting of what he saw and heard. Of incomparably greater interest were other things: how the debate was launched, how it developed, how one intervention triggered off another and how they fell into sequences, how the contributors determined whether they were in disagreement, etc.

Popper was incensed. He thought he had been *discussing* something, or, to say the same thing, he thought he had been discussing *something*. The anthropologist apparently did not.

Popper's story can be matched with another told by an economist. A prominent member of that school of economics which postulates the market as the universal basis for social relations, and advocates the strictest adherence to the market for satisfaction of all wants, retired to an institution congenial to his principles. He was ignored and, when finally, in some desolation, he complained to another member of the faculty that he had no friends, he was told, "Why don't you go out and buy some?" There is meaninglessness in the one story, and isolation in the other; the two are connected. Both meaninglessness and isolation are precipitated by the adoption of the methodologies that had their great sway in the nineteenth and early twentieth centuries, the period from which we are now emerging.

The standard method of legal analysis is quite different and always has been. The contrast, as well as the methodological connection between meaninglessness and isolation, may be illustrated by a third story. A psychologist gets up and seeks to persuade an audience to the view that mind is intrapersonal and that an individual must be a behaviorist as to all others than himself. After listening to him in silence, one of his audience suddenly asked, "Are *you* behaving before us, or speaking to us?" The behaviorist said, "I am behaving, from your point of view, of course." A puzzled look came over the face of the listener, who said, "But I thought you were saying something to us." The behaviorist replied, "I am. That is my behavior, which you must process." His listener exclaimed, "If you are behaving, then I must be interested in *how* you have come to act this way, not in *what* you are saying. For you aren't saying anything. In fact the very notion of agreeing with you, or being persuaded by you, is quite foreign." The behaviorist looked at him and said, "But you are a process too, processing what I am throwing out up here." The listener said, "You say that, I don't. Actually, I gather that you don't *say* it either. If you are a process, then I cannot hear you, and can only investigate you. We can do nothing together."

We could enter into a discussion of the problems in justifying a view that treats legislation as only the product of a process. That the ends of political actors conflict does not mean that a system must "choose" ("choose," because the word "choose" must be used figuratively here: systems do not choose because they produce outcomes; they just produce outcomes). Conflicting though the ends may be, they still may be shared by all the participants. Some participants may be pursuing particular values at one time, other values at another; and other participants may be doing the reverse. The conflict may be one of timing rather than one between values. The question of interest may be not so much Which will succeed as How all can be realized, if not simultaneously, then over time. *Others* may not be adversaries at all. They may be seeking what one could easily imagine oneself seeking. And if they are not adversaries, the appropriateness of bluff and lack of candor is not so evident.

But instead of entering such a discussion, let us turn to the way the legislature is treated in legal analysis.

TO THE LEGAL ANALYST, the outcome of the legislative process is a statement. It certainly looks like a statement and has the form of a statement. And the question for the legal analyst is what to make of the statement, what to do with it, how to respond to it. No response can be made to it if it is gibberish. It can have no effect unless it makes sense, and so sense must be made of it. If the statement is, "Automobiles in reverse gear must go forward," the mandate will be ignored, or it will be treated as a mistake and an inquiry will be made. Or it will be interpreted, and automobiles in reverse gear will turn around and move forward with their rear end at the front, or one will always be searching out a place where one can turn around without using reverse gear.

Most statutes, of course, are not such single sentences. They are elaborate affairs, with many sections, and they are placed into books which contain vast numbers of statutes. During interpretation, one thing is put with another, section with section, statute with statute, to build up a consistent whole. There is a counterpart to ignoring a statement. It is called "narrow" construction, or "gutting" a statute. There is a counter-part to making an inquiry, what has been denominated the "legislative remand" (analogous to courts' remand of administrative decisions and opinions back to agencies). But in general there is simply continuous interpretation. The multitude of sections and clauses in a statute and the multitude of statutes spread over time is not greatly different from the multitude of paragraphs within opinions and the multitude of opinions spread over time produced by judges, and the treatment is similar.

If one looks at what lawyers say while they are going about their work, it will be found that their questions are in the form "What did Congress mean by this?" or "What was the purpose of Congress in enacting this?" and legal conclusions arrived at from the reading of statutes, and introduced into the course of legal reasoning, are couched in the form "Congress intended this," or "The purpose of Congress was thus and so," or "There is evidence that Congress meant by this provision not this but that."

Notorious exceptions highlight the general practice. For example, in state corporate law, which more and more has seemed meaningless to analysts (Bayliss Manning's oft-quoted quip is that corporations statutes are "towering skyscrapers of rusted girders, internally welded together and containing nothing but wind"), the supreme court of Delaware has purported to follow what is called the "equal dignity rule" and to view different sections of the state corporation statute as if they were without context and stood independent of one another, each with "equal dignity." If corporate management is forbidden under one section of the statute to achieve a certain end, squeeze out a minority shareholding group by amending the corporate charter and reclassifying their stock; and if it appears possible to achieve precisely the same end under another section of the statute providing for reclassification of stock in mergers, which says nothing about whether a merger can be effective between a corporation and a shell (or dummy) corporation set up for the purpose of producing the appearance of a merger; then the object may be achieved, in Delaware, under the latter section. The first section says nothing about the second.

The effect on a statute of such an approach is to render it a purely formal utterance, without substance. It becomes pure procedure, a setting up of hoops to jump through; in short, a charade, as the ready acceptance of dummy corporations, phantom mergers, and other fantasies of the corporate bar might suggest. But generally courts do not attribute an absence of intent or a ridiculous intent, or inconsistency. To the contrary: tiny evidences, which presuppose absolute consistency in syntax, tense, and number, and authorship so punctilious with language that Dr. Johnson himself would stand in awe, are marshaled as grounds for conclusions about the meaning of a statute, and it is supposed that the Congress enacting, for instance, the securities laws, had fully in mind the relations between those laws and all of labor law or all of law governing insurance.

Is this personification of Congress—or any other legislature— merely a manner of speaking? Is it serious and meant to be believed? Or is it figurative expression, pointing to something else not said directly either because it is unwieldy and inconvenient to say it directly or because judges, lawyers, and others initiated into the truth of the matter must never say out loud what they know for fear that things will fall apart if ordinary folk are not kept under a spell, or fall apart perhaps even in their own lawyers' minds if they do not keep themselves half under a spell?

These are wretched questions. Begin to answer them by asking another. When we refer to the statements of an individual next door, and speak of him as intending this and that, is it likewise only a manner of speaking and a shorthand reference to all that historically produced the statement at the time it was made? Do we dissolve the individual next door into his blood and bones, his mother, his father, and his education? If we do not, because he is *there*, in what sense is he *there* different from the sense in which the legislature is *there*? Well, it could be said that he is there in a sense akin to, though perhaps not exactly the same as, the sense in which the child cuddled in bed, the woman embraced, the friend between whom and oneself even silence is charged, are not abstractions but commanding realities. They are like the stars, bright points of light that have remained bright points of light whatever picture we have drawn of them after reading the instruments we have designed to gather their signals. Individuals, it might be said, are always different.

But if this be so, why the mimicry?

Is there any difference between saying "Congress passed a statute and sent it to the printer to be published" and saying "An Angel gave the Book of Mormon to Joseph Smith for publication"? In the case of the statute, we might say that we know what we are talking about because "Congress passed a statute" refers to the happening of a series of events, amendments, votes, conferences, more votes and so forth, whereas the phrase "An Angel gave a book" does not refer to anything that happened, or at least need not. But note that we do not say merely that something happened when we speak of Congress. Something may have happened, true, but that is not what distinguishes the cases. If we were told "Something happened," we would have to go on and say "And so?" for that something which happened does not affect us without more. It is not a happening like a volcanic eruption. So some people did do something in a room, did raise their hands, were counted, voted. They set up no air currents thereby that reached and fanned our faces. What *happened* does not affect us. We must add something more. We cannot reduce "Congress passed a statute" to that which happened when Congress passed a statute, any more than the music we hear can be reduced to what happens when we hear it. Angels and Congresses may be different. There may be more reason to hear one than the other. But the difference and the reason, the greater comfort some of us may have in following the commands of a statute than the commands of the Book of Mormon, do not lie in the fact that Congress is a being whose inner processes are a little (but only a little) better known to us than the processes within angels.

F ROM TIME TO TIME courts and lawyers speak of the "intent of the statute" rather than the intent of the legislature. This is quite evidently figurative since the statutory words sitting there on paper have no more intent than words typed out when a mouse runs across the keyboard of an electric typewriter. When a lawyer or a court reads a statute, tries to know a statute, understand it, see what it *says* (and we likewise refer to a book or a poem, and quote "it" as *saying* something), the lawyer is trying to decide what to do with it. He will respond to it in carrying actual life forward into the future. The historian and scientist are not deciding what to do with what they study, certainly not in carrying life forward. To know how a particular provision of a statute got into the statute tells one nothing about what to do with it (except as the tracing of the how reveals that the thing crept in unintended, in which case one might know to try to extirpate it). The question "Why is it there" is not the question "How did it come to be there?" If judges and lawyers are debating what to do and are looking for authoritative guidance, if, that is, they are not just looking, like bad boys, to see how likely it is that they will be hurt if they do what they already have decided they want to do, then the question "Why is a provision of a statute there" is the question "What was intended by it?" and that passive "What was intended?" carries an implicit active: "What *who* intended?"[3] If such phrasing, with both a what and a who in the same question, seems grammatical nonsense, we leave a blank, and say "What _____ intended?" The tongue in fact leaps to say "What someone intended," and we should note that there is a one or a unitary in someone. If there is no who to see and contemplate, *there,* next door as it were, the who must be constructed.

The lawyer cannot look to the drafter, or the amender and reviser, or even to the voters who voted upon the measure. Drafters and amenders often write opinions, and lawyers hungrily reach for them even though they must often eventually put them aside because reports to the legislature accompanying a bill are often not authentic documents at all but patchworks of inserts by individuals without responsibility who have gained access to the drafting process. But it is not the drafters, amenders, or revisers that matter, in any case. It is the legislators. The legislators themselves do not write opinions as judges do in making statements of law. They may agree only on one thing, to vote Yes, like the committee that issued the report "This Committee is unanimous for reasons impossible to communicate, each member having a different and contradictory reason for joining in the recommendation." And without written opinions, the writing of which as well as the analysis of which is designed to overcome the situation where an outcome of deliberation rests on grounds that cancel each other out, all the judge or lawyer can do is to construct, from the animating values alive in the air, a person to say what the statute says.

Even though that person may not exist.

Could it not be that the legislature is a special case—an illusion, admitting which does not make illusory all our other personifications? We may be allowed one sleight of hand. We may need to play one trick upon ourselves, to have a thing which does not make sense introduced into our thinking as if it did make sense, with which we struggle rather than simply tossing it back out. For it must be recognized that there is an authoritarian streak in all we have said about judges and lawyers going about their business seeking the legitimate and the authoritative, and in the suggestions throughout, which are impossible to avoid, that the judge or lawyer is doing little more than the ordinary citizen does in daily life, so that, *mutatis mutandis,* the ordinary citizen *is* the judge and lawyer of whom we speak. The authoritarian and the authoritative are, within their world, polar opposites. The one is pejorative, the other, I have tried to show, is not. But there is no joyful anarchy in either of them. In seeking the authoritative, in acting with faith—good faith—in seeking coherence, one is trying to tie things down, to control them, to fit and lock them together. There is a backward looking quality to the search for the authoritative. The techniques involve running over all the evidence, which, if it exists, exists in the past. However clearly willing obedience may be shown to be obedience to oneself, it is still obedience, with all its ancient connotation of surrender and turning back, away from the delightful and the fascinating. A regime to which a formal center or a pointed hierarchy is even helpful, though they be not necessary to it, is not exactly one to rejoice in. And so we make the system open-ended.

We introduce a rough-and-tumble, and jumble things. We joke about serious things. We do the absurd. The whiteness, the silence, and the motionlessness of the ultimate unity do not attract us. Instead of searching for the agreement and the oneness beneath our contentions or trusting ourselves to a dialectic which zigzags off into the mists, we set up a game, the field for which, unlike that for any other game, is *not* set apart, so that there is no beginning or end nor any boundary from which we as players can step back into a surround of real life. It is the Game of Life, in which reality and illusion are confounded, and it is ultimately self-assertive—like the act of suicide, only not so dangerous. The fact that we have no terms to describe its outcome, other than those reserved for meaningful creations of the human mind, the fact that we must personify, insures that we do not isolate it and lose the benefits of the paradox we have created.

Legislatures need not be this way. The size and complexity that make the legislative outcome so apparently a product of something other than joint discussion, as the product of a large bureaucracy is so apparently not the work of a responsible mind, are not necessary attributes of a group of legislators. The size of legislatures is obviously affected by historical circumstance, by territorial boundaries (as in the division of the United States into its fifty states), by cultural identifications, and by the numerical possibility of access to a representative by constituents. But admitting this, still we are left without sufficient explanation why the overwhelming consequence of size and complexity—making legislation a game—is so readily accepted; so readily accepted, in fact, that it is rarely discussed except surreptitiously in outbursts of despair about the decline of authority, alienation, loss of individual dignity and sense of worth, loss of control, and loss of community. There are choices that have been made.

The legislatures that are set up, and whose statements we are all instructed to treat as authoritative, are designed. They continue to be designed. The United Nations created the General Assembly. The European Common Market has established and elected its Parliament. The situation is not one of utter unawareness, for it is striking how commonly such legislatures are held in disrespect and even contempt—the same attitudes we can see budding as a bureaucracy judicial or administrative grows in size—and how pungent is the language used to castigate them, which are, after all, our own handiwork, for being "ineffective." But they are not ineffective, if they are an antidote to authority itself and the control it produces. The unreviewable discretion of the attorney general and the absolute power of clemency in the chief executive may do the same for us. Most gods, in fact, have a capricious streak in their natures.

The chance product of the legislative process is not confined to cases or instances. The statements that emerge are not "yes" or "no," win or lose. They are general, complex in themselves and cast in the terms used by individuals making meaningful statements. Thus for decision makers outside the legislative process, persons trying to decide what to do, who are spinning their webs of understanding and putting this with that, they appear suddenly, as a hand might appear to a spider spinning his web, to cut strands and tangle and tie them in knots here and there. And it is striking how frequently the attitude toward legislative enactments is one of having to deal with them or get around them, as if they were obstacles rather than guides. Why are they not ignored? They are, after all, only words. It may be that we like obstacles, we appreciate the freedom of a tangle, we don't like spiders.[4]

THE SECRET LEGISLATOR

Sometimes a presupposition of mind is possible, or at least not glaringly impossible. Deliberation has taken place, however cumbersome and by whatever fits and starts, and the outcome is its product.

More often the presupposition of mind is indulged, for legislative statements, on quite different grounds, that the statement, in the particular instance, is congruent with the spirit of the age. To speak of the spirit of an age is not to surround oneself with a cloud of unspecified references. Cultural historians rigorous even by the standards of modern historiography are drawn to such a view. Judges and lawyers may be allowed the same instincts.

When this latter is the case, the mind that justifies the statement is not the mind that produces it, if any did. The statement simply appears, as from a hidden loudspeaker, and evidence not about its making but about something else is used to determine whether to seize upon it, as an *objet trouvé*, and use it as a surrogate for the statement of a mind. We do this too as individuals. Mind—our own—may lie behind our preservation and adoption of words that emerge from our mouths, even if we cannot say that mind lay behind their initial utterance.

But when the presupposition of mind cannot be made with respect to legislative process, and there is no ground for faith that the outcome happens to match what we are hearing by other means, then we are exposed to risks, that must be laid beside the benefits.

ONE OF THE risks is entrusting human life to chance on such a scale. This is a danger appreciated the more, as it appears the more frequently that the material system of the world is not homeostatic and that huge irreversibilities can occur. It is not just such matters as species destruction, atmospheric heating, or radioactive waste that seem too serious to be played with. The prospect of a constitutional amendment that would insert economic constructs such as the gross national product or a balanced budget into the Constitution is of a similar order. The American mechanism for effecting legislative change of a constitutional kind, which does not involve debate and passage of a resolution in an assembly but rather proceeds directly to the fifty state legislatures, is sometimes perceived to be the equivalent of asking the Fates to rewrite fundamental law.

The attitude of many when at risk in this kind of situation is naturally to assume that any such changes can be handled; that they are after all only incremental; that what can no longer be done one way can perhaps be done another; that the concepts themselves—the notion of "gross national product," for instance—can even be transformed. And they can. The risk lies in the possibility that they cannot be handled in time. Irreversibilities might occur, outstripping the capacities of our method, which we might call in this connection (drawing an artificial but appealing parallel) the technology of dealing with texts. Getting around legislated words is usually possible in the stream of life if our attitude toward them is cool enough and we see them as mute obstacles. But like getting around a post in a stream on a canoe trip, this takes time. (A lawyer with ample resources acting for some particular one of us can usually buy time for the purpose, but a society as a whole has no one to buy from.) Much can happen while a text is being reduced to a dead letter—unless we decide simply to ignore it. But can we, if we have made a pact with ourselves not to break the illusion? Not "Can we?" because we have promised, but "Can we?" because the illusion would be broken all at once, and with it would go the freedom from ourselves we gain from it?

Another risk is the risk of capture. The human instinct to master the machine is great; it is the instinct to bring order to chaos and put control in the place of chance. The fact that the machine is one made by human beings for the purpose of introducing disorder and avoiding mastery would not necessarily lessen the temptation it presents. Looking carefully, the observer often discovers that legislative power is in the hands of a few men, not by delegation but because they are in strategic positions. Organized parties, party leaders, the bosses of political machines, the chairmen of powerful committees determine outcomes and maintain coherence. They are few enough to deliberate. If they do deliberate in smoke-filled rooms and use power for substantive ends and are not wholly manipulative with one another, the mind behind the legislative utterance is their mind. The difficulty is that they present the very picture of a tyrant. They exercise power without responsibility. They work without method. They need *persuade* no one. And they do not have office. They do not have the goad of office to make them act, when inaction is the equivalent of action; they do not have the role of office to expand and guide their vision. Indeed, invisible and unexalted, they may pursue with every sense of justification the minor office they formally hold, and accentuate their irresponsibility by attributing outcomes not to their own decisions but to the body whose head they have become.

B UT IF THESE ARE the risks raised against the contribution of the legislative process as such, it will be said in response that there are risks just as great in entrusting ourselves to deliberation—not the straw man of mechanical deliberation but any deliberation.

Mechanical deliberation is that exemplified by the British commission that computed where a third London airport should be built. One possible location was the village of Stewkley in Buckinghamshire. Confronted with arguments against the loss of a Norman church in the village, the commission gave the church a value in their calculations, a numerical value, of course, the only numerical value they had, which was the amount of the fire insurance policy on the building. That was hooted.

But any deliberation, even the purest kind, consists of argument, looking at factors, putting factors together, not giving some too much weight, not relying on others at all, not missing factors that should be relied upon, hearing what is said, reading what is there, rousing oneself and taking initiative when tired, controlling passion. What reason do we have to think that all this will be done, done at the right time, done well? Suppose the telling argument is not made, or is not made at the right time? Suppose trains of thought are started from which the participants cannot escape in time? Think of the entirely reasonable fear so many have of a Constitutional Convention where deliberation might be possible as an alternative to the machinations of interest groups in fifty state legislatures.

Besides, the response continues, here becoming more soothing, it is the outcome that counts. The individuals who find they have their hands on the levers of the legislative machine do quite well. They acquire a sense of the importance of their position and take responsibility often enough. Things work out in the end, and if they do not appear to be working out well enough, we can always fiddle with the system, as has been done recently, for instance, with electoral reform, and see whether that works out better. To the practical and pragmatic man of affairs almost any decision-making system will do. It can be made to work.

Thus, the outcome of deliberation cannot be defended on the ground that it is less chancy, at least outside the procedures of the judicial process, which are designed in contemplation of the deficiencies and difficulties of deliberation. And what real difference would it make if the Equal Rights Amendment to the United States Constitution was finally adopted, not because it was thought that there should be equality for women but because the motel industry in one State was particularly vulnerable to a boycott by organizations pushing the amendment, and financed the campaigns of candidates for the state legislature that motel owners knew secretly favored it? We would still have equality for women, which is a good thing, and which we would have had in any event ultimately in some other way, such as a proper interpretation of the equal protection portion of the due process clause.

THIS IS THE counsel of what may be called the institutionalist. It is frequently said that baseball is an American institution, and one can characterize legislating as the activity of an institution rather than as a game. What distinguishes the analyst who fixes his attention upon the institutional aspects of an activity is that he is not interested in any particular product. He is, instead, interested in the run of outcomes. Like the chemist working with molecules in a gas, or a traffic engineer working with the behavior of drivers in automobiles, he is interested in regularities appearing over time. About the individual instance or outcome he cares very little. It is always marginal—his setting of a time span of appropriate length ensures that it will be marginal. If it were not there its absence would make no difference to the large picture. Or, if *it* were not there, another instance or outcome would be, and whether that instance or outcome was different would, again, make no difference. Whether you or I decide to turn left or right in a traffic flow does not affect the traffic engineer's perception of the traffic flow, nor is the behavior of a gas different if a particular molecule vibrates to the left rather than to the right.

It would not occur to the engineer to criticize any individual product or to change any individual product. The traffic engineer does not go down and argue with an individual driver any more than the physicist would think of arguing with an individual molecule; and an automobile manufacturer rarely thinks of arguing with an individual worker on the assembly line. What he does is to change the conditions and then see what the consequences, again in general, are. The traffic engineer makes some streets one-way and inserts some barriers and stoplights. The chemist changes the diameter of a tube. The manufacturer divides one task into two on the assembly line. The conditions may be physical or they may be in the form of rules. It doesn't matter (and, as a matter of fact, the physical conditions of legislating, the distance from the floor of the Senate to the senators' offices, the heat or cold of the Senate chamber, may have quite as great an effect on legislation, in this view, as any quorum or voting rule or arrangement of committee jurisdictions). Consequence is all. Unless it appears that a particular twist or change or turn which has been followed and can therefore be associated with a desirable change in the run of outcomes has some undesirable consequence on another front, it really makes no difference what the turn is. It makes no difference what the reason, or cause, for a desired change is, so long as the change occurs. Who cares whether traffic congestion is eliminated by a one-way street or by a stoplight unless the elimination of congestion through a one-way street causes some other problem? If a train between the Senate Office Building and the Senate, a change in the filibuster rules, or mandating senatorial attendance at seminars on economics or ecology, will have the same consequence of producing better legislation—that is, legislation with better consequences—then it makes no difference which is chosen.

And lest it be thought that an institutional view of things is the preserve of the social engineer, we might recall that parents often take the same stance in raising their children, at least in the modern era since an individual bad act ceased to be viewed as an irredeemable sin or invitation to damnation. Parents are often tolerant of any particular instance of a child's behavior, regretting it or reprimanding it perhaps, but not wholeheartedly. They know that what is important is behavior in general. The instance is either unimportant, or it begins to raise the question whether some change of conditions is not desirable, a later bedtime, a part-time job, a larger allowance, a new set of books, a summer away from certain companions, even (if it were not destroyed in the programming of it) more engagement and attention from mother or father.

THERE IS NOTHING necessarily cold about the attitude of the institutionalist. He may be quite warm about the consequences on which his attention is fixed. The problem with his counsel, and with viewing legislating as either a game or the activity of an institution, is that the outcomes are statements. They are statements in the form of statements of law. They must be heard and attended to if they are to have effect. They must be understandable and have meaning if they are to have effect. At the least, the effect they have will differ according to the meaning they are taken to have and how they are understood. As statements in the form of statements of law, their consequences will differ according to whether they are treated as authoritative or resisted, whether they are internalized or left external by the listener, whether the listener commits himself to them or remains detached.

The legal analyst cannot set about to compare the consequences of what is said by an arguing group of men and women who come to a conclusion, and what is said as the outcome of an institutional process. The institutional process is not *saying* anything. The analyst may as well be remarking, "You have stated this, and here is a stone. Let me compare what you say and this stone." Or, better, "Let me compare what you say over a period of time with a series of stones that are tossed up to my notice." Molecules in a gas producing their regularities, drivers turning left and right producing their traffic patterns, even the child's behavior over time in the sight of his parent, are not *saying* anything to the observer that the observer is meant to follow (though it must be admitted that every action of the child, the child being an individual and being loved, may in the end be a communication asking something of the parent). In drawing conclusions about statements the use of methods developed for the analysis of physical actions should tickle one's sense of the odd, and provoke one to ask how this could have come about, rather than lead one to assume and accept the equivalencies presupposed and go on to quibble about the details of the execution of such methods.

F OR THERE IS something intriguingly secret about what such an analyst is doing. He cannot have others see as he sees for, if they did, his subject matter would vanish. If they saw statements as stones, they would respond to them as stones. They would not hear them and there would be no consequences. And is not the natural reaction to coming upon a secret to ask why it is being kept?

As for the unacceptability of the consequences (if the secret be kept), which spur the desire to change the design of the legislative institution and to select particular modifications, the institutionalist is of course forced to look somewhere other than legislation for guidance. Critical and self-determining as he is, he may look very much within himself. There is something indeed parental in a view of the world as a collection of interlocking institutions, tended, repaired, corrected, and rebuilt by a few who have the fortune, or misfortune, to see them for what they are. But look where he will, he must look. The consequences upon which he fixes his attention do not speak to him, or have tags around them, like those Alice found saying "Drink me." How is he to think about them, by what concepts and categories? What is he to take into account and what not in his work upon the rules, the design of the machinery? What is he to seek and pursue?

Often it is found that those who think there is only process pursue peace as their only goal and guide. Consequences are good or bad according to whether they lead toward or away from peace. Acceptability becomes an end in itself, the sole end. Whatever is accepted, for whatever reason and by whatever means, is good. Whether the nineteenth-century British Parliament legislated correctly and according to the will of the people is to be known by whether there was rebellion and disorder. Whether the Supreme Court makes proper decisions is to be tested by whether those decisions are accepted.

But this radical skepticism, so typical of the international diplomat today, and so much a part of the psychology of the threatened aristocrat who was the usual statesman in the generations just before us and who set the tone of the role into which the institutionalist today has stepped, is more a sign of weariness than anything else. Almost any *acting* skeptic, who has not retired into a cave, can be aroused by particular consequences, and when aroused and tinkering with and adjusting the mechanism for any reason other than to avoid an explosion, he finds himself asking questions that do not have immediate answers and on which he must turn outside himself for help.

Does he not listen to another, a secret legislator? And if others are deliberating, now not about legislation but about the design of the system that will produce legislation, and he must persuade them to his conclusions (or what he thinks might be his conclusions if they were confirmed by discussion), rather than presenting his conclusions in the form of an order in the name of an authority which he believes to be fictional, then that secret legislator will emerge.

The institutional designer and all those who are working with him on the processes in their hands cannot say that they are guided by History. Many, perhaps including Marx, have been inclined to think—largely for want of an alternative—that History legislates for mankind and that they are listening to History. But one cannot wait for History to speak. One is in the present and must act in the present, not in the future from which one could look back and see what one and one's fellows in fact valued as revealed by what they sought and what they did. If they say, "We, too, are but part of a process of institutional change, all-embroiling and rolling on beneath us, which continuously gives us the values that guide our hands in designing mechanisms for reaching them, and which continuously changes those values, which are themselves nothing more than outcomes of processes—we are but links in the chain of events, actors playing useful parts in producing the ultimate outcome, which is History"—if they say this, they run into the hard fact of present existence. The historical view omits the present. One can conceive of oneself as part of the process of history if one looks back into the past or forward into the future. But one is dead in the past and not yet alive in the future. One does not exist there. One exists now, this instant.

10

DEMOCRACY
The Democratic Connection

WE BEGAN Chapter 9 with the question whether the legislature was an a fortiori case. We bow before it. It ordinarily has the last word. There is about it an aura of power which judges would shy from ever claiming. It seems to have authority, it seems to have the most authority; yet when it speaks what it says is seen most transparently to be the result only of a process. We turned and wondered whether the legislature, far from being an a fortiori case and a model, might be instead a special case, a useful illusion against which reality is known by contrast as the waking world is made more substantial by the knowledge of dreams.

In our discussion we said almost nothing of what might be thought the legislature's principal source of authority in the modern state, that its voice is the voice of a sovereign in a way other voices are not; that it represents the people, Demos; and that its conclusions are given legitimacy by the first principle of public life, which is democracy.

We have said so little of democracy, to this point, because the problem of the legislature and its apparent difference from even a multimember court is met whether or not there is any assertion that the legislature represents the will of the people. The great Councils of the Christian Church from Nicea to Vatican II, operating as legislatures, have remained sources of governing texts of the Catholic Church despite the development of the Papacy; the problems presented by such texts are not unlike those of texts coming from Congress today. The American Law Institute is a large self-perpetuating body. Its executive and board review and approve Restatements of Law. But a Restatement does not have the authority of the Institute until it has emerged from the parliamentary processes of the

Annual Meeting of the Institute. Recall that the British Parliament asserted sovereignty long before universal suffrage. Its conclusions were presented most forcefully as the conclusions of Parliament itself.

Furthermore, there can be democracy, or not, within these legislative entities, these Councils, Congresses, Parliaments, Institutes. Neither the phenomenon of the legislature, nor the phenomenon of democracy, is confined to the translation of the will of the people into decision and text.

But the fact that legislatures are met at every turn, are special, and present a special problem quite apart from the special place of the legislature in the modern state, is not the only reason for having waited to advert to political democracy. Democracy should not be prominent in our thinking and search for the authoritative, if the reason for making it so is an assumption that its outcomes are closer to the will of the people. Democracy should be prominent in our thinking—but for another reason.

THE QUESTION REPRESENTED BY CALIGULA'S HORSE

Vox populi may be vox dei. The question is, in a phrase, the democratic connection. The people are sovereign: whether the outcome of a democratic electoral and voting process has any special claim to be connected to the preferences, values, and will of the people is another matter.

There is no doubt of the importance of the connection in our talk. When the president sets himself in opposition to Congress, his first claim is that he also is elected and speaks for the people, as much or indeed more than Congress since he alone has been elected by all the people. When the authority of the Supreme Court is attacked by academic lawyers, their first claim is that the Court is not democratic. Parliament may be sovereign, but in Parliament's conflicts with labor or the queen it relies ultimately upon its connection with the people. In the state of Michigan, the legislature, the governor, the judiciary, and three of the universities all have what is termed constitutional independence. Every generation a university goes to court to vindicate its independence from the legislature in its internal affairs. The force of the university's claim lies in its direct connection to the sovereign through the election of its regents. It is the sovereignty of the people that gives the very idea of independence, from no less than the legislature's own power, its persuasive force in current argument. Without the democratic connection we would certainly have to revise our manner of speaking.

We would not, however, be in a new world. The issue we have been addressing is what authority the statements of the legislature can have for us. When and how does one obey? What stance does one take? Does one accept its statements, really accept them and go forward with them, not resisting them, not manipulating one's way around them, but internalizing them and making them one's own as one moves forward? There is such a thing as resistance and even massive resistance to a legislature's decisions, of the very kind that was directed at the United States Supreme Court's desegregation decisions. If it seems that questioning obedience to the legislature acting within its jurisdiction is questioning an axiom, then we should remember Caligula's horse. That Emperor made his horse Consul and ordered the Senators to obey the horse. The question that can be raised about Caligula's horse can be raised also about the legislature. How can one even think of *not* obeying to the full the democratically elected legislature in the modern state? How can one think of not obeying a horse? The question is what connection there is between the sovereign will, the imperial will or the will of the people, and what we are being asked to obey.

THE ARGUMENT FROM THE ALTERNATIVES

If the question, Why obey the legislature and treat its utterances as sovereign and authoritative? is put to the most worldwise, who are often also the most skeptical, the answer will likely come back that to do so is better than any alternative. Churchill is the most prominent of those in recent history whose spirits are summoned to give weight to this disarming view. Democracy is a terrible system, perfectly terrible. But any other system is much worse.

And this may be true, depending of course upon what we mean when we refer to democracy and when we refer to other systems. The problem is that this fact is no reason for obedience. It gives no positive authority to the outcome of the electoral and legislative process, except as we may delude ourselves or, as an articulate elite, wish to foster illusion among those for whom we care.

People who say this and say no more, the worldwise, the skeptical, are in fact detached. Their hearts are full of reservations. Usually *they* do not accept the authority of the legislature, except as it suits them or matches what they hear a secret legislator saying. Their stance is generally one that in fact denies true authority to the outcome of all that terrible tumult. They do not accept it as their own decision.

But passing that, we know that resignation with a shrug and a sigh of *faute de mieux* is not the same as acceptance and recognition of authority. A horse might be better than any of the other possible prime ministers.

The point remains that there is no reason to obey *if the reason to obey is that the voice heard is the voice of the sovereign.*

THE ARGUMENT FROM MAJORITY RULE

Then the fact that democratic decision making usually involves majority rule is focused upon, and it is said that one obeys because one must. The majority could force the minority to its will. That, however, has never been a justification of obedience and has always been a foolish explanation of it. The fact of majority rule is quite beside the point. There is no reason to think that fifty-one can defeat forty-nine, beyond bare-handed combat between gangs where mere numbers of hands that can grip, pin, and punch might be important. Too much depends upon the degree of organization, and upon strength, cunning, access to weapons and technology, and all the other sources of power that have nothing to do with authority. There is also no reason to think that the fifty-one will hold together. "The majority" is a construct which is not an entity in most cases. It has no substance, and is not meant to. It appears for an instant when a vote is taken, and disappears thereafter. Fear is no reason to obey—it is only reason to appear to obey—and besides there is not sufficient reason to fear.

Nor is there reason to obey because the decision of the majority *is* the decision of the whole in the same way that a boat laden with stones will, as a whole, roll over on one side if there is just one more stone on that side than the other. The fact that some democratic systems operate by supermajorities is enough to dispel the thought, attractive though it may be in an era accustomed to thinking of human beings and other entities as physical systems. When the question whether to replace a liturgical term read by some as gender-specific was debated by the Conference of Catholic Bishops in the United States, the resolution in favor of replacement was adopted by something just under a two-thirds majority; it did not pass and all the papers said that "the bishops" rejected the resolution, because the bishops operated by a two-thirds majority rule. But even without supermajorities we do not operate like boats or scales. There is no reason to think that, in your ambivalences and conflicts when in fact you want to go both ways, you decide which way as it is decided for a boat laden with stones, or that in fact going one way it is *you* going that way.

THE LEGAL STRUCTURE OF POLITICS

Majority rule does not supply authority. But it does not foreclose willing obedience either. It should not be supposed that majority rule is the difficulty.

We have spoken of accepting what is presented to us rather than created by us. An individual who loses on a vote taken after full participation and candid discussion can still accept the decision as his own. Individuals do it every day. But the reason for actual acceptance of a decision which is a product of a vote on principles of majority rule—we should describe it in this way to avoid the impression that there is such a thing as a decision of the majority, as if those voting in a particular way were ranged on one side of a field with linked arms—is that the outcome is understandable and appeals to at least some part of the mind of the individual who found himself in the minority.

The decision may be viewed by him either as losing only on a question of means, or as not losing at all—as instead simply disposing of a decision that must be made in order to go on in the effort to achieve all the ends that in fact contend for recognition within him and within others. If one end or state of affairs is to be achieved now, in this way, as the vote has turned out, then the minority (and the majority) know where they stand with respect to achieving those other ends that the minority focused upon in objecting and opposing what turned out to be the majority position. One must begin somewhere, somehow. The total outcome will not look the same or have the shape that it might have had otherwise, but then no one really knows what precise shape the total outcome might have had anyway (and we have noted, in connection with the drafting of an opinion by a multimember court, the difficulty of determining the degree to which a joint statement, bargained out in a situation of mutual trust, is less a statement of what one believes than a statement of one's sole devising would be).

There is, too, a sense, surely experienced by all men with open minds, that if more individual minds whom you respect come out, after full consideration, in a way different from the way you come out, there is more reason to doubt that what you think you believe is what you really believe. Their votes are evidence of what you really believe, and while you may not admit it, the thought is at work within you. This is at least the beginning of acceptance.

But none of this can be said of a situation where the outcome is quite evidently not the determination of a majority after full discussion, but rather is the product of the workings of rules upon the contingent givens of the world and of factors that are not the sorts of factors deliberating minds take into account in deciding what ought to be said and done. Then the result is simply served up. It is not entirely the product of chance, for the rules, as we have seen, are subject to design and continuous readjustment. But it is not the decision of the electorate either. Just as we have experience every day of accepting decisions of majorities as our own, from the deliberations within a family on up and out in the various multimember groups to which we may belong, we also have experience every day of facing results which are merely tossed up. We see them both in the choice of the persons who are to make decisions as representatives, and in the choices of the statements to be made by those elected representatives as they participate in the smaller democracies we call committees and legislatures.

WHETHER OR NOT the politics of election are more complex than the politics of legislation, the contingencies of electoral politics are more clearly evident to all.

In any election year in the United States the press is full of analysis of party convention rules and how the choice of the candidate will turn upon the application of one or another rule. Strategists calculated the effects of John Anderson's third-party entry into the 1980 presidential campaign as if an odd part had been added to a machine. Would Anderson drain votes from this side or that side, or from both sides? Charged with being a spoiler and thwarting the expression of the will of the people, Anderson responded, "What good would it do Jimmy Carter to be elected in a two-man race if maybe forty percent of the American people showed up at the polls?" He would not be troubled, he said, if his independent candidacy knocked President Carter out of the White House and Ronald Reagan was elected. But he further acknowledged that even if he wanted to end his candidacy, federal campaign law would force him to continue, on pain of owing millions of dollars for the rest of his life, for the Federal Election Commission had said that Anderson was eligible for government campaign aid after the election only if he won at least five percent of the national popular vote.

So, too, even the least analytic of political actors know that the absence of any particular rules of quorum or notice of party meetings can be the very foundation of a political machine. A few of the faithful can turn up at a meeting secretly announced, to begin the process of election of representatives leading up to the election of the boss, all perfectly according to the rules.

But rules such as these—and rules on independent candidacies, rules on primaries, caucuses, and delegate discipline, rules on finance, patronage, corporate involvement, and access to mass media—are but a small part of the structure of politics.[1] Beneath the party structure is a substructure of associations, clubs, and other organizing entities, all sustained by rules. If parties weaken or structure is deliberately removed, other forms of organization move in or are uncovered—corporations, churches, unions, family trusts.

As courts struggle with a challenge to a rule or its administration by a person in a decision-making position, they do not find any prior definition of democratic process. The design of the process is continuously created by their decisions and the decisions—strategic or deliberative—of those they review or decline to review, or the design of the process is a given of history, change in which some are in a position to block given the system as it stands. The *sovereign* cannot be asked how his vocal chords should be constructed while his vocal chords are under construction, and they can be seen to be always under construction.

Decisions on design are made quite as much to insure that an outcome is possible as that all be heard. Parties conceive it their function quite as much to win as to be representative. The outcome of an electoral process is not connected to the will of the people or a majority of the people by the process: choices must be narrowed if there is to be any outcome at all. An election begins with a world of alternatives, and it is party structure or some other system of rules that finally brings the electoral decision down to a bipolar one. But it is the rules that have produced the substance of whatever there is at the apex of the poles, in the same way that the mechanisms of the physical body or of a machine see to it that one or another alternative is excluded in the course of arriving at organization rather than chaos.[2]

And once selected the elected face the question of how they are individually to make decisions *without* voting and elections, just as do judges. When elected officials make decisions, respect may be given those decisions for the same reason that respect is given to the decisions of unelected officials, and may vary along the same lines, according to whether the official had full information, listened with concern to all considerations, meant what he said, and so forth. The electoral and selective process itself has simply produced organization, produced a decision maker. The outcome just is, in the same sense that the people who happen to be around us just *are* until we begin talking to them and become connected with them. They fall from the sky around us, or we fall from the sky amidst them. So it is that the structure of a political system deposits decision makers with particular given names among us. The work of connecting the outcome of what they do to the will of the people begins after the election.

THE FACTORS PRODUCING legislative outcomes are not hidden either, and the production of outcomes can be seen to be similar to the electoral process that places individuals in legislative office.

The quorum and membership rules of the White Panther Party were adopted as part of the widespread effort to achieve participatory democracy in the early 1970s. Meetings were held on sunny days out-of-doors in the middle of town; anyone strolling by could stop and vote; questions were frequently put and decided by majority vote. Ordinary lay observers of the process did not fail to note the importance of the rules, and the sunshine. Not very long after this, the American Law Institute voted on whether a Restatement of the Law of Future Interests was to treat unmarried persons living together as if they were married. The vote was taken at the annual meeting after discussion in a large room. The halls outside were filled with groups of members renewing acquaintance and discussing other matters. Members streamed in and out of the room. The question was put. The decision was made, 132 to 107. The figures were carefully put into a book, and the result was announced as a conclusion of the Institute, which had 1500 members.

These are bas reliefs. Let us consider the problem in an example less sharply etched. In a college or on a faculty there may be a voting membership of fifty. On a given afternoon ten may be unable to participate, sick, or out of town. Of the forty remaining, twenty-five may choose to come. The discussion may drone on during the afternoon and individuals may begin to go off to relieve their baby-sitters before supper or play their games of squash. Finally the vote is taken among the fourteen left, and a resolution passes eight to six. How should the loser treat such an outcome if the matter is one of great importance to him?

He can seek to have the matter reconsidered. He can spend time showing his delinquent colleagues how important the matter is. But there will be a period of delay before he can get the matter reconsidered, and parliamentary rules make reconsideration difficult. If any substantial number of such issues builds up he must begin to ration the time he can spend fighting old battles. And he must decide upon his stance, whether to treat the resolution as authoritative or resist it.

Why should it have any legitimacy for him? It is the outcome of the process, but that is all one can say of it. Did he agree to it in agreeing (if he did) to a quorum rule that allowed fourteen to continue the meeting? In all likelihood the quorum rule as such was never put to him; but even if it had been, he would not likely react very differently to the resolution whether he had voted yes or no to that rule. In the same way, if shareholders are successfully squeezed out in complex and ingenious maneuvers taken to merge two companies with a squeeze-out as an ultimate object (one of the companies perhaps being created solely for the purpose of merger and known to the corporate bar as a "phantom corporation"), they do not always accept, nor do courts who hear their pleas always accept, the argument that this is after all the outcome of the decision-making process, including the process of changing the decision-making process, to which they implicitly agreed when they purchased their stock.

Unless those of the college who remain at the end of the meeting, the eight and the six, are viewed as making a decision of a kind like that made by any other group holding office in a multimember body, there is no decision with which the individual member can identify. There is a decision of eight or of fourteen people: that is not a decision of the college. But if the decision of the fourteen *is* viewed as virtually indistinguishable from that made by any other delegee on behalf of those who have neither the time, nor the information, nor the current interest to participate themselves, then an individual must look to something other than the process to give it legitimacy and authority.[3]

Some decisions of substance which are the outcomes of rules operating upon contingencies are viewed as simply absurd. There is no purely conventional, or procedural, or what we may call definitional recognition of the sovereign. Our laughter is testimony to this, and we laugh before we roll up our sleeves to begin the serious business of dealing with the decision. Absurd outcomes are also viewed as occasions for adjustment of the rules. But the relative adjustability of the rules in a given situation (a quorum rule might not be adjustable upward without having the effect of transferring power to an executive because of the difficulty of assembling and keeping a quorum) is not an index of authority. Even if the rules cannot be readjusted and it appears they must remain as they are, the outcome may be given no authority. It may be resisted and fought, and the system will be manipulated to reverse it insofar as it may not have become irreversible by reason of its effects.[4]

RATIFICATION AND ACCEPTANCE

None of this is to say that there is no will of the people, no sovereign. Nor is it to say that the outcomes produced by the electoral and legislative process are never "ours" in some sense, or that we cannot make them ours. Acquiescence and ratification can indeed be substantive rather than wholly formal. Comparing something previously made with what one might believe and want, and coming to the conclusion that what is presented is what one does believe and want, is different from creating what one wants from ingredients not yet put together. But the difference is no absolute impediment to embracing what is given from without.

It may be easier to make our own the materials presented to us by chance than materials chosen for us and presented to us by another. They may be more our own precisely because they are not someone else's who claims authorship of them and therefore authority over the recipient as his creature. Particularly if we pull back, stretch ourselves out over time, stretch the sovereign and the people out over time, we can see the larger picture over time ratified and accepted, just as individuals make their own the careers and the homes that come to hand and are more fallen into than chosen. Men do not find their loves empirically by testing every alternative: friends and marriages are made from the materials that come to hand, and of course their children are presented to them entire. Individuals and peoples are changed by the results of a process regardless of its initial authority. The constitution of an undeveloped country adopted by an illiterate population in nonsecret voting, the Fourteenth Amendment put on the books under duress and without ratification according to the rules contemplated for amendment of the United States Constitution, the desegregation decisions of the United States Supreme Court in the 1950s whose authority was initially denied, all mold those who grow into adulthood under their influence.

No: the only point is that it is not democracy as it works in the modern nation state, not political democracy, that gives to an individual in office, to a decision, or to a text, the authority that any of them may have over us. Authority they may have and expressions of the will of the sovereign they may be, but not by virtue of the fact, the objective fact, that they are the outcomes of the process we call democratic.

The Democratic Connection

If democracy as it entered men's and women's lives in the eighteenth century and developed thereafter is not the provision of a necessary connection between the will of the people and the outcomes of the decision-making process, then what is it?

Democracy is a negative thing, a denial, more than a positive. Democracy was, in the eighteenth century as in its ancient antecedents, and is still, the denial of authoritarianism, which, when done, leaves us still with the search for the authoritative. That a denial of the authoritarian comported with biblical Christianity and removed a major contradiction in the organization of the world made it appear immediately to be progress; but it was, in a way, a moving back, or down—a stripping away. There is in democracy a positive, to be sure. There is affirmation of the equal dignity of the individual, equality not of the kind that integers or billiard balls have by reason of their separateness, for integers and billiard balls have no dignity, but an equality coupled rather with fraternity. But this affirmation that each individual has claims upon us, shares and is a source of our very thinking and all that we seek, is only the ground of the search for the authoritative to come.

PART III

The
AUTHORITATIVE
and the
AUTHORITARIAN

Then said the shepherds, "From that stile there goes a path that leads directly to Doubting-Castle, which is kept by Giant Despair; and these men (pointing to them among the tombs) came once on pilgrimage, as you do now, even till they came to that same stile. And because the right way was rough in that place, they chose to go out of it into that meadow, and there were taken by Giant Despair, and cast into Doubting-Castle; where, after they had a while been kept in the dungeon, he at last did put out their eyes, and led them among those tombs, where he has left them to wander to this very day." . . .

Then I saw in my dream that the shepherds had them to another place, in a bottom, where was a door in the side of an hill; and they opened the door, and bid them look in. They looked in therefore, and saw that within it was very dark and smoky; they also thought that they heard there a lumbering noise as of fire, and a cry of some tormented, and that they smelt the scent of brimstone. Then said Christian, "What means this?" The shepherds told them, saying, "This is a by-way to Hell, a way that hypocrites go in at." . . .

By this time the pilgrims had a desire to go forwards, and the shepherds a desire they should; so they walked together towards the end of the Mountains. Then said the shepherds one to another, "Let us here show to the pilgrims the Gates of the Celestial City, if they have skill to look through our perspective glass." The pilgrims then lovingly accepted the motion: so they had them to the top of an high Hill called Clear, and gave them their glass to look. Then they essayed to look, but the remembrance of that last thing that the shepherds had showed them made their hands shake; by means of which impediment they could not look steadily through the glass; yet they thought they saw something like the Gate, and also some of the glory of the place.

—Bunyan

143

IN THESE LAST FOUR CHAPTERS we leave our guiding question. Chapter 11 recalls what we have seen. Chapters 12 and 13 explore the hope that the lawyer's dilemma is in part self-imposed. Chapter 14 looks forward to the aid that may be hoped from others in sister disciplines who also hover between the authoritative and the authoritarian.

11

DILEMMA
Faith and Failure

S O   W E   C O M E to the lawyer's dilemma. It is presented not just by a Supreme Court whose staff is increasing. It is met at every turn. Trained to see law as system and process, aware more than others how much legal commands are merely the outcome of processes, knowing how often there is nothing behind the mask and that what is heard is only the imitation of a voice, put in this position by the very part he plays, the lawyer must nonetheless, by virtue of that same part, be the first to ask for willing obedience and the most assiduous in cultivating it. He must be an illusionist, a magician, when he had thought he was entering the most rational of professions. The pain is not in the charge of hypocrite or tool always made against him. The pain is in his practice, the work he does day to day. The pain is in playing his part, whether others clap or sneer, and however aware they may be. His position is worse than that of a courtier of the emperor who wore no clothes, passing a sock to him knowing all the while that there was no sock. At least there was an emperor.

But it is this pain, these grains of sand in the mantle, that must ultimately drive the lawyer to make the law's commands in fact authoritative and to realize in the world the presuppositions of legal method. He is not in a situation where he knows there *can* be nothing behind the mask. He is not even in the position of the Grand Inquisitor, whose certainty that there is nothing is merely put into some slight doubt by a prisoner's kiss. There is indeed mind and there are indeed real voices. The problem arises because there is not always mind and the voices are sometimes false, and the problem is peculiar to the lawyer because of the lawyer's greater awareness of this.

But, comes the retort, what is this mind that is placed in opposition to process? Is it not a process itself? We are met with the legislative and asked how we are to explain the fact that legislative statements, quite obviously the product of factors which are not the sorts of factors that deliberating minds take into account in deciding what ought to be said or done, are nonetheless treated as authoritative and as the statements of a speaker, the expression of a will, and the conveyor of intent, the Legislature's or the People's. We can transform this question into a question whether a view of government as process has within it a secret thing which is not process and does not escape making an appeal to a speaker with a mind like our own. But think back over the way this mind has been described. The process of deliberation, the methods of arriving at understanding, the process of decision making, the arguments that proceed along: Are these not the realities of the mind that lies behind statements accepted as meaningful? They may be complex and relatively unillumined. We may not have models of them or ways of analyzing and describing them. But they are still processes.

They are indeed. The difference is that they are processes inside us rather than outside us. We ourselves, and other individuals around us, cannot be eliminated in the one. We can be eliminated, and are, in the other. The difference resembles and is perhaps the same as that between a system that treats us as if we were objects, and which we therefore resist and push against and rightly see as one in which we have no place and which therefore cannot be part of us, and a system which, instead of manipulating us, seeks to embrace us. What are we to make of the fact that we do personify mindless systems? The response is another question: Can anyone escape an appeal to mind even analyzing law as a system? Law is a process and a system,[1] but it is a system depending for its very existence upon assent. It is not unique in this regard. Language is also a system, a way of doing things from which certain outcomes follow. But though apparently even less a matter of will than law and more a given in the world into which we are born, language too rests upon assent. If a computer were the model of man, we would have to use the language we have because it was built into us. There would be no question of assent. But with us, language can cease to have meaning. One can cease to understand it, not as a machine might cease to register and process it but because one does not agree with the only things it allows one to say, or believe that others agree with them either. One may not like it or accept it, down to its very roots. One may have to talk and think in a particular way, because there is no other way to talk and think; but that does not mean that one has to talk or think. Of course a man who does not talk or think, *refuses* to talk or think, is reduced to utter isolation and madness. Even more would a society for whom its language had lost meaning be mad and disintegrated. But we know there is no law of nature that prevents us from going mad.

A system that rests upon assent; assent that rests upon perception of a mind and a person in place of the system. The final question is whether this perception is illusion, not in some special case but generally.

If that which produces law and statements of law is a mindless system, how can we see it as something else without deluding ourselves, deluding ourselves and maintaining the delusion by a vast network of mutually supporting fictions introduced into the language in such a way that individuals cannot escape their use; making use of the worst and only inescapable limit upon our hopes, time, by ensuring that the use of a language free of any reference to mind and personality, the substitution of a description of the reality of what it is that mind and personification refer to, would take too long and be too burdensome; because we know the terrible consequences of awakening and facing the reality of things—no God, no Nation, no People, no Legislator, no Court, no Law, only a system and a process in which we play our parts so long as we dream?

This is a bit like asking whether we must live in delusion and listen to voices that are not there in order to save ourselves from a state of such utter solitude and silence that we might be driven to hearing voices and seeing visions that are not there. The question seems a mad one. How could we do such a thing? Does not the question answer itself?

But we cannot dismiss the question, for there is no doubt that the presupposition of mind is made and that it is assumed that a person is speaking when the evidence points to the contrary. When words which come in the guise of a meaningful statement and "in the name" of People, Legislature, Court, or Committee are presented to a judge or a lawyer, he does not always ignore them, treat them as if they are not there, hear them as he might hear thunder or the rustle of leaves, if he knows that they are not the product of an engaged decision. Sometimes he does ignore them and treat them as if they are not there, or are just noise. That is when courts vacate the statements of agencies and remand the decision to them, insisting that it be made again and saying, "This statement is not the statement of the *agency*. This is just a form of words, masquerading as the agency's statement, but really the product of bias, money, individual whim. We cannot understand the agency to mean this, we cannot understand how the agency could mean this: therefore the *agency* did not say this." But as often the judge or lawyer does not ignore them, and the examples are legion, not just the treatment of the statements of legislatures but of courts, corporations, and administrative agencies making a great host of decisions. "No inquiry into motive" and "Do not go behind the words of the statute" are two of the expressions taken off the shelf of legal maxims when an irrebuttable presumption of mind is made.

Now in part this is simply a refusal to demand perfection. There is, again, the constraint of time. There is the fact that individuals are deceptive and self-deceptive, full of hatred and self-hatred, short-sighted, fearful, in pain. It is not just the rare individual who experiences such agonies but the run of individuals. If what was said was treated as not said if it could be perceived to be the product of these, there could be little communication between men. Instead of waiting for perfect materials, one works with the materials one has.

And in part the presupposition is made because things would fall apart if men challenged each other at every turn, not just because they would spend too much of their time doing that but because passions are aroused by challenges which are, after all, accusations. There is this much of the authoritarian woven into law.

But one of the consequences of this accommodation, of which everyone is at some level aware, is to threaten the very integration for which the accommodation is made, and it is this that leads to the push to adjust systems of decision making so that such presuppositions will not have to be made in the future. The consequence of a particular design of an institution before which all others pale is its ultimate promotion or destruction of a sense of meaning in the world. In fact, though the methodological presupposition of mind be made, authority does not thereupon flow from it. We have noted from the beginning that authority is a matter of degree. Courts cannot help themselves any more than individuals can. As understandability becomes more difficult and the perception of an integrated mind behind a statement grows dimmer, the lawyer becomes perceptibly more objective in his treatment of it. Good faith becomes less a question because there is less to internalize. He begins to fictionalize it and thus to dissolve it. He pays attention to it only when he cannot avoid paying attention to it. This is obvious where the document does not hang together internally or cannot be fit into other statements, and the presupposition of mind fades after analysis. But it can equally fade before. A thing is understood only if there is a will to understand it. It may even be said that a thing is understandable only if it can attract the attention of an understanding mind. If the supposition is known to be false from the beginning, the will does not respond as if the supposition were true. The will does not respond. It cannot.

Or can it? If the meaningful statements of an integrating mind can be imitated to a high degree of accuracy—put aside the thought that such imitations usually fail in the end—why could not the will to understand be activated and the techniques of understanding be applied, objectively? If, the less authority there is, the more alone in the world we are as individuals, and the more alone, the closer to the madness we see in those who feel themselves utterly alone and begin peopling their silent, empty worlds with private visions and voices, why is this not goad enough to the will? Beyond the individuals whom we know and love and who know and love us, why are not the minds and persons to which we so readily refer obviously the results of a conspiracy with the facts, to which we are all parties—a public illusion rather than a private illusion, which is better because we are all in it together, a comfort which we have created for ourselves? In the end there are only individuals. Every other person is a useful fiction. Insofar as these other persons are not merely a convenient mode of reference, so that when a statement is issued in the name of Congress or the Court that is to be taken to mean in the name of the particular system that produced it, and insofar as they are not simply atavistic remnants in our language of an earlier day when men were not so adult and listened to gods to tell them what to do, greater persons are parasites on the experience each of us has with other individuals. And we can certainly make our experience with individuals bear the weight and provide the necessary nourishment, if sanity and life are at stake.

But in the end there are no individuals. Individuals die. We are going to die, you the reader, and I. If we survive long, such lovers and friends as we have known, if we are among those who have truly known personal love and friendship, will die around us, and we can expect to be left alone, without that experience from which the persons whom we might propose to conceive as parasites would have to draw their nourishment.

Yet we continue to live, and live actively, most of us, to the death that nature brings.

Life in the face of death. That is the great fact always asking to be explained, and always there also as the source of explanation. Does not life in the face of death suggest who we are, and does not who we are explain life going on in the face of death? The persons of whom we speak do not die when individuals die. We can plan and argue in and through them right up to our deaths, and they carry on our hopes. Perhaps we think that we do not then die either, whether or not we individually have children. We may create these identities larger than our own lives just to avoid facing death. But what if we do? Are they not real? Who is to say they are not as real as anything else we know, even death itself?

Forlorn! the very word is like a bell
  To toll me back from thee to my sole self!
. . . .
Adieu! adieu! thy plaintive anthem fades
. . . .
  Was it a vision, or a waking dream?
  Fled is that music:—Do I wake or sleep?

The Necessity of Explaining Legal Method

Let us return to legal method.

Lawyers do much that is odd. The oddness of it, demanding explanation, is what spurs inquiries into method. If what lawyers did seemed more natural, methodological questions might be put aside for a rainy day, and everyone could turn to the harvest. But that is not our situation. Lawyers are continually asked, "What ought we to do in these circumstances, how ought we to think about this matter?" They have to explain, to themselves and to those who are on other business in the world, why they do what they do in going about answering these questions of moment so continuously put to them.

Asked by others what to do, what the law would want a person to do, American lawyers will go off and find what a few old men scattered about the country thirty, fifty, a hundred years ago, sitting on intermediate appellate courts in Pennsylvania or in a town in the mountains of Kentucky, said they thought the law was at the time they spoke. They come back, put it all together, and say, "*That* is the law. That you ought to obey." They expect to be paid for producing such an answer and do not expect their inquirer to exclaim "Ridiculous!" and turn on his heel and stalk away.

A commentator writing an article, still much looked to, on the question whether business corporation directors are liable for negligence when they undertake to make decisions for the corporation, finds four opinions from different jurisdictions at different times and at different hierarchical levels, and proceeds to pay great attention to them. Professor Bishop concludes, "[T]o my mind none of these cases carries real conviction." One he decides is a decision on pleading. Another he regards as a "sport"; there was a cogent dissent, and "it does not seem to have been followed in any subsequent decision of the New York courts." In another he examines the facts as stated by the trial judge; weighs a fact, that the trial judge's conclusions from the facts were rejected by his brethren sitting en banc, against the presence of phrases in the state supreme court's opinion suggesting that the supreme court agreed with the trial judge; and ends by categorizing the case as "one of those in which 'negligence' is a euphemism for dishonesty." He concludes from his inquiries that he is "very skeptical of the proposition that directors of industrial corporations run any substantial risk of liability for ordinary negligence." There is no suggestion that the commentator is not serious in spending such time with what these men said in these cases. The implication is that if one statement had not been a sport, a second about procedure, a third euphemistic, and so forth, then directors of industrial corporations today, great mercantile princes, would indeed run a risk and ought to be concerned.

In a 1978 opinion Justice Rehnquist begins an inquiry into whether political advertisements by business corporations are protected under First Amendment guarantees of free speech by stating, "Early in our history, Mr. Chief Justice Marshall described the status of a corporation in the eyes of federal law. . . ." Justice Rehnquist's assumption is that all who read his opinion would think that they *should* ponder what this man Marshall had taught nearly two centuries before. In a 1980 case not far away in the *United States Reports,* involving definition of securities fraud under federal law, Justice Blackmun refers to a trend toward a "more flexible, less formalistic understanding of the duty to disclose," and to the "steps [that] have been taken" to that end. He then cites a 1963 California intermediate appellate decision, a 1959 Kansas decision, a 1949 Missouri decision, and a 1947 Tennessee decision. This appears to be the trend and these to be the steps to which he refers.

John Hart Ely, arguing in 1978 that the Supreme Court is bound by law to frame constitutional issues in terms of democratic procedure rather than substantive value, devotes much time to an examination of the words of the justices in *Calder v. Bull,* a 1798 decision which "[Professors Brest and Gunther have] cited as the 'least equivocal' Supreme Court reference to the possibility that a statute could be held unconstitutional because it violated natural law." He asks his readers to "note carefully the last three words" of a sentence in one of the four opinions in *Calder,* the phrase "of the State," and goes on to say, "The context makes fairly clear that by 'State' [Justice Chase] meant one of the political units that make up the union; he tended to use 'government' to refer to 'the state' in its more abstract sense." And he concludes that *Calder,* this collection of opinions from the eighteenth century, "far from being authority for the view that natural law is enforceable in the name of the Constitution, appears on a close reading as strong authority against it."

THEN THERE IS what lawyers do when new men speak, men or women who may have been their classmates in law school.

"Is this course relevant after *Chiarella?*" was chalked up on a blackboard by a student before class in a course on corporations at a law school on the last day of the 1980 term. *Chiarella* was a 1980 Supreme Court case which came down (as the phrase is) at the end of the school term. It appeared vastly to cut back on the scope of federal securities laws' prohibitions against profiting on the stock market from special access to information, to be a turn away from concern with corporate office, obligation to larger entities, distributional equity, and economic efficiency which had been held out as central to the securities laws, and a turn back to a prior common law world of concern only for those with whom an individual man dealt face-to-face or with whom he was connected through relationships recognized by the law of property. The case itself did not do this, and we shall not pause here to go into why it might have been thought to wipe away so much in the law, or why it did not do so. What was important and striking about the question scrawled on the blackboard was the thought that the action of four living men sitting in Washington, joined by one more in a confused concurrence, could wipe out all that had been said during the previous forty hours of classroom discussion, without precursors that would have been the subject of analysis during those hours. It is an odd thought, but that it was entertained by lawyers generally was evident from the spate of articles pouring from the pens of commentators and the seminars for practicing lawyers immediately organized across the country. Two images, both false, are projected. One is military, that of a general giving orders to a regiment marching in one direction to change course. A majority of the Supreme Court speaks, and 300,000 lawyers march in the opposite direction. The other is scientific. The scrawled question on the blackboard appears to be of the form "Is this course in physics relevant after the discovery just announced that matter can travel faster than the speed of light?"

Dean Ely, again, could observe of the 1857 *Dred Scott* decision that "only two other Justices concurred in Taney's opinion" and that "the path of the law had not been altered," implying that if two more had joined, the path of the law *would* have been altered; but attention to just what sitting justices say is even more meticulous than that paid to the actions of their predecessors. A flavor of the kind of attention given generally to the *Bakke* decision on reverse discrimination when it appeared in 1978 can be provided by Dean Ely's conclusion:

> Immediate media coverage of *Bakke* gave inordinate attention to Justice Powell's opinion. . . . It . . . seems he was the only one who said that

special scrutiny was constitutionally appropriate, though four others (Justices Brennan, White, Marshall, and Blackmun) seemed to settle on the view that an in-between standard was proper. (The reason for the cagey language is that Justice White joined both the Brennan opinion, opting for an in-between standard, and part III-A of the Powell opinion, requiring full-blown special scrutiny. I have resolved it this way in deference to Justice Powell's footnote 34 . . . criticizing Justice White for disagreeing with him on this issue).

There seems little danger that either standard will be difficult to meet. Justices Brennan, White, Marshall, and Blackmun found their in-between standard satisfied by the Davis plan. (To the extent Justice White thought special scrutiny appropriate, he obviously thought it too was satisfied.) Justice Powell did not think special scrutiny satisfied, but made it abundantly clear he would be satisfied with the sort of cosmetic change it would take to convert the Davis plan to a "Harvard-type" plan. That's five votes. . . . [I]ndeed at least at certain points in their careers on the Court, each of the [dissenting] Justices joining Justice Steven's . . . opinion has apparently stood ready constitutionally to sustain at least certain types of affirmative action. . . . Of course differences may be perceived, but it seems likely that some of these votes will be added to the five already committed to sustain a plan like Harvard's. . . .

The image again is military, the officers' mess gossiping about the attitudes of the general's staff.

And always subtle, yet forthright, is Donald Regan. In his discussion of abortion he comments, "If the ultimate test in the equal protection area is whether a reasonable American legislature could have passed (or in some cases, could fail to repeal) a particular law, then there comes a point at which the judgment of persons imbued with and sensitive to our traditions is worth more than hypotheticals and distinctions." He concludes:

[T]he most important fact about the decision in *Roe* is that seven Justices, including some not known for their activist tendencies, were impelled to strike down abortion laws even though they must have realized that their arguments were not very persuasive. In this case, given the nature of the issue, the fact that the Court held abortion laws unconstitutional is evidence for the proposition that they *are* unconstitutional, even though the Constitution does not simply mean what the Court says it means.

LOOKING UP what some old men said, jumping when some new men speak—these things need to be explained. They need explanation, as a mother jumping when her child calls and a scientist looking to what an experimenter said long ago do not, at least in the modern world. So, too, does lawyers *poring* over what these individuals say, whether new or old, need to be explained. The examples set out above will give some sense of the degree of it to the nonlawyer. The lawyer knows how meticulous the analysis is because he does it; but sometimes he needs to step back and see what it looks like. Whether brief or fulsome in the statement of their conclusions, lawyers dwell upon what has been said. In this they are like Isaiah Berlin writing on Tolstoy, Marx, or Vico, only the men whose words lawyers turn over in their heads are not Tolstoy, Marx, or Vico. They may be excellent men, but they are rarely so excellent as obviously to warrant such attention.

In the late 1970s, discussion of the authority of Supreme Court decisions reviewing actions of Congress swirled around a short footnote in a 1938 opinion. In his 1979 inquiry into the American judicial function Owen Fiss begins his analysis with the statement, "The great and modern charter for ordering the relation between judges and other agencies of government is footnote four of *Carolene Products.*" Professor Fiss is fully aware that focusing discussion upon the footnote is a matter of choice. He treats its decline and resurgence in the legal mind. But the fact remains that he and others writing on this grandest of issues pore over the few sentences contained in that footnote. He refers to "a new and highly suggestive commentary on the footnote" by one of his colleagues. He asks how a "view that declares supreme the people's preferences" can be "reconciled with the very idea of a Constitution" and follows his question with, "There is, to be certain, another part of footnote four, one that I have not yet described." He speaks of the "preferred status of legislatures under footnote four," but concludes, "Footnote four is prepared to recognize [specific constitutional] provisions as a limitation on legislative supremacy. . . ." He infers that the free speech clause is an example of textual specificity "from the citations," *Stromberg v. California* and *Lovell v. City of Griffin,* "two early Hughes Court decisions heralding a new era for free speech," and goes on, "In discussing the theory of specificity the footnote speaks of the entire Bill of Rights, giving us a further insight into what that Court actually meant by textual specificity."

Dean Ely, though disputing Fiss, is no less willing to dwell upon the footnote. He begins the analysis of his "On Discovering Fundamental Values" by stating, with a citation to the footnote, "Generally speaking, the Warren Court was a *Carolene Products* Court, centrally concerned with ensuring broad participation, not simply in the processes of government but in the benefits generated by those processes as well." He goes on, "So far as the first of the *Carolene Products* themes is concerned . . . the record of the Burger Court is mixed but generally consistent with that of the

Warren Court." He explains his reference to the *Carolene Products* themes as "two" by stating, "Actually, the footnote's first paragraph strikes an interpretivist theme, adverting to the 'specific prohibitions' of the Constitution. It apparently was added to gain the concurrence of Chief Justice Hughes and historically has received less attention than the two succeeding paragraphs" (and he thus presents an example of a lawyer withdrawing the force of a statement by making it the outcome of a process, all the while maintaining his attentiveness to just what was said by five particular men who did agree and thus spoke for "the Court").

Or listen to a passage from the text of Professor Regan's essay on the legality of abortion laws to which we referred above, as he argues that imposition of pregnancy is imposition of serious bodily harm:

> It is interesting to note that one of the comments in the *Restatement* *(Second) of Torts* includes an illustration which strongly implies that a broken arm is serious bodily harm. The illustration in question does not *say* that a broken arm is serious bodily harm, because the primary object of the illustration is not to define serious bodily harm but rather to indicate the legal effect of a mistake on the part of the attacker about the extent of harm he is likely to cause. Nor does the illustration specifically say that deadly force can be used to avoid the broken arm, since what force can be used depends in part on how much force is actually necessary in the circumstances. However, the illustration appears in connection with the basic section on the use of deadly force in self-defense, and it would lose its point if it were not intended that a broken arm should represent a higher level of harm than the harm which justifies the use of non-deadly force.

The legal reader is assumed to be interested in this, and he *is* interested. Delicate analysis is lavished upon an illustration to a comment to a section of a restatement, drafted and approved by individuals who were themselves relying upon a collection of legal texts from disparate times and places, upon which they had lavished similar analysis.[2]

PERSONIFICATION IN LAW

This is what lawyers do when asked to find the law. It is not exclusively what lawyers do. It may not take up the bulk of their time. But it is what lawyers distinctively do, and what others see done when they ask about the *law* rather than the effects *of* law, the sociology *of* law, the philosophy *of* law, the economic analysis *of* law, and so forth. It is the core of what is taught in law schools.

As we have seen, the explanation and the justification of these things lies in understanding the method of legal analysis. For it is lawyers' method that produces law. Hard and practical men are generally impatient with methodological questions and inquiry into presuppositions. Just tell us what the law says, they growl, and forget the jurisprudence. Thinking themselves realists, they are in fact just the opposite, magicians, believing that the written or spoken word has an independent power, that *it* can command. But it can issue no commands. Statements of law are not formulae to be conjured with. A client of a lawyer hears of a Wyoming case in which a school board loses on a question whether it must teach minority children in their native tongue. He is in New York and deeply involved in litigation there on such an issue. He rushes to the law library to find the advance sheet and read the opinion, saying excitedly to a colleague he passes along the way, "They lost in Wyoming." Why is he interested in what happened in Wyoming? Why does he rush to look at the case? Because what happened in Wyoming affects the law. But it has no effect except as lawyers' method gives it effect. It is made part of the law by lawyers' method in a way akin to though not the same as the way the truths of natural science, not being given, are made by the scientific method. Any theory, indeed any conception of system in human affairs, contains an unstated and usually unexamined assumption that people will follow the law. That is a given. If people don't follow the law, they could be required to. All maximizing and exchange theories, as in economics, assume this structure. But what is the law? That is supplied by the lawyers. How? Through their method.[3]

But the method lawyers use involves a presupposition of mind. And as we have seen, it is this that produces the dilemma of being a lawyer and the dilemma of much other modern social thought. Lawyers are to be blamed in part for others' dilemmas in this regard, for they have kept their method something of a secret, perhaps because of its incompatibility with the scientific tenor of the late nineteenth and first part of the twentieth century. Return again to the problem of jointly building up in multi-member court, agency, or legislature a statement that is to have legal effect. One can imagine a sentence or a paragraph of a statement of law being built up by a number of persons, and words exchanged as interests are exchanged. But it is not a word but the *consequence* of a word—for the interest in question—that is exchanged, gained, or forgone. The consequence depends upon lawyers and the presupposition of mind, which is at odds with an objectivist view that words are bargaining chips and things to be exchanged like bolts of cloth or bushels of grain in a bazaar. The objectivist must presume, if he expects a statement to be respected rather than combated, to be obeyed, to have authority, that the listener will take a stance quite the opposite of that which he, the objectivist, is taking, that is, that a sentence or paragraph is like a machine and that he and the others who are to build it are each sitting on a cushion before their own boxes of parts, dipping into them, passing parts back and forth and adding them here and there to the machine or replacing parts that have been added before as they bargain away. The objectivist's dilemma, that others must proceed as he has not, is all the more painful when he himself comes to listen to what he has helped construct.

What speaks? If we are spoken to, it is by a person. Widespread complaints today about the impersonality of bureaucracy are accompanied by widespread observation that a sense of the authoritative in society is collapsing. The authoritarian opposite of bureaucracy, the man on the white horse, also mimics the source of authority and relies parasitically upon it, and his mass appeal, though always temporary, is a result of his greater immediate success in doing so. In law personification can be seen on the surface and in the depths, in the dress of the law, the conclusory metaphors and turns of phrase in which legal thinking is expressed, and in the very structure and process of that thinking.

There are of course periods in history in which the urge to escape the demands of perceiving a person speaking is very obvious. The law becomes laden with fictions, which we find easier to laugh at the further we are away from them in time. We can join Dicey, for instance, in wonderment at the early nineteenth-century action of ejectment, but find it more difficult to join John Noonan in his wonderment at the replacement of plaintiffs and defendants with algebraic symbols by the very judges we were taught to revere in our youth. That is too close, and does not seem so odd though it is of quite the same order.

These periods in the development of law have been associated with escape from the tyranny of personal authority, from the institution of slavery and its associated states, including wage slavery and the various devices of rural social control. Tyranny they may have been an escape from, though one must be careful with the rhetoric of even a century ago; it is doubtful, however, that they ever saw an escape from personal authority or personification, or that they represent a breaking, even a temporary breaking, of the link between personification and authority. Personal authority need not be tyranny, but impersonal authority necessarily represents chaos. It is doubtful that arbitrary personal power, pure power, tyrannous power ever was legal. We could summon the greater Portia, Antigone, to testify to this, but the prophets of the Old Testament and the insistent position of the medieval church are probably better evidence that the tyrant at least in the West did not really have authority—power, yes, but not authority. Merely as a matter of language, the two phrases that describe the two polar states men struggle against—the *tyranny of personal authority* and the *anarchy of impersonal authority*—are internally inconsistent and paradoxical. The law cannot be said to swing between them over history. Impersonal authority is no more authoritative than is personal tyranny.

Indeed, these periods of legal history in which there seems an urge to escape the demands of personification are being recharacterized and presented as periods of legal formality or formalism, which is a very great advance. When characterizing them in the usual way as periods in which the "rule of law" held sway or in which "liberalism" or "individualism" was in the ascendency one must always keep in mind the Pickwickian and technical sense in which such terms have been used. The record of our experience in history never does put the necessity of personification in question. The attempt to depersonalize reflected in the fiction and formality of the law we inherited from our immediate predecessors is a longish experiment, an experiment with defining an abstract person, a person without content, a Euclidean point of a person, a person who is a source of pure energy only, unapplied and without purpose, an entity exhibiting only the form of a person, drained of substance and meaning. No doubt the provocative idea of this experiment runs far back and can be seen at work in various societies at various times before its dominance in the time of our parents, grandparents, and great-grandparents. But we are standing at the end of that experiment. Running through legal discourse as a constant, dictating even the form of its opposite, is an insistence upon seeing, hearing, and feeling a person behind what is said.[4]

THE DIFFICULTY OF BELIEF

The lawyer must be a believer. But it is not easy to hold fast against the dissolution of things.

There is evidence all around that we do believe, both in the large and in the small. The individual who says he is consumed with doubt, believes nothing and knows nothing, has particular delights. He believes in those. There is the evidence of our language, what we say, the terms we use. "We," "our society," "the Court," "the corporation," and the "individual" pepper the talk and the writing of the most determined reductionist. There is the mode or stance or tone of arguments made whatever their content, including those made in favor of doubt, the earnest attempt by the determinist to persuade another and seek his assent to the proposition that all is determined, the behaviorist who acknowledges the existence of his own mind and only his own but who is not satisfied with his views until he has brought others to share them and who expects others to listen to what he says rather than simply observe what he does. There is our own behavior and the behavior of others around us in the face of death. There is the experience of love and the connection we recognize truly looking into another's eyes, the brief flash of mutual openness. There is the perception and rejection of madness. Why is authority associated with willing obedience, and both associated with law in the very structure of thought? Why must one believe this, why will not unwilling obedience do? Ask why not madness, the isolation of utter silence or the hearing of voices others do not hear or life perpetually in a raging storm.

But the believing, the actual believing itself, is hard. To some extent we must put this down to flaw, imperfection, sin, what you will. Every reformer has wanted to sweep away the authoritarian and replace it with the authoritative; this is the constant thrust, the ebb and the flow of history—and we do not know whether we reach higher and higher as the waves crash around us, or what is on the shore and beyond. The problem of being a lawyer and doing the work that must be done before asking for the obedience of others is not peculiar to law. It is met in history, in perceiving a historical process which is produced by historical actors who were acting in what for them was the present with an indeterminate future, and who could not and did not conceive of themselves as part of a process anymore than the acting and choosing contemporaries of the historian do. Like biologists, historians have difficulty with man as the outcome of a process alone, as the product of minuscule increments of change in a directionless, mindless interaction. But for biologists, man just appears, once. For historians man appears every instant. The problem is met in art with the arresting of time which should produce the present, there being no change, no development, no past or future, but which instead produces a form of death and silence. It is met in the practice of psychiatry, where the therapist must have the trust of his patient to succeed, and to obtain that trust must eschew manipulation and base his authority upon the authority of greater knowledge, and who yet must have responsibility for one who is, after all, a patient, and must (given the shortness of time and money) guide, surprise, choose his remarks, time his remarks, emphasize or not, comfort or not—and is expected to do so by the patient and by his profession. He must calculate the effects of the words he speaks and the actions he undertakes as a result of his knowledge while respecting his patient as a self-determining and self-creating person and asking the patient to respect him with an openness that will also be openness with self; and, like the lawyer, he is always threatened with the loss of the sense of the person before him as he analyzes the person's behavior and statements as the outcome of a process within the patient and within the therapeutic relationship. Indeed, the presupposition of his success—his faith—is more at war with what he thinks to be the facts than is the lawyer's and his dilemma is that much greater. The problem is met in the sense one has of one's own life, the reality of which waxes and wanes as one thinks of it as a continuous present graced or haunted by memories and hopes, or as going on over time, a journey of which the present is an instance. We can make a rock, indeed the entire universe, dissolve and become an instance, a passing outcome of a continuing process that disappears as it is formed, by simply shifting our units of time from hours and years to millennia and eons. Both seem true. Whether we exist seems very close to a matter of naked choice, and thus to depend upon our own affirmation of the fact, our willing assent to the fact.

The choice to exist, if it is a choice, would not be entirely arbitrary. If we believe in a thing, a value, a work of art, if we believe in the present, then we have only a difficulty and a puzzle. All the rest, the future and the past, the process of change, causation and that which might have been and might be, become only metaphors and attempts to express what we experience, and not very good ones. Our sense of all the rest becomes a miracle and a gift—an endowment of novelty, change, liberation from the death of the static, freedom in a way, imagination of what might have been and contemplation of possibility.

But if we perceive, believe in, only the process, then we are lost. We, who might be as real as what we see when we look directly into another's eyes, do not exist. We are contingent, we might not have been. Nor does the present exist, nor the work of art, nor our loves or achievements. Then it is not the future, the past, and process, but instead the present and the person that are the miracle and the gift.

There might seem only a miracle and a gift on the one hand, and a miracle and a gift on the other. But there is a difference. A gift is that to which we have no claim, and a miracle is that in which it is hard to believe. We know which of the two is harder to believe and to what we have more claim. Is it so hard to believe in ourselves? Do we not have at the least a claim to ourselves?

The lawyers' problem is *the* problem. We will not solve it here. What we should see here is that within it is the problem of authority, and that it is linked to the problem of bureaucracy today and to the difficulty of the search by law today, as science is being put aside, for what it is, what it is for, what it is about, and what legal method should be. In the end, of course, the problem is a religious one. A question of meaning always is.

12
IMAGE
The Self-Imposed Dilemma

A T THE END OF the last chapter we noted that the lawyer's problem is a religious problem. This does not mean that an answer lies at hand. Recall John Bunyan's dreamt-of pilgrims, who accompanied so many to the New World. Seeking the Celestial City, on a rough path, they passed the place where a smooth and easy way led to Doubting Castle. If they had gone in there and stayed, Giant Despair would have put out their eyes and left them to wander among the dead. Then they saw a door through which went hypocrites who did not say what they believed or believe what they said; it led to hell and torment. Many like them had gone in. Finally they reached the top of a hill called Clear, from which, through a perspective glass, they should have been able to see the Gates of the Celestial City. As it was, because of the dangers so close, their hands shook when they each held up the perspective glass to look, and none of them could look steadily through it.

But even though their perspective glass was shaking, "they thought they saw something like the Gate, and also some of the glory of the place." So it is with lawyers. The lawyer's perspective glass shakes in his hands today, and perhaps it always will, for the same reasons. But something can be seen. And Bunyan wrote in the seventeenth century at the beginning of the time when equality was to do its work. We have gone forward, and can go forward further. One way is through our language. The lawyer's problem is not helped by the metaphors of legal discourse. We do not help ourselves as much as we could in the way we speak.

In particular there is the metaphor of making legal decisions and statements by taking factors into account and giving them weights. This is central to our concern, for it focuses directly upon mind, and it is through this description of the legal mind in action that mind dissolves so easily into process. Legal texts are written using the imagery of taking factors into account and giving them weights. Rule or guideline, commentary or legislative history, opinion of judge, administrator, or lawyer stating, explaining, justifying, or integrating—any of these may use it. It is very much with us. It is part of legal thinking, and we have reflected this in our own discussions in earlier chapters.

But while one cannot think without tools of thought, and must use those that are at hand, one need not, as we have seen, be entirely committed to them. One can conceive their replacement even if one cannot conceive what that replacement would be. One can believe in mind but not necessarily in a particular description of mind. For while we search to express ourselves, there remains a difference between the expression and what we are seeking to express; and certainly when it is mind we are seeking to represent this difference becomes a most important one.

Metaphors are, in a way, worshipped as their implications are unfolded and followed by the devotee. "The death of the animal is like the death of the motor car" was a late nineteenth-century aphorism, and more than we like to think may have flowed from it and its like. Some legal arguments about abortion today begin by replacing the image of a mother giving nourishment with the image of a dependent person being plugged-in to a healthy person, as if to a kidney machine. Henry Adams suggested that the age into which we, our parents, and our grandparents were born could be projected from a shift in the image of worship, the Virgin to the Dynamo; Adams was certain that this shift was quite as much a determinant as a consequence of development.[1]

Whatever our materialist leanings, if it is of very great importance to sanity and will we might well take pains not to be too beguiled by our own images. And sanity and will are at stake.

THE LANGUAGE OF AUTHORITY

We have asked whether the processes of the deliberative mind could be imitated and what reason we had to think that we could not personify the imitation quite as well as its model. But is taking all relevant factors into account, excluding irrelevant factors, and giving factors their proper weight what is being imitated?

We have asked what makes us take into account or exclude factors and give weights to them, and wondered whether that might not be the hard ground of the law and whether we might not be bound by it even if we were ignorant of it. We pointed to the problem of infinite regress. All this assumed that taking factors into account, and so forth, was what we were doing, and that what *makes* us choose to take a factor into account is the important real question. But is that what we are doing?

Judicial and administrative procedure, whether in connection with the decision of particular cases or the issuance of rules, is designed to exclude from consideration irrelevant factors. It is designed, further, to insure the consideration of all relevant factors through doctrines of standing, intervention, notice, reopening, issuance of intermediate opinions, and a host of other devices. And it is designed, so far as it can be, to prevent the placing of undue weight upon particular factors, through such measures as separation of prosecutorial and decisional functions and prohibition of ex parte argument and secret witnesses. Then on appellate review there is undertaken an identification of the factors actually ignored or actually taken into account, and the weights given to them. But these carefully designed procedures, with the details and application of which much of the litigation over a great issue may be concerned, do not reach the putting together of the factors. Nor does appellate review. There is an indeterminacy of result, which appears to be inconsistent with the "rule of law," and which is so troubling that it leads either to disillusionment or to more and more elaboration of procedure, to the distress of all, it seems, but lawyers who have no concern for time or the substantive objectives of the decisions being made. This is an aspect of the twin specters of arbitrariness and discretion that have loomed larger and larger in discussions of modern law and government.

But the problem may arise as much from the metaphors we are using as from conflicts of ends, the intractability of the world, or the ultimate limit of time. All these various problems may have the same source, at least in part. The metaphors of mind, the definitions of what it is to make a legal decision or to make a decision legal, may still be too mechanical.

In fact, they may be quite crude.

They have replaced and represent an advance (except, perhaps, as there can be no advance upon a situation that has uniquely served a dialectical function) on the language of rights and the geographical metaphors that spread throughout the law from the law of real property. Traditional legal discourse was organized as if there were a thing between two antagonists. The talk was about that thing. Talk was organized spatially and territorially. Rights were rights *to*: a chain went out from the right-holder and attached itself to the thing. There might be a struggle over a chain, or a snarl of two chains that had leapt out from the antagonists. One antagonist could walk away and give up his grip. Chains could be tossed from one person to another. The picture of what lawyers were doing was a picture of disentangling or sorting out, and of building walls, restoring the status quo principally on the appealing criterion of priority in time, who was there first. The images were drawn from cattle and farmland, and, indeed, the classic cases through which law students were first introduced to law and the terminology of rights involved cattle and farmland.

But while legal discourse was organized and dominated by the language of rights, it was clear, even in reading about land and cattle, that this was not at all what was happening in legal thinking. It appeared that the right existed (just as a thing might exist) before the judge's conclusion that he had found it, but quite obviously the right emerged at the end of the case and was a result, or expression, of what the participants in the case had said and done. It was always a *decision,* by someone else, that was being challenged in the adversary process of producing legal texts, and the search for "rights" or the right answer was a review of that decision, to determine whether it was authorized, legitimate, legal, authoritative, and to be obeyed by the challenger and others.

Thus the language of decision making and the analysis of mind always lay intertwined with the language of rights. But the language of decision making too was, and is, earthbound. Geography, place, and the gravity that goes with place are all there in the imagery.

It is not just the notion of a *factor* having weight. *Decisions* are "weighty" depending upon their importance. A factor taken into account is a "ground" of a decision (including, it should be said, a decision to make a statement of law as well as a decision to act or order action). A good decision is "well-grounded." A decision "rests" upon factors, or considerations, or, if the language of fact is being used, upon "evidence." Factors, considerations, or grounds "support" the decision. The "weightier" or more important the decision is, the more "support" it must have, the better "grounded" it must be.

If, on analysis, the decision rests upon factors that cannot be used and a court removes those factors, the decision may "fall," as the Eiffel Tower would fall if its supports were removed. The decision "cannot stand." If the supports for the decision are not of sufficient "weight" to support it the decision will also fall and so also if there is a failure to support a decision with a consideration that should have been taken into account. But, if there is more than one support, if there are multiple independent grounds, then the calibration becomes more complicated. The decision need not fall if only one or a few of them turns out to be weak or bad and are therefore removed. This is the doctrine of harmless or nonprejudicial error, and is matched by the doctrine of blatant illegality if a decision has only one ground and that is removed because it itself had absolutely no support.

So also, when we move from the challenge to the challenger, we find that to make arguments against the legality of a decision, to reach out and pull at its supports, a challenger has to have *locus standi*, standing, a "place to stand." The language of jurisdiction continues to be used. And this usage continues when we move back to the decision maker after a particularly successful challenge. A decision maker is often said to be "beyond" or "outside" his or its jurisdiction, with an implied reference to a territorial lord stepping outside the boundaries of his geographically defined domain, where what he would say would have no legal effect. He is beyond support, in a field not his, where he has no place of his own to stand.

Now what I want to suggest is that we should feel no more bound by the metaphors of process than we feel bound by these echoes of real property still at the very center of our description of the legal mind. We also say, in place of saying that a decision "without support" falls, that it is simply "not there"; and in response to the fact that of course a decision *was* made in the sense that something happened and that processes did occur, we say that the *decision maker* has not made the decision.

Some individual, who perhaps thought he was acting as property owner or executive of a corporation or commissioner of an administrative agency or judge, was not. The illegitimate decision, the decision without authority, is to be ignored, paid no attention to, taken as no guide by others in deciding what to do, not because *it* has no force, has fallen and is not there, but because the decision maker that purported to make the decision cannot be understood to have done so. If the decision maker had made *that* decision it would have been acting out of character. It would have lost its identity to the senses of the listener and would therefore not be seen or heard. So it is that the king can do no wrong. Wrong may be done, but the king does not do it.

There are evident difficulties with this way of stating the experience of authority, which find their expression in the doctrinal difficulties of the sovereign immunity of governmental units, the effect of ultra vires corporate acts, the criminal liability of corporate entities, even diminished responsibility and legal insanity. If, that is, an individual makes a decision not as an individual but as a corporate or administrative official, and if the decision cannot be attributed to the agency or corporate body, who did make it and who is responsible? Or if an individual does wrong knowing that he does wrong, does he not disobey himself? How then can he, as a whole, be condemned and confined any more than the corporate entity can be condemned as a whole for the actions of an agent who was disobedient and outside his authority? On the other hand, if one does *not* know that what he is doing is wrong, is that not the very definition of legal insanity?

Where money is involved, as in the case of contract and tort, these problems of perception and conception have been successfully ignored; but where condemnation or structural remedy are in question their presence has been somewhat paralyzing. If one cannot do anything to remedy matters, one cannot go forward. There is an ebb in the ebb and flow. Authoritarianism creeps back in: that the king can do no wrong also means that one cannot challenge and must obey, regardless of what one believes and even if one cannot understand. This is to be expected. Paralysis and authoritarianism accompany a failure to integrate one's own mind or to share an integrated mind with one's fellows.

Here the failure is a failure of the legal analyst, and one reason why law, like mathematics, continues to challenge. Nonetheless, in admitting or saying that it is not the administrative agency, the corporation, the parent or some other personified decision maker who would do such a thing or make such a decision or make such a statement as is put before us, and that our first reaction is to "vacate" it (with all the overtones of emptiness and abandonment that surround the word), we are closer to our own mind. To say that the decision has no authority, was not authorized even though as a matter of fact it was made, takes us one step away from the historical facts and one step closer to what is important to us. It puts us linguistically into more direct contact with the problem of understanding.

To say that the agency has not made the decision when a decision most certainly was made and issued in its name is to say that we cannot understand it. We cannot understand it as a decision of the agency. To take an egregious case, an individual making a decision on behalf of an agency but taking into account the interests of his family and kinsmen may have made a perfectly understandable decision, as a parent or as a head of a family; but it was not a parent or head of a family that made the statement. It was the agency that made the statement and if that was so the statement does not fit. It is as if in Old Testament times a prophet thought he had heard God commanding the worship of Baal. The command would not have fit. As a command of Baal it might have been understandable, but not as a command of God. The prophet's first reaction would have been to think that it had only appeared that God had made the statement. The actuality was that He had not. Identifying the speaking voice and understanding what is said are the same.

Again, once past the thought that what one heard was a delusion, one need not deny that *something* was said and that *someone* said it. One might, of course, deny this, as in the case of mechanical speech. Roald Dahl has introduced the notion of a Great Automatic Grammatisator, the control console of which looks like an organ, with stops marked Gothic, Tragic, and the like, and which established authors can use to write whole novels in a matter of minutes. One might say in the case of mechanical speech that no one at all *said* what made the sound waves in the air or the marks on the paper, and that the sound waves in the air or the marks on the paper were not, in any understandable sense, making a statement. But one need not go so far. An inability to identify the speaking voice is enough.

THE FAITH INVOLVED IN THE CHOICE OF IMAGE

It is enough, if one is being asked to give willing obedience to the statement and therefore not just to listen to it but to act upon it in one's own life, that the statement is as one coming through a hole in a sheet from an unknown speaker, a speaker, yes, but one unknown. There is no reason to obey what just anyone says. A man would have no mind at all if he responded first to this voice, next to that shout. He would become a butt and a lightning rod for cruelty, a less than human creature from Jean Genet. Obeying a cacophony of voices would lead to madness as inconsistencies piled up and he had no way to choose. The voice one obeys has special qualities.

One *would* not obey a voice without knowing who the speaker was because one *could* not without running into frightful difficulties, and this would be reason enough; but there is a further, somewhat separable, and perhaps more important reason why one would not obey and could not obey. Without knowing who the speaker was, one would not know the meaning or the intent of the speaker, because one could not place what one heard in a context of other things said over time. It is partly because of this that one tends to conclude that "nothing" has been said when the speaker is unknown and one has not been able to construct a sense of the speaker, personify the speaker, even working on the assumption that there is a person behind what is said speaking it. Meaning and intent cannot be constructed from a statement without something more. An isolated statement is like one hand clapping. Without more it is nothing to understanding. It may be the beginning of a cacophony beside which the sound of two hands clapping is sweet and meaningful; cacophony can come out of one mouth as easily as from many.

Understanding, personification, and authoritativeness are thus linked. Without personification and understanding, there is no authority. Again, this does not mean that a decision has not been made or a statement issued, or that the decision or the statement will have no factual effect, no effect on history. It does mean that the hearer will not be actually guided by it and instead will work against it or around it.

But a statement is not worked against or around, only to the extent it is internalized. It is part of one to that extent, animates and directs one's affirmative seeking: one cares about it, believes *in* it, is committed to it. Indeed, the authoritative statement is a clue to what one oneself believes. Personification, understanding, authority, and internalization flow together. But if one is to be committed to and care about and affirmatively and imaginatively seek what the authoritative voice seeks, one must believe, or assume, that the voice means what it says, that *it* cares about what it is asking another to seek, that *it* believes in what it is asking another to believe in. Thus authenticity joins personification, understanding, authoritativeness, and internalization in any sketch of a statement of law or a decision that is to have the force of law—again, not just force, which it may have regardless, but the force of law immediately and thereafter. And with authenticity comes openness, speaking out loud, revealing one's purpose, not holding back and keeping secrets, not manipulating, all that goes under the name of disclosure and that underlies the production of the justifying, explanatory, and integrating texts that are the material for the exercise of legal method.

But then, if this statement is to be spoken by an understandable person, who cares about and believes in what he is saying, and if what the person says is to be internalized, and if with internalization there is to be a joining of the speaker and the listener, the statement cannot be only the outcome of a process, its epiphenomenon if you will, as an abstract formula for a legal statement or decision in the language of process might suggest. To say it is only the outcome of a process is simply to deny the experience of the thing one is seeking to define and express. And if, in one's own individual situation, one has no sense of any very direct experience of what one is seeking to express, or senses that one has only barely experienced it—if one does not know one's own mind, much less that of others; has not really understood a statement as part of an integrated whole; lives with personifications that are hazy and with confirmed suspicion that what one hears are statements not meant or cared about—well, then, one is proceeding on faith, the kind of faith that underlies the practice of legal method, faith that seeking understanding is worthwhile, that there is understanding to be had, that there is a mind. Even where an individual finds the tools of his own thought most poor and his direct experience least clear, faith is not unfounded, for every individual has intimations, visions, epiphanies: on these, the eyes of another looked into even if only once, the experience however brief of love and openness, much is built, on these and the fact that down the other road lies death, and we do not take the other road.[2]

THE STORY OF ABRAHAM

Let us use a well-known example to illustrate what is missing in accounts of legal decisions and the authority of law which fail to include authenticity, internalization, personification, and understanding. The experience of mind can be captured and imprisoned by expression through an inadequate story as well as an inadequate formula. One of the great stories of obedience, and of faith, is that of Abraham and the sacrifice of Isaac.

God commanded Abraham to sacrifice his son Isaac as a burnt offering, and Abraham obediently proceeded to do so. He had bound Isaac and was about to plunge in the knife when God commanded him to stop. Abraham sacrificed instead a ram which he found nearby. It is not recorded what Isaac thought of his father after this, although God so rewarded Abraham for this ultimate demonstration, according to the story, that Isaac may have been fully occupied in reaping the fruits and there was no occasion for the son to wonder in any concrete way what it means to be a father.

The reason why the story of Abraham and Isaac will not do as a source for further development of an understanding of authority, as a tool of thought in the way a metaphor is a tool of thought and source of development, is twofold. The first is that the identity of the speaker in the story is a given. The situation faced in life by even the most obedient and faithful listener is that he must address the first question of authority, which is to decide who is speaking. It is never suggested how Abraham could be so sure that it was God who was giving the command that he kill his own son.

The second and related aspect is that the command given, though dramatic and memorable, is so very simple—thrust a knife—and it is followed by an equally simple counterorder—hold the thrust. It is simple, physical, mechanical. And here we may bring in the specific experience of lawyers with such orders. The orders to Abraham are like the orders and commands contemplated for the master-servant relationship in the law of agency. But lawyers who have practiced the common law of agency know that such orders can be only contemplated in that body of law. Its doctrine still asserts that the master (often today an organization) controls the detailed physical movements of the servant and that this control is what makes it a master rather than a contracting principal. But in fact the master does not and even in concept it does not.

The authoritarian definition of the master-servant relationship in legal doctrine—the relationship that produces what is called respondeat superior and the liability of organizations for the acts of their agents, upon which so much of the risk-distributing operation of modern law is based—breaks down upon analysis, just as does the process definition of a legal decision. An infinite regress is met when the analyst comes to the point of deciding at what level of decision—"dig a ditch," "dig a ditch *with a shovel,*" "dig a ditch with a shovel *maneuvered in a particular way,*" and so forth—control must be exercised before the analogy of the serving person to an extension of the master's arm, a "hand" in farm and factory parlance, will be triggered. Criteria for choosing the level of human action and decision making that will trigger the analogy of a human being to a hand are found to be lacking in the law, or inexpressible, as might be expected. In their absence there is, in discussions surrounding the continuous determinations of whether there is a master-servant relationship in particular cases, a revealing shift over to the language of status and to the identities of the persons involved—expressions of and explanations of distinctions based upon whether the activity is to be viewed as an end in itself with a form and an art to it—and an equally revealing search for and summoning up of organizations of responsible actors directed to a common end and bound by duties of openness to one another.

The order to Abraham, Thrust the knife, thus sidesteps the second standard question the faithful and obedient listener faces, which is the meaning of the command. What does the speaker really intend the listener to do over time? To make a mechanical order a paradigm and draw conclusions from it would be like making a traffic regulation, or the statement "A will must have three witnesses," the paradigm of a legal rule. In matters of ethics and religion, the command "Love thy neighbor as thyself" is far more representative, just as the statement "Causing the death of a human being intentionally and with malice aforethought is murder" is the better paradigm of a legal rule.

Now there are many uses to which the story of Abraham and Isaac can be put, and there is a different way in which the story can be interpreted. When Isaac questions the absence of any animal to sacrifice as the two of them set off for the altar, Abraham replies, "God will supply the burnt-offering." It is entirely possible that Abraham obeyed because he believed, had faith, that his hand *would* be stayed, just as a child goes along with the parent's obsessive idiosyncrasy of the moment, foolish though it be, in full faith that things will turn out all right. But if that is the interpretation, it makes the meaning of the command complex. It draws the story closer to the truth of authority and all that is involved in the creation of authority, and it makes the story quite unfit for use as a central example of simple obedience.[3]

There is a better, more developable intimation in a short phrase than in the much-used story of Abraham. The phrase in ordinary language defining the other side of authoritarianism is "blind obedience." It is a pejorative, obedience which is not the product of seeing and understanding. Blindness is the very image of loss, disablement, and darkness. And when coupled with obedience it suggests instability: for what happens when the blindly obedient regains his sight and looks to see?

13

FAITH
Evolution of Legal Descriptions
of Mind

T HE METAPHOR OF mind as a taking into account of weighted factors, and all the other perceptions of law as process, leave a hole at the
center where the substance should be, and regress away when they are
grasped at, dissolving either into processes of change in processes, grander
and grander, or tinier and tinier into processes of formation of factors
taken into account at the stage in the process just above, down and down.
Current metaphor and perception pose a dilemma and a problem. There is
no doubt of that. But they do not pose *simply* a dilemma and a problem,
that is to be overcome in part by continuing faith and in part by working
toward change in the structure of thinking for those who come after us.
Our organizing descriptions of mind fail to go as far as they could even
now. They do not reflect what is already there in our thinking and imagery. What is missing from them is not simply something one might wish
for, but something that one can *see* is not there. To see the limitation of a
thing, its border, one must be able to see beyond it, and that is the case
here if one reads and listens to what even just lawyers say.

FALSE MARGINALISM

There is a marginalism about the descriptions we use that we can perceive
as false, just as we can perceive a false marginalism in any description of
the aesthetic decision as a progressive taking into account of this or that,
step-by-step. It does not describe, or explain, or help us to understand, or
help us to do it ourselves, to picture Mozart as achieving the perfection of
a phrase through a decision made at a point where he places a note up on
the scale rather than down on the scale, that one note, the placing of
which seems to the listener to have made the phrase and given it its beau-

ty. What is often called a decision tree can take a composer, a decider in matters of music, to a point—weighing a particular set of factors to produce a conclusion on one aspect, weighing and taking into account another set of factors to produce a conclusion on another aspect, then putting together those aspects, weighing them, taking them into account, to produce yet another decision of a higher order, small things feeding into larger and being organized therein as leaves feed into twigs, twigs into branches, branches into limbs, and limbs into the trunk of a tree. But a decision tree will not take a composer to the real beauty of a phrase.

If, when he reaches that "marginal" decision, to go up, or to go down, he concludes that neither produces beauty or perfection, he *starts over*. It is a characteristic of analysis of decision making focused at the margin that a fixed context is assumed. The alternatives are givens. That, however, is not true of the mind, as young students of English literature have the opportunity to learn when they memorize Marvell,

> The mind, that Ocean where each kind
> Does straight its own resemblance find;
> Yet it creates, transcending these,
> Far other worlds, and other seas;
> Annihilating all that's made
> To a green thought in a green shade.

The composer would start over, and make earlier decisions with an eye to putting himself in a better position to strike for perfection of phrase when it came to the point again of deciding whether to go up or down (a decision that admittedly must be made and made in sequence). In fact, the question what it was that the composer was seeking, what shape, what color, what mood, could be expected to emerge more and more clearly (if only through increasing certainty that he had *not* got what he wanted and did *not* believe in what was unfolding under his hand) in the course of his repeated runs at the sequential, individual-note-choosing process of writing out the music.

Something of the same happens during the making of a legal decision in a hierarchical system of appeals and reargument, and, as we have seen in Chapters 6, 7, and 8, making this possible is one of the functions of a supreme court and one of the justifications for concentrating so in legal method upon particular texts and the words of particular individuals, which without justification seems arbitrary and obsessive. We cannot venture here into whether the aesthetic decision might not be made as a whole and in advance. Nor would we want to assume that the aesthetic decision and the legal or authoritative decision are the same. The economic, rational, or calculated decision, the aesthetic decision, and the

authoritative decision may all be different from one another (although I
wonder whether "economic" or "calculated" decisions are made except in
theory and on paper), and the legal decision may in particular be different
because it animates, pulls, commands us to act and think in a way that,
though I hate to say and think it, music and perfect form do not, allowing
as they do more of the satisfaction of contemplation than of decision and
action. What we should note is that marginalism is *no more* descriptive of
the legal decision than it is of other decisions that are most certainly
decisions and most certainly made.

Indeed, if one really probes what is meant in law by "taking into account," both the marginalism and the mechanical quasi-quantified weighing and balancing suggested by the descriptive formula fall away. Consider
the decision making involved in designing the Ford Pinto automobile,
which was challenged in a 1980 criminal prosecution for reckless homicide
after a series of deaths from gasoline tank explosions in rear-end collisions.
The law was phrased statutorily as a prohibition of "conduct in plain,
conscious, and unjustifiable disregard of harm that might result and the
disregard involves a substantial deviation from acceptable standards of
conduct." In analytic terms, the value of human life was to be taken into
account and given due weight when one was aware that the value of
human life was threatened.

In designing the Pinto there was assumed to be a set of givens supplied
not only by gravity and energy but by competition. Though competition
could never be empirically tested beforehand, it was reportedly assumed
for purposes of design analysis that the car could not go over two thousand
pounds in weight nor two thousand dollars in price. These did not set the
alternatives open to the decision maker. Marginal analysts sought to make
them such. The problem that precipitated the deaths in the case in which
the design of the Pinto was challenged was the gas tank. It appeared that a
part costing a few dollars and weighing a pound or so would have substantially strengthened the tank and reduced the risk of explosion and that this
was known to the corporation. The corporation decided not to strengthen
the tank and thus to cause the deaths.

What else could the corporation do? How could this be criminal, condemnable, illegitimate, unauthorized indeed if a business corporation is
not authorized to commit crimes? The car could not go over two thousand
pounds. The decision was being taken at the margin. Add a pound and the
Pinto went under against competition, and, in going under, jobs, a domes-
tically secure source of transportation, and a host of other characteristics
of a life worth living might be eliminated also. If told to take a pound off or
reduce the cost by a dollar elsewhere, decision makers would say, "Where?
Off the hinges of the doors? In the mechanism of the doorlocks? The

quality of the windshield glass?" Those are marginal decisions, too. The doors could be strengthened and lives could be saved. Or the doors could be weakened and lives could be lost. If a pound and a dollar is to be added to the gas tank, why not to the doors, and if to the doors, why not to the windshield, and so forth into the impractical and the impossible. "Here," they might say, "you design the automobile."

But that is not what the inquirer into the legitimacy of decisions is doing, comparing the outcomes of decision making with a conception (in the inquirer's head) of what they should be, or telling others what decisions to make, after the manner of an electrical impulse running from the brain to the hand. The dissolution of the design of the Pinto into a thousand marginal decisions is a way of eliminating the question whether the value of human life was taken into account and, at the same time, eliminating the actual experience of design. For the design of the Pinto did not consist simply of decisions whether to use two-dollar doorlocks or one-dollar doorlocks, or whether to put a strip of chrome here or there or both places on the hunch it might attract customers. It included also decisions about the time to be allowed for the design and the timing of the production process—particularly the ordering of machine tools for parts—in relation to the design process. It appeared that the gasoline tank might also have been set in a different place in the car to eliminate the discovered risk of explosion, as opposed to adding the six-dollar part of one-pound weight to the tank placed where it was in the design at the time its riskiness was discovered. But shifting the location of the tank could not be done because the tooling up for manufacturing the car with the tank as it was had already begun. Why had the tooling up already begun? Because a decision had been made to accelerate the tooling up. Why had not more time been taken on design? Because a decision had been made to shorten the design time.

Throughout these decisions the question would be whether the value of human life was being taken into account. Was there concern about it? Did decision makers care about it, or did they exclude it in their decisions of consequence? Did it affect those parts of their action that were not mechanical? The search for legitimacy is the search for a state of mind, which is evidenced in the process upon which mind operates, a rolling process, linear only in time, with loopings back, anticipations forward, and continuous testing of initial premises against current outcomes and the dilemmas they have helped produce, all in light of the guiding objects of the decision-making process itself. The business executive's control of the design of the Pinto was said to be very tough-minded and hard-headed. So was General MacArthur tough-minded and hard-headed in the Second World War in designing amphibious assaults on the Pacific Islands. He was also bold, flamboyant, and daring. Yet it turned out that he was most efficient with lives. The preservation of the lives of his soldiers was perhaps a factor that he took into account in making all his decisions. He cared about it, or, to say the same thing, about them.

This drawing away from the margin, this elusiveness about just what decision it is that is to be analyzed in terms of taking considerations or factors or values or consequences (however that which is taken into account is denominated), is found not only in the application of the criminal law, which is always dramatic, but quite evidently in the civil law as well—in the law of torts, or of equitable remedies. If, in a case of negligence, it cannot be said that one ought not to have done what he did at the instant of time he did it, it can be said and often is that he ought not to have put himself into the position in which he had a Hobson's choice. If, in a case of segregated schooling, it cannot be said that a municipality now wishes to exclude black children from white schools, it can be said that the municipality ought not to have engaged in certain housing zoning practices before.

Shiftings back of this kind are sometimes obscured by the division of legal analysis into cases, which focus upon different parts or points or times in a continuous decision-making stream. Some fizzle out. Some are openings to an understanding of the decision-maker's mind: if, for instance, there is nothing to be said about an administrative agency's application of a particular rule, shifting back to that same agency's decision not to reopen the question of the rule itself may spark a full debate. There is always a search for the point at which taking a consideration into account would have made a difference; and, since outcomes are so very unpredictable (legal opinions being full of warnings against second guessing, taking advantage of hindsight, and forgetting the difference between quarterbacking and Monday-morning quarterbacking), the search becomes one for a point at which evidence of a state of mind can be expected to appear. The division of legal analysis into cases may obscure, but it does not prevent or even greatly hinder this search. Within the confines of a case broadly drawn (or, in the view of the practicing lawyer, before the boundaries of cases are drawn up), the decisions of a corporation, being analyzed, let us say, under the law of antitrust; or the decisions of a school board or municipality being analyzed under laws against racial segregation or environmental degradation; or the decisions of an individual being analyzed under the law of murder, are like the decisions of a court spread out over time. Each is like a text (in the case of official bodies, private or public, a decision may *be* a text), and what the analyst is doing—the method he is using—in working with these decisions is not very different from what he is doing in working with texts of courts, finding some revealing, some not, some wanting, and some not. To do this, of course, time must be elided. A corporation run by a succession of different people, a school board whose seats are occupied by a succession of elected representatives, must, like a court, be seen as a single institution with a single mind.

The inapplicability of marginalism to legal analysis is indeed what makes precedent seem unstable. It is often said that the law changes as the circumstances of the world change. What was not negligent a decade ago is held to be negligent today. Courts do not, it appears, follow the case of a decade ago in which precisely the same thing done was accepted. But often all that has happened is that a way has been discovered in the intervening time to achieve the values to be taken into account in the situation, values that were equally taken into account before. In law school an old case holding a tugboat negligent under common law for not using a radio when radios became available, despite the fact that the very same actions earlier (not of course involving the nonuse of a radio because radios did not exist) were not negligent, is used to illustrate the point. Courts rarely say yes to the loss of a value. They use language that does not tie them down. So, if a prototypical calculator comes into court and says, "Now, you said that we could do this in this case, and therefore cause this harm, and from this we conclude that this value is to be given this weight, and therefore we assume that we can treat the value in the same way in this case," the court will be seen to leap about and say, "No, now we think you can avoid the harm. You took the value into account as best you could before; we want you to do the same now." So too in the debate on the value of human life. Marginal choices are made, what are rightly called tragic choices, in which it appears that the value of human life is being weighed, numbered, and placed in a balance. But then, in the next case, or when pressed for a definitive general statement of the value of human life to be used in the run of decisions being made, that value does not stick, there is evasion and obscurity, and texts taken as a whole seem to say, "Act in good faith toward the value," rather than, "Give the value this weight and proceed to make your calculations."[1]

ANIMATION OF LEGAL THOUGHT

All this flows from the fact that when one truly takes into account a consideration or an end or a consequence or the avoidance of a consequence, one does not weigh it so much as one seeks it. What is authoritative does not so much restrain one as it animates and feeds one's thought. And it is this that the metaphor of mind as *weighing* and of analysis as supplying or discovering *grounds* for decisions, with its various geographical and gravity-derived associations and images, fails to convey. The value, the end, the consideration, feeds into the imagination, the cunning, the resourcefulness of the decision maker. The value might as well be a dead thing from the description of it in the common metaphors of the process of decision making—one speaks of a "dead weight"—whereas it is a warm thing, living if you will, and the authoritative decision maker is warm toward it.

Values are not realized by giving them their due, to use an old phrase from property that may be echoed in the phrase "giving due weight," by treating them as something outside and weighing on one, to which attention is paid because it must be paid, as one respects the weight of one's leg and takes it into account because the gravity outside oneself requires that one pay attention to its weight. Values are realized in a changing world only through the use of imagination, experimentation, trying. Everybody knows that, where anything they really care about is concerned. And the link in imagery between the warmth of a thing and its entering into the imagination as a driving and guiding force, which is not calculated with but toward, can be seen over and over again. Lawyers in modern American legal discourse, discussing the applicability of probabilistic thinking and argument to legal decision making, speak of the "coldness" of a gambler's posture when they undertake to describe the difference between obeying the law and calculating the risk of being held to have violated the law, and to the "hardening" of hearts that attends the introduction of probabilisitic calculation into a criminal trial, which is also described as "losing *sight*" of the person before the court. Sight, warmth, and perception of persons come together in contrasting what is distinctively legal to what is not. The way in which a court chose to describe the decision making of a corporate official charged with civil antitrust violations, who, the court concluded, had no "respect for the laws of his country," was to emphasize its coldness: "In analyzing the likelihood of civil prosecution at some time in the distant future, he coldly weighs the consequences on the one side, together with the penalties that might be exacted, and the ultimate financial gains on the other side." In literature and ordinary language alike there is cold respect and warm respect. Cold respect is based on fear and is expressed in wariness. With warm respect there is a joinder of minds and hopes. There is pleasure, desire, feeling, a thing positive rather than a thing limited.

It is this warmth and this animation in legal values that helps, if only a bit, in holding the inquiring analyst back from infinite regression in his attempts to understand and work with a statement of law. The making of a statement is an action with consequences; a speaker must *decide* to make a statement. Legal analysis does begin to dissolve statements of law into the factors that went into the decisions to make them or the objects the speakers had in mind in making the statements. This can go on and on, the factors or objects being themselves dissolved into further factors and objects that went into their making; until it is remembered that the thing being analyzed is a thing said as well as a thing done, and, if a thing said, with its force dependent upon its authority and its perception as authoritative, then perhaps a thing only said and not done, certainly not done *to* anyone; and until it is realized by the analyst that the analyst too will make a like statement which he will not conceive dully, externally, and coldly as the passing outcome of a process, but to which he will be committed. There is a snap when the new statement is made, as there must have been when the old statement was made if it too was authentic, summing up, organizing, and pointing. The act of making an authoritative legal statement is the act of making values come alive—a phrase law can safely borrow from painting, where there is a nice ambivalence about whether the painter, in making a thing come alive, is accurately conveying the truth of a thing outside himself or, instead, creating it. Since the value is warm, alive in the present, and pointing to the future, it is saved —or saves itself—from fading into its antecedents and the past.

THE INTERNAL IN LEGAL THOUGHT

There is, finally, in that summary account of mind which *faute de mieux* lawyers presently use, no reflection of the emphasis on being inside that runs throughout legal analysis. We have spoken of the internalization that accompanies the recognition of authority in the listener.

It may be that all that is said by reference to insideness, as opposed to outsideness, can be said by reference to the nature and warmth of the values and factors that are taken into account in the process of making authoritative decisions and authoritative statements. But legal discourse uses a number of ways of getting at the truth and reality of what discussants are talking about, and to neglect any one of them may be to miss some of that truth. If one asks a lawyer what is the law on a subject, let us say the law of partnership or labor law, or what is the law on a particular question, he will go off and come back with a series of texts—opinions, statutes, reports, restatements, committee commentaries, treatises—and spread them out on the table, point to it, and if he does not say, "*There* is the law of that subject, it is contained within the four corners of that table," he is sure to say, "*There* is where I will begin to find for you the law of the subject and myself move toward making a statement of the law for you"; and if those writings he spreads on the table contain notions and images of withinness and insideness, he ignores them at his peril.

There is a thinness, if you will, about a picture of factors feeding into relationships with one another as if they were factors feeding into equations or into industrial processes, and that thinness is recognizable as the absence of a depth the picture should have. There is both a presupposition and a perception of mind in the recognition of authority and the exercise of authority. We describe mind in images of depth and withinness. On judicial review (other than constitutional judicial review of statutes) there is pursuit of the factors that actually went into the decision, a rejection of post hoc rationalization, pressure to see the full record on which the decision or statement was made, and construction of various requirements of legal procedure with reference to the taking into account of appropriate factors and with an eye to ensuring that one or another is not given undue weight and that all are brought out (for instance through concepts of notice). But this is not sufficient to produce the mind that is presupposed, or to give the statement or decision, that appears to be the result of the process, its authority. There is in the expression and in the recognition of mind also a sense of being inside, which this does not convey at all.

In law, *wanting to achieve an end* that is taken into account in decision making, which we have variously described as being warm toward a consideration or believing in it or caring about it or as the end's having warmth for the decision maker or animating him, and *being inside an entity*, are connected, if they are not indeed one and the same. One sees this in extreme form in the law of conspiracy or aiding and abetting, in which what associates an individual with organized activity, makes him an insider rather than an outsider, a *member* of the conspiracy, is not his causal contribution to the furthering of its ends nor even his knowledge that what he is doing has the result of furthering its ends, but rather desire that the ends be achieved; and evidence of this desire is described alternatively as evidence of an individual's having associated *himself* with the action. The entity is a distillation of desire. The merger of the self with the entity takes place through desire, not through knowledge and most certainly not through cold calculation on the basis of knowledge.

It may be said, however, that conspiracies are accorded no legitimacy. Consider then foreign law. The connection between desire and being inside an entity, on the one hand, and legitimacy, on the other, is seen whenever an individual approaches the law of a foreign country. Except where one translates the law of the foreign country into the law of a larger entity, it is exceedingly difficult to deal with the law of a foreign country except as a force to be reckoned with. The question of interest to an individual is the reaction of officials of his own country to a finding of a violation of foreign law. Often there is rejoicing if an individual can escape or be traded out of a foreign prison. It may indeed be impossible to make the law your own and to approach it in any other than a calculating and manipulative way, if you are not yourself a member of the entity whose law it is; and this is sometimes expressed in anthropological terms as being a "consequence" of not being a member of the culture of the country or group, so that one cannot truly understand it—which recalls the connection in legal analysis between understanding and authority. The problem is currently of largest practical importance for the multinational corporation. It is not at all clear that the solution lies in making multinational corporations citizens of each country in which they do business, for they may thereby become citizens of no country. Since they do regard themselves as an organized and (however organized internally) a *single* entity with a center, if they have no home country they may cease to regard the law of any country as having any legitimate claim upon them at their center, or, to say the same, they may come to regard the law of all in a manipulative way. Home, after all, is the place where manipulation is in principle to be put aside.

The internal quality of a legitimate command is thrown into sharpest relief at various points in the administration of the criminal law, which presents to the lawyer and the nonlawyer alike what appear to be the most enduring dilemmas. Criminal law is, on the one hand, the law that demands of individuals most unequivocally that they make its values their own (the similar demands of civil law being muted by those definitions of individualism that have experimented with the abandonment of substantive value). Yet criminal law introduces also the most unequivocal authoritarianism through its special sanctions and its total condemnation of the individual as a whole, rarely making the distinctions between the various aspects of an individual's life or the various times of his life that emerge naturally in noncriminal law. There is no meaningful connection between these two sides of criminal law. Their being found together is a product of history (in fact, totality of condemnation, expressed in the reduction of convicts to nonhuman status, may begin to lose its habitual association with criminal law analysis as criminal law is more and more applied to corporations and other institutions not vulnerable to its traditional horrors). The acuteness of its dilemmas, which is produced by this, makes them the most revealing.

We have mentioned the dilemma of insanity, where true lack of knowledge of wrongness or belief in wrongness (usually evidenced by lack of capacity to understand wrongness) or a persuasive demonstration that one was not oneself leads to the impossibility of condemnation. This, the demand indeed the necessity of an internalized voice, appears also in the testimonial privileges that are so distinctive a feature of criminal procedure. Consider the problem of requiring a parent to testify against his own child, with prison for the child as a likely consequence of doing so, and prison for the parent, or for both parent and child, as the consequence of perjury. How a parent might be expected to act if forced to testify against his child is closely associated with whether lying is condemned in that situation—or instead found justifiable—and with whether a witness in such a situation will be formally and legally relieved of his dilemma through recognition of a privilege not to answer a question. It is not, of course, at all clear that lying would be the best course for the parent. The horror of being personally involved in the infliction of the unspeakable upon one's own child (which is what prison so often represents in this day in every country) would not be the only consideration. A parent con- templating perjury would want to consider the likelihood of getting caught for perjury, whether he could do more for the child staying outside prison himself, what the likelihood is of prison as opposed to probation for the child or for him, whether, indeed, a short jolt of a certain sort of prison might not be a good thing for the child in the circumstances. But what might be expected not to enter the calculation at all is the ought-notness of lying itself. The command, "Do not lie," may have no weight whatever for a *parent* in this situation. He may approach the matter entirely objec- tively. And knowledge that a *parent* is likely to take such a position and, perhaps it is the same to say, as a good parent arguably *should* take such a position—again, not that he inevitably will lie but that he will engage in a calculation whether to lie—may lead people generally to conclude that the parent cannot be condemned for lying. It cannot be claimed that he is doing wrong because it cannot be claimed that the command has any legitimacy or authority over him as a parent. It cannot be claimed that he disobeys *himself,* which is, perhaps, what we do claim when we condemn. We cannot claim that he disobeys *us,* for we would, we suspect, do the same in his dreadful position. Therefore serious consideration is given to a privilege.

The privilege against self-incrimination may be similar in its ground- ing. We expect another, like ourselves, to act in a certain way, to see no legitimacy in a command that we condemn ourselves to the status of a convict. After a person becomes a convict, we may inflict greater or less pain upon him according to whether he confesses and admits. But that is after he has lost his status as a free and equal individual. Before and during the trial we recognize the privilege, surely for reasons in addition to the lesson we have learned, we think, from history, that the absence of a privilege against self-incrimination leads to awful tortures because we can- not restrain ourselves individually or institutionally. We actually do not like putting someone in jail because he refuses to condemn himself, we do not like that in itself. We are even uncomfortable with immunity laws which have that effect. The reason is that in the case of one's self, as in the case of one's child, the command is *outside*. It does not come from within. It does not come from within because we would not condemn ourselves were we in the other's shoes, and only then can we condemn another. The command does not come from within when we are commanded to sentence ourselves to the unspeakable, to slavery and to treatment as a thing of no account. It does not come from within when parents are commanded to condemn their own children, because the parent and the child are one, flesh of flesh, apple of the eye, creation of the heart. Friendship and love between unrelated individuals can produce the same situation, and tragedy. Perhaps this is a large part of the reason why we have and continue to maintain such a large purely discretionary or alegal element in criminal matters in the operations of juries, prosecutors, sentencing judges, and executive clemency.[2]

Indeed, shadowed as it is by its bloody remedies, its prison houses, and the total condemnation that follows its determinations, criminal law advances an understanding of law in the same way that study of a body reacting to disease advances understanding of the conditions of health. The intractable pathology of the prison and the foundering of all efforts to erect any system of legitimate authority there or to administer prison rules on the model of legal systems outside prison reveals the strength of the connections and presuppositions we have been discussing throughout. Absurdity results when they are ignored. The strenuous effort to treat the crime of escape in the same way as any other crime and to fit the prison into the ordinary fabric of thought gives one the best and most direct sense of what that ordinary fabric is.[3] But what that ordinary fabric is can be perceived without turning to criminal law. A legislator, asking what his duty is, is told "Don't leave anyone out," which flows directly from the child's cry "I was left out." And this in turn is translated into taking the interests of everyone into account. Every reference to good faith in the law is as much a reference to internalization and insideness as it is to authenticity of belief and forgoing calculation and gaming, and references to good faith run throughout the law. The duty of directors of business corporations is defined in large part by the sole term "good faith." The meaning of acting in good faith and taking ends into account for their own sake in decision making is often best and most succinctly conveyed by a reminder of the difference in one's feeling and attitude if one considers oneself an insider rather than an outsider to an organization. The legal terms "loyalty" and "allegiance" do not mean blind obedience anymore than does the legal term "trust." They mean the recognition of authority, the sense of being inside. A claim to loyalty is quite inconsistent with outsideness and is never made: it would be like a bully demanding scrupulous good faith from his victims and punishing them for not pursuing his interest in hurting them. The question, Is this person inside or outside? is a constant refrain in litigation over business and economic relationships, which is very largely litigation over the definition of the circumstances in which manipulation and a manipulative frame of mind will be countenanced and the outcomes of manipulation accepted and enforced. This party says he is a creditor of the organization rather than a partner in it. Which is he? This person says he was acting as an individual rather than an employee. Was he? This person says he was a customer giving an order to an enterprise rather than a principal giving an order within an enterprise. Can he be conceived as a customer?[4] This person says he had only a contractual relationship and was not required to deal openly or fairly. Was that the relationship he had, or was he instead a fiduciary? However often issues cast in this form are translated into issues of the distribution of wealth and the distribution of the risks of loss of wealth, and apparently resolved in such distributional terms in particular cases, they are inextricably bound up with the drawing of lines between persons and interests who are inside and persons and interests who are outside. And requirements that automobile manufacturers work in good faith with their dealers, or that insurance companies settle insurance claims in good faith, or that employers discharge employees-at-will in good faith, or that corporations act in good faith toward former employees drawing pensions, each raise the question whether the persons toward whom faith must be practiced are not thereafter and to that extent pulled inside the organization and must be viewed as part of it in any comprehensive attempt to describe and convey what the organization is.[5]

A COURT LIKEWISE ASKS that it, speaking on behalf of the law, be treated in good faith. It does not say, I order this, and now I shall bargain with you, keeping my secrets as you keep yours, to see if I can extract compliance from you. It does not say, Obey or not as you please, I do not care, I have superior force to reduce you to my will. Courts ask instead for a putting aside of calculation. They know they have no access to physical force save through a recognition of the authority of their orders and a belief that they should be followed. They know that their force waxes and wanes with the degree of their authoritativeness and the degree of belief that what they say should be followed. They know, indeed, that there is no sense in which the law, or they speaking for the law, *have* a will except as that will can be found through an understanding of what they say. They ask for willing obedience, not for obedience based upon habit and unthinking reflex—the jerking of the hand to the forelock at the sight of a feathered hat—which could find nothing to be triggered by or latch onto in the spread of legal texts taken as a whole and which in any event would be as exasperating and unpredictable as the behavior of any literal-minded flunky. They ask for willing obedience, not for obedience based on fear (however much they may dally in fear), which would have nothing to do with a sense of obligation.

In this insistence upon willing obedience to the law's commands and in the fashioning of statements of law that can be willingly obeyed lies the merger of speaker and listener which saves the legal mind from dissolution into process. Process it may be, but it is a process within us and we each know that we can exist in the present. The metaphor of process works well for analysis of what is outside us, but we know it is inadequate to express what is inside us, the life within us, and we would know that we had left ourselves out of the picture were we to describe ourselves as process alone. What happens in the recognition of authority happens as much in the mind of the listener as in the mind of the speaker. A statement of law incorporates and conveys what is to be done by the person asking, What ought I to do—or say, or think? And that statement of law is a statement of a person to a person. It is a responsive definition of the person asking out loud how he ought to act and think and speak in this vast, complex, and changing world if what he does and thinks is to have meaning for him. It is also a definition of the person speaking the statement, and as the statement is understood and internalized and the ends that animate the speaker come to animate the listener and be his own, the two are pulled together, the one undying and speaking over time, the other very much in time, individual, mortal—but undoubtedly living.[6]

But in the end, after all is said, it is the listener's grip on the present that saves the mind behind statements of law from dissolution. We are the listeners, and we listen as individuals. Meaning helps retain a grip on the present. It may be essential to a sense of the actuality and presentness of things. But meaning is not all there is. There is something more, that which saves meaning and makes meaning possible. There is more to life than the language through which we seek to integrate and order our experience of ourselves and the world. The problem of being a lawyer, of searching for the authoritative and staving off the authoritarian, is not just a matter of inadequacy of expression and poor summary metaphors handed over from one generation of professionals to the next to be struggled with, improved a bit, and passed on. The problem of the lawyer is not restricted to lawyers nor indeed to professionals working in their professional roles. It

is a problem of personal life, which can appear in a mild and gently rock-
ing way, a rhythmical blooming and drying, or in a devastating way.

There is a form of self-consciousness that can afflict an individual, a
pulling back and observing of oneself in action, which can be destructive
to the point of madness. If it becomes chronic the will is known to fade.
One observes all, and all is a thing observed. Even what one says becomes
a thing one observes oneself doing, with one's third eye, from the outside.
Since one is outside, what one does seems moved by the hands of another
or by forces unknown, with secret intention or no intention at all. This is
the loss of affect, in the modern description of it, the loss of feeling,
affection, being affected.

An individual tears himself from this state, if he can, only by ceasing to
observe untouchable, and undertaking to act and speak himself, to say
what he believes and commit himself to it, to act with responsibility for
pain and harm, vulnerable, affected by the consequences of what he does.
When one says one loses oneself in a thing, or a person, or in what one is
doing, one means curiously that one loses not oneself but one's self-consciousness, that implacable unblinking third eye looking down on oneself.
One does not lose the substance of oneself. One gains it.

Now just as an individual can lose the substance of himself, so in precisely the same way can he lose, so is he in danger of losing, the substance
of others by pulling back and observing them from the outside. So too do
they seem unreal, gripped by something beyond and secret as ghosts are, in
the hands of forces that do not disclose themselves, unreachable, irresponsible, uncaring, unaffected, separate, only doing, never speaking. What
frees an individual from this is what frees individuals from paralyzing self-
consciousness where they look down upon themselves from above but do
not see themselves there. One embraces rather than observes, one ceases
to stay outside, one commits oneself to them as to oneself, one is affected
by what happens to them and by what they say as one is affected by what
happens to oneself and feels what one says. Indeed, since the way is the
same, it may be true that one cannot find oneself without finding them,
feel substance oneself without seeing their substance, love oneself without
loving them. It may be that one cannot find the authoritative for oneself
without also freeing others to will and to act. It may be that one can find
the authoritative only by ceasing to look down, that one finds meaning
only by looking directly into another's eyes.

14

RECOGNITION
The Neglected Metaphor

THE PRACTICE OF LAW AND THE
PRACTICE OF THEOLOGY

IN THIS LAST CHAPTER I want to raise the possibility that the practice of law today is most like the practice of theology. If the traveler were to say, "I do not know what the practice of law is, tell me what it is like, or a branch of. Is it physical science? social science? the practice of history? literary criticism? the writing of literature itself?" The answer may in fact be theology.

I hesitate to suggest this. Ever since Thomas Huxley defended Darwin against the bishops, the practice of theology has become progressively less familiar to the general run of educated and thinking men and women. It may not be a useful metaphor. Theology does not occupy a place in the standard curriculum, the newspapers do not run accounts of theological disputes, and books on theology are not found on coffee tables as they might have been in the eighteenth and nineteenth centuries. I think it fair to say that theology is seen more as the activity of a cult and less and less the perfectly natural thing to do and to follow. Its very vocabulary has become almost incomprehensible to one who is not an initiate. Worse, theology is often a thing of ridicule among sensible, practical, active men. The word has become a pejorative, along with *metaphysics* and *jurisprudence*.

But there is one group of thinking, educated, sensible and practical men and women who should be able to see the affinities without difficulty. That group is the legal profession. It might be thought they are the one group that does not need a metaphor for law. To the contrary, they are always reaching for metaphors and revealing that they are no exception to the general observation, that much of the bringing into consciousness and reflection upon a thing of which one has direct experience is achieved through the use of metaphor. Indeed it is in part through the use of metaphor that one stands off from and affects the thing in which one is involved. Certainly the adoption of the computer as a metaphor for law would have perceptible effects upon the practice of law, if it were thought desirable to proceed in that direction, and one can think of other examples: History has wanted to be like Science, until Science began to be like History.

The parallels between the practice of law and the practice of theology are too striking for the lawyer not to see. They are also comforting, which makes them easier to see. For lawyers are required by the customs of the profession in which they are imperceptibly trained from the first day of law school, as well as by its discipline, to behave in ways that any adult, self-respecting, and free man must think either offensive or mad. If the lay citizen faces a dilemma in obeying what he is told is the law, lawyers face it even more. They are taught that they must be more obedient than other citizens, and this is reinforced by etiquette. They stand when an individual in a special robe enters the room where they are to do law, and takes a seat on a raised dais. They stand when that individual leaves the room. The architecture of the room and of the building containing the room is designed to produce respect, even awe. They are punished for anything resembling contempt in their gesture or phrasing, and say, "Yes, your Honor," when reprimanded. They accept reprimand and correction given in a tone that only children experience outside the courtroom. They address this person to whom they speak, who issues reprimands, corrections, and statements that must be obeyed, with an ancient title, a title of the kind otherwise eliminated from American mouths, beginning with the word "Your" and followed by a word which might be Excellency, Majesty, Reverence, or Grace. In the case at hand, it is Honor. Even the most prominent lawyers appearing before the Supreme Court speak in tones of deference and in elaborate circumlocutions which hide the fact that they are instructing, guiding, or disagreeing with the justices before them; the most careless, ill-informed, foolish, or malicious questions are treated with an elaborate show of seriousness. If lawyers lose the habit of self-effacement and self-abasement they lose credibility and the ear of the judge to whom they are speaking, who turns away if he is not treated with the respect he thinks his due. Lawyers engage in overt and elaborate supplication, as does almost no one else in modern society. They begin, "May it please the court," and in the end they "pray" for relief. And everything they say must be backed by authority. Indeed, they do best if they say a thing not in their own words but in the form of a quotation from an authority, as if the ultimate end of and best demonstration of obedience and self-abasement is to eliminate themselves from view. Despite the seriousness of it all, which bespeaks a conviction that what they decide to say matters, and despite the heat of the argument the words they speak are never claimed to be their own. (And when a man in robes speaks he will say "We" or much more often "The law" or "This Court," referring not to himself or himself and his colleagues but to the Court speaking over time.) When they get down to business, after their forms of greeting and stationing themselves and in between their modes of address and before their prayers, what do lawyers do? They hurl quotations at each other.

In law school a student is asked a question of law. To his reply, the professor says, "Ah, but Mr. Justice so-and-so said *this*," with an air of having demonstrated, in the most conclusive possible way, the error of the student's statement. If the student is not silent (as the professor at some level hopes he will not be), or if another student takes up the argument, the other student or the professor will say, "But in another case Mr. Justice such-and-such said *that*." The professor will then ask, "How can we reconcile these statements?" implying that until we are absolutely forced to doubt we must take the position both are right, that it is our task to figure out the order which is being given, and that it will be our ignorance, laziness, or stupidity that will lead us into error and disobedience. Faith is demanded at the beginning of discourse. It does not come at the end and as a result of discourse. There is no waiting to be persuaded. There is *seeking* to be persuaded, and a seeking less to be persuaded than to understand. Faith is a premise, built into lawyers' method.

After law school, lawyers in court marshal their quotations and piles of books on either side of the room before they do battle. Legal research is commercially described as a search for the right quotation, and lawyers use digests, indexes, commentaries, and glosses upon the words of these old men, in an effort to find just the right statement that will strike home. These statements and opinions lawyers use and professors expound are themselves interlaced with quotations and references, often to the point where the page looks like a collage. Denying the authors of opinions use of quotation marks, brackets, and omission signals would be tantamount to plucking the pens from their hands. The difficulty of expression that frustrates them appears to be less the intractability of language than the absence of punctuation marks for more than one internal quotation. If quotations within quotations, within quotations, within quotations could be written, they would be.

And this seems the central foolishness. Most of the rest can be dismissed as quaint, even though it is well known (and the military continuously demonstrates) that being forced to engage in outward acts eventually molds the inward disposition. The rest can be thought mere form, but this exclusive focus on the words of old men! this paying *attention!* The statements quoted in opinions are the statements of old men, often dead and separated from the author by the gulf of generations. Their treatment in opinions is as deferential as lawyers' treatment of them in the flesh. Instead of "Mr. Justice Butler was wrong," or "Mr. Justice Butler spoke nonsense," or "Mr. Justice Butler was mean-spirited," it is "I do not read Mr. Justice Butler as saying that." And, with notable exceptions, the words to which lawyers thus bind themselves are not even the words of good men. They are the words of vain, unliterary, ambitious, and successful men, politicians and friends of politicians, men with whom princes and politicians feel comfortable. Gather together in groups the senators, the novelists, the nurses, the chief executives of large corporations, the carpenters, and the judges, and it is not at all clear that the judges would be chosen as the group to whose words the closest attention should be paid.

Where else do free, grown, thinking, and sane men and women behave in this way and in such an atmosphere? Where else do individuals in robes sit on a raised dais in the center of a room designed to evoke awe and respect? Where else do men conceive of themselves as supplicating, and say explicitly that they are praying for relief? Where else can be found men and women dressed in their best and most sober clothes engaging in self-abasement, where respect enforced by custom and discipline, where absence of direct challenge, use of titles, faith demanded at the outset? Where else but the church?

Now of course there are many churches, and the behavior of men and women in them varies in the respects just enumerated and thus in the degree of their resemblance to the legal profession. But in one respect, I think, they do not vary. They all look to authoritative texts. This they do not do just for the regulation of their ritual behavior, for which the authority of the text is almost a matter of definition. At least in the Western world questions about what to do in the world and how to think are settled by appeals to authority. If the authoritative statement is uttered by an official, it is made after reference to an argument about written texts. The agreement of religions on this point, this point of method, and their identity in this regard with law, is remarkable. It matters not whether the religion be hierarchally or pyramidally organized, like the Roman Catholic or the Protestant Episcopal or the Mormon, organized in more horizontal fashion with occasional convocations to settle issues of basic doctrine, like the Presbyterian or Calvinist churches, or not formally organized at all except through educational and social institutions, like the Jewish, radical Protestant, and Muslim groups. All value learning in the ancient sense of the term, as lawyers do. They think naturally in terms of authority, as lawyers do. Indeed they have the same difficulty lawyers do in bringing other disciplines to bear in education—the same fear of teaching something other than "the law"—or, in argument, in making reference to psychology, sociology, or even ethics. And they have the same difficulty lawyers do in deciding what the materials of discourse appropriate for analysis should be. Is what a priest or minister says in preaching or counseling evidence from which understanding can be drawn? Is what is said in arguments before courts, in letters of opinion, in counseling or in negotiation, material for legal study? Or would the inclusion of some or all of these make the practice of legal method or theological method impossible and lead to the loss of the legal or the divine?

In fact, a traveler coming upon the United States would have to wonder at the frequency and vehemence of the assertion that ours is a secular state. He would look round at the temples in the centers of towns, containing men in long robes and disputants arguing about, commenting upon, and organizing a canon of received texts, and then observe that there is no tolerance whatever on the question whether individuals shall be subjected to this regime or required on occasion to attend its ceremonies in person. Of course, what he would find on close observation is not slavery but a high degree of belief and willing obedience and an insistence by many, not at all paradoxical, that their freedom depended upon their belief. He would conclude, I think, that the term "secular" was being used in an odd way, and that the Founding Fathers' aversion to a certain kind of Christianity inconsistent with human dignity, to the silliness of the eighteenth-century English established church with its condescension, corruption, and entwinement with a hierarchical social order, to the Catholicism of the Medicis, Richelieu, Bloody Mary, and Philip, all of which may be thought to have produced the First Amendment, was not, for all that, a rejection of the theological heritage.

If the charge of foolishness stands, it stands against both lawyer and divine. How can they spend their time doing what they do, and respect themselves for it? The theologian has the claim, which the lawyer does not, that the statements to which he confines his attention or pays particularly close attention were made by men into whose ears God was whispering. But this does not in itself produce meaning or understanding. With the exception of sitting popes or convocations, the texts were written by men separated from the present listener and user of them by even more of a gulf, of time, culture, and language, than separates dead and aged judges from the lawyers who appeal to their statements. Why pay such attention to what a smelly, querulous old man, in goatskins, said three thousand years ago if what he says does not command attention by its intrinsic beauty and insight? Why pay attention to passages that are obscure and dull, in a constitution, a statute, an opinion of the justices, or a book of the Bible? Why write commentaries on them, and commentaries upon commentaries? The very selection of religious texts may be conventional, the result of human decisions, perhaps even bargains, threats and pressure in the legislative sessions of ancient convocations. Where is the profit in all this?

Might we not be generous and self-confident enough to say that what lawyers and divines seem to be doing is not what they are really doing? If theologians are asked why they do what they do, they respond that they are trying to save the world and redeem us. They are seeking knowledge of meaning, purpose, the hidden, the invisible. They do it in the only way they know. No one has ever supplied a better. Lawyers are too shy to give the same response, or too wedded to the bravado of tough-mindedness. But it sometimes seems that in a modern, secular American university the law school is the one place where meaning and purpose are discussed in a systematic way. Science cannot allow the presence of mind. But men, law, and theology, not to speak of literature and art, cannot do without it. And it seems to be true of our existence so far, that the presence of mind, the experience and acknowledgement of authority, and a special method of argument and analysis, are all bound together, with authoritarianism and its reflection in institutional and linguistic form tagging along, as imperfection is always known to dog man, perhaps indeed serving as something of a shield against the blinding demands of the fully authoritative. Both lawyer and theologian argue from texts because otherwise there is nothing particular to talk about. They cannot do without texts any more than the novelist can do without life. But there is always something behind the texts. There is no understanding of them without interpretation, and no interpretation without creation and imagination, reaching behind to what is *there* for us now.

In the Concourse of Disciplines

Scores of institutes and programs, formal and informal, exist now devoted to scanning economics, social sciences, history, and psychiatry for whatever help they may yield, not only in changing and forming the law but in understanding what law is and how it yet remains separate from them and not translatable into any of them. There are few if any that have turned to theology. Perhaps the very commonness of source stands in the way, the erstwhile association with priest-kings, the descent from magicians, the memory of authoritarian religions which were not of the mind and heart but of external form, religions of fear. The pain of the struggle for liberation may be still too great for a rapprochement.

But there has been a struggle for liberation in theology as well, perhaps always, and certainly from the time of Aquinas through Protestantism to the present. As late as 1878 the Catholic papacy, claiming infallibility, was asserting, "The inequality of rights and of power proceeds from the very Author of nature." But then the *Dred Scott* decision was of the same era. Pope Pius IX (1848–78) was opposed to universal suffrage, but then in the United States it was courts of equity who enjoined strikes and inhibited the organization of labor at the same time they were devising new and more effective ways of organizing owners of capital. Everything may have had its place, and there are in any event happier tales to tell. Both law and theology are always being measured against the ideals they set for themselves. The serious question is not whether law would be tainted but whether there would be enough gain in a detailed scanning of theology of the kind that economics and the social sciences have received in the United States and history and psychiatry receive in Europe.

T HE FACT THAT something has not been done or not tried is not in itself a reason to try it if very considerable effort is involved. But the stakes are large. It is not clear that evil and chaos, doses of which may be thought useful, will not triumph in the world we know. Things may become unglued. The day is past when it could be said that those who are in the position of receiving orders obey because they have agreed to obey the individual issuing orders and that the explanation and justification for obedience is the motive or value of keeping promises. This might be true within very small groups. It is impossible in the mass. As an explanation and justification it is no better than the metaphor of the social contract which provides so little help in understanding why civil society hangs together. An agreement to obey an individual has virtually no meaning, for one never, unless one is a slave, agrees to obey an individual except as that individual is in a given role. If the modern corporate employee, for instance, is to be viewed as agreeing to obey anyone at all, it is the corporation, and the interposition of the entity opens to the full the question of the authority and legitimacy of the commands that are issued.

Nor can obedience be explained today by fear of sanctions. There is no doubt an enormous amount of pure arbitrariness and the wielding of purely personal power by individuals in official positions within the various corporate hierarchies of modern society. There are also imperatives of organized life that give obedience as such a certain attraction, even if it cannot

be valued in a society of free men, and especially where evil must be met
with evil. But in a society of free men fear is not the reason and not the
answer. We know too much. We know that it is the executioner who kills,
not just the judge or the law. A choice may be commonly presented between losing a job and participating in responsibility for enormous harm;
but the engineer ordered to throw a switch to put a nuclear power plant on
line, who is informed that the inspections of welds in the plant are false
and that their falsity has been suppressed, knows that there is a question
whether the order he has received is a legal order. He can say seditiously
and effectively to the person above him in the chain of command speaking
the order, "You do not have to obey either. You are stepping out of your
role in issuing the order, you too are responsible." Fear is what the social
movement of the last two centuries has been eradicating as the cement of
society. There can be no pride in fear or the fearful, nor resignation to it
any more than there can be resignation to nausea. Those who advocate
fear and urge its eternal desirability do not like it in themselves or in those
around them. Fear is what man has been escaping from, and however
much fear may explain obedience to authority, it cannot in any way justify
it, and if it cannot justify it, it cannot be relied upon to explain in the
future. The revolutionary in man will always out and appeal even to the
heart of the tyrant.

There is always habit, the urge to say yes that rises in the throat at the
sight of a visored hat or some other insignia of rank and authority. That
must have been very strong in society's past. The very elaborateness of the
pomp, the ceremony, the dress, and the handling of sacred objects and
decorations that represented authority has to be comprehended in some
way. But the modern world is ordered in a different fashion. The breaking
of such habits and the smashing of such symbols, the elimination of the
regalia of caste, rank, position, and status, has, along with the elimination
of fear, been such a major thrust of social development for so long that one
cannot easily think it just a passing phase. While there are certainly echoes of class dress today—the businessman, the executive, the union official, the factory foreman has his tie or his tie and coat (and the coat is a
military tunic), the judge has his black robe, the professor his tweed
coat—there is too much confusion for such signals to have much effect
upon behavior. As far back as the eighteenth century Continental trav-
elers were complaining of the English that it was getting difficult to tell
them apart by their dress. And the nature of the commands being given
and carried out is far too complex for habit. A command must be understood to be obeyed. Complex commands cannot trigger reflex responses
and are too easily frustrated by tiny reluctances.

Without contract, without fear, without habit, authority has only itself to fall back upon. What authority is and what produces the authoritative in the eye of him who acknowledges it has become the more important to address directly as time has passed. Lawyers' discovery of theologians may not be quite like man discovering another form of intelligence, or writers of the Renaissance discovering the classical texts, but there is no reason for lawyers to cut themselves off from a source of help. And the best help has always come from a co-worker.

RAPPROCHEMENT

There will be difficulties in reaching out to explore the connections between law and the other learned discipline that works with authority, for we would not look to the connections between secular law and religious law. Secular law and religious law may be hardly distinguishable. We would look rather to the connections between what transpires in the schools, offices, and chambers of law, and what transpires in the schools, offices, and chambers of divinity. And lawyers will no doubt find an oddness and an off-puttingness in the language of much theology. But they may reflect that the language of such theology is hardly odder than lawyers' language with its own pious fictions and equally reverential tone. Mature lawyers need only put themselves back to their situation as first-year law students; what they could to then they should be able to do now.

It will also no doubt be difficult to go beyond or across sectarian concerns and through the formulaic language which expresses sects' uniqueness and is designed in substantial part to separate them and keep them separate. It will be difficult both for the nonbeliever and for the believer in the language of one, for whom the language of another bristles with implicit hostilities and heresies. But surely any lawyer who has been exposed to the adversary process should be able to do this.

And the views of one's friends? Moral and political philosophers with whom lawyers consort tend to have a view of theology as authoritarian, trading on mindless and fearful obedience, very much the kind of view, it should be said, that theologians have of law. But it is not clear that moral and political philosophers do not tend to have a rather authoritarian view of law as well, assuming that once they decide (or a decision is made) what the institutional arrangement or the formulaic statement of law is to be, then that is it: obedience follows because they have linked their thought to the field, the phenomenon, the discipline of law. This is mistaken. Lawyers know any such view of law in the back of the minds of theologians and political philosophers alike mistakes what the reality of life in the law is like. By the same token, lawyers and political philosophers may come to know of theology what lawyers know of law.

Consider here, as we end our walk through the problem of legal authority, just one way theology can be of aid. Any disciplined search for authority must deal systematically with emptiness, what in law is called legalism and what in theology is often called law. Isaiah invokes the spirit of legalism in his lament, "No man sues with just cause, no man goes honestly to law; all trust in empty words, all tell lies. . . ."

For example, judges, scholars, litigators, and advisors all wonder, in their quiet moments, at the degree of their manipulation of texts in their own practice of legal method. Theologians face the same problem of methodological emptiness. Theologians' chins may sink upon their chests, like lawyers' in their armchairs, as they entertain the doubt that they really are drawing anything from their texts or being guided by them, but instead are making their decisions for other reasons and only then turning to texts.

Such a skeptical view of interpretive activity might be thought, at first, less troubling to lawyers than to theologians. It might be thought, at first, not a matter on which lawyers would be inclined to seek help, particularly if the seeking of it involved a degree of embarrassment and difficulty. The reason this might be thought is that a skeptical view seems particularly congenial to a view of the world as based upon property—where the power of individuals is exercised for reasons private to themselves and is enforced without question as long as it is exercised within their separate spheres, where all questions of legality are therefore questions of jurisdiction viewed in a geographical way, and all those affected by the exercise of power within that jurisdiction can no more be heard than cattle or slaves can be heard, and law really is a matter of confining power from the outside and has nothing to do with what goes on inside.

But this is not the lawyer's view of the world, or of law. The skeptical view may be congenial to the structure of thought with which our grandfathers and great-grandfathers toyed. But lawyers know that structure does not work and never did. Lawyers especially know that from the beginning, in one way or another, law has been concerned with what went on inside; that the jurisdictions with which lawyers work are generally not geographical but are rather subject-matter jurisdictions whose content is defined by joint purposes; and that those affected by the exercise of power are not to be viewed as cattle or slaves. One does not have to spend much time around lawyers to learn that the mere fact a decision is confined in a negative way is no reason to obey or follow it in any positive way. The authority of such a decision, if it is to have authority, must always have come and must come today from some other source.

The situation may be in fact the reverse of what might at first be thought. A skeptical view of interpretive activity may be more troubling to lawyers than to theologians, not less. At least some theologians may suppose that in making their decisions and coming to their conclusions for "other reasons," reasons that are not talked about or admissible in their method, they can be directly inspired and that their texts are there serving as a confirmation. Lawyers do not easily think in these terms about themselves, except perhaps as they listen to a secret legislator.

The act with which the lawyer is familiar in making a decision for "other reasons" and then turning to the texts is the act of holding texts and what they say outside oneself. The methodological emptiness which this produces is very much associated with the emptiness to which we have referred in our discussion of the dilemma of the lawyer generally in the modern world. For the legal statement or text that the lawyer himself then makes in this frame of mind is like the statement that might be expected to emerge from an institutional arrangement in which those who write are not themselves responsible, not themselves thinking and deciding, but instead are told to justify in a post hoc way a decision arrived at by others. The statement made by the lawyer holding texts outside is not a text that is itself a contribution to the law, that integrates, sums up, points, and gives life to the values that define us. It is not an authentic statement. It is not, one may say, a statement of law. It may be expected to disappear, to be dissolved by careful legal analysis and then ignored as all statements that have no real content or meaning are ignored when one is seeking help in deciding what to do. Lawyers are well aware that "other reasons" which cannot be disclosed and are not talked about are paradigmatically illegitimate. They are not justifiable, or they would be brought out and justified or at least subjected to the beginnings of justification. They are the dark reasons, reasons of class, sex, race, and politics in the partisan sense, reasons of an expediency not thought through, embarrassing consequences of atavistic structures of thought which could not survive analysis if revealed.

And this is a great trouble, one on which all help is needed. Now theologians may be less troubled by the way they often work with authoritative texts, allowing themselves to think as they do of inspiration and confirmation. But this is at worst a matter of degree. It does not mean that lawyers' method and lawyers' doubts and difficulties are set apart and that no help can be forthcoming from theology. Theologians may be less troubled, but they are not untroubled. Furthermore, there is a form of confirmation that goes on also in the practice of legal method, and which brings the situation in law close to that in theology. It is this: to the extent other reasons are brought out and are accepted as justifiable in light of the meaning of the forward-pointing expressions of the legal mind surveyed as a whole, they become not "other reasons" at all. If they survive analysis and are incorporated into a present statement of law they become part of the developed meaning of the guiding values and organizing structures of the legal mind. There is confirmation—of the validity, truth, legitimacy (words often used as substitutes for one another) of a statement or decision of law—that proceeds from the act of integration. Assurance proceeds from understanding. The confirmation is in consistency, but it is not in the consistency conceived or achieved by a man trying to maneuver a thing in from the outside, who may even twist and bend the whole to fit the part. The consistency and assurance achieved to a greater or less degree by the effort at integration is the consistency of a caring mind. Theology knows this very well.

The contrary of methodological legalism has posed equal difficulty for lawyers. The contrary of legalism is requiring and respecting true belief in what one is saying. Requiring true belief, in oneself and others, and then respecting it when it is perceived, seems to lead to disobedience and disorder. The response of law has been to deemphasize belief. But without belief, with the relativism and nominalism that takes its place, law falls apart and becomes the plaything of the clever, a thing not to be taken seriously. The church has had hardly fewer difficulties with true belief. Respecting it in practice has toppled hierarchies and splintered communities. But the church must at least begin with belief, must require belief, and cannot take the relativist's escape so easily. Theologians' connection of belief with authority, and of requirement of belief with respect for belief, must therefore be of enormous interest to lawyers. In seeing how far away theologians are from the Grand Inquisitor, lawyers may sense how far away they can be. Theologians will have something too to learn from lawyers. For one does not enter the contemplation of true belief without entering into personification, both in the large, and of the individual and the two persons in one who must be found if the individual is to exist. The law is a fabric of personifications, and in the West, through its inchoate respect for the individual, the law pursues the mystery of the individual in swirls of life that theology is known sometimes to hold itself back from entering.

The aid of what may be law's sister discipline does not end here. The problem of emptiness is also a problem of idolatry. Quaint though it sounds, lawyers can at least turn the term over in their hands, for it may shift their thought from the methodological emptiness and pretense which they know, to that emptiness of substance which they also know but for which they have no ready word. The words of texts may be held outside and manipulated. One may also fall back and try to bow down to them and worship them, and force others to do so too.

One may try to bow down and force others to do so; but a word is only a signifier, pointing to the signified. A metaphor always points to something else, just as legal evidence is always *of* something. That something is the actuality, the truth, what it is that one is talking about. And it is when one tries to wish away, ignore, or forget the thing itself, and treat the signifier, the metaphor, the evidence as all there is, that one runs into the great difficulty, with results so serious that in religious discourse extreme measures have sometimes been taken to avoid them. The Old Testament God, for instance, had no name. "I AM, that is who I am. Tell them that I AM has sent you to them." There were ways of referring to the supreme being, but the language was not to include a signifier that could take the place of the actuality.

Of course in general one cannot approach the signified except through another signifier. If we give up one metaphor we must adopt another. But this does not mean that we cannot know anything other than signifiers and metaphors, or silence, any more than it would be true to say that one cannot learn a foreign language without a dictionary or engage in translation from one language to another seeking the common what of their signification. We are not in closed systems. A language does have its own rules, guiding the moves one can make, as in a game. But to say that language is like a game does not mean that language is a game. A game is quintessentially process, the outcome of which is insignificant. The winning of a game is nothing more than the end of the game, after which there is, for a game player, only the beginning of another game. Do we believe that a person cannot speak through language to something beyond it, that he plays only a game signifying nothing? Do we believe that a person cannot be seen through language, that he is only a player, nothing real, a manipulator of the rules going round and round?

All lawyers have experienced the movement of legal discussion toward a definitional game as some particular evidence is less and less treated as *of* something else, and becomes more and more itself the object of concern. When evidence does become, by definition, enough for a conclusion that a thing is so every time one meets that evidence, what lawyers call a legal fiction emerges. At that point the law, or an evidentiary hearing, or mere discourse between lawyers, comes to have an especially formal quality about it that signals its unreality. It is, for instance, a common and understandable legal criticism of a proceeding that the proceeding is an "empty shell." If asked "Empty of what?" lawyers might be hard put to it to say what they have in mind that such a proceeding is empty of, but they know its absence. Consequences may flow from moves in the game and, from manipulating definitions, conclusions may be drawn that have effects in the world of affairs. But the law itself, the hearing, the arguments, are devoid of substance, unreal, only a game, and the conclusions drawn and

actions taken on the outcomes may be and usually are thwarted and resisted with various degrees of success in the world of affairs, even wiped out
as if they never were.

Whatever our ultimate conclusion on this question of disciplinary affinity,
our larger inquiry must go on. What we point to when we seek to describe
mind or a person—the truth, the reality, the whatness, of mind or a person—may be meaning itself. To the extent there is no such reality beyond
or behind what we say and the word games we play moving from signifier
to signifier, to that extent we may live without meaning and on the edge
of despair. And so faith in the possibility of meaning, and belief in one's
ends and identification with them, may be necessary. Faith and belief may
be necessary not just to legal method and for lawyers and not just to theological method and for theologians, but to all active life, all hard work,
all pushing forward. Faith and belief may be necessary to life itself, as
necessary, dare we say causally necessary, as any of the other ingredients of
human life. And very nearly all of us do believe, often. It is not that we
experience belief. We believe. This is what makes us care when we care
and take responsibility for what we do when we take responsibility.

Yet time, change, and process are always with us, and how one can
believe while keeping a mind open to the persuasion of others' and one's
own reflection and acknowledging that one may be persuaded otherwise,
change one's mind, and not believe or think a thing forever, how what
one believes he believes and thinks can be what one actually believes and
thinks if this is the case, is no simple matter to understand.

We cannot conceive of ourselves as a changing system believing nothing, for that is not true to the evidence of our experience and our lives. To
be told that one cannot believe anything now if one agrees that one does
not have a closed mind and may change one's mind is little different from
being told in a crisis of one's life (whether at the age of sixteen or twenty-
two, or thirty-five or forty-five, or sixty-five) that in a few months or years
everything will be all right. Knowing that things may change is no more
reason to doubt present belief than it is reason to doubt present agony. If
one's belief changes, one must change, oneself. If one is in a stage of crisis,
there is no help or comfort in being told that one is merely a system.
Though systematic analysis is helpful, the individual must himself still get
on to the next stage and go through the transformation that getting on
involves. He cannot sit out and wait as a mere system. If he thought
himself merely a system he would not get on to the next stage. He would
stop. Perhaps it is the same thing to say that if he were merely a system, *he*

would not get on to the next stage, for he would not exist in his own contemplation or that of others. What will happen, will happen in him and by him as well as to him.

I do not know how far we can go beyond this. What can we say we know that is more positive than knowing what cannot be? Ordinary people turn to children for help with the problem of emptiness. Those working in disciplined inquiry need not think of themselves as so out of the ordinary. A child can be a joy at twelve, and not just in anticipation of the man or woman of forty, and the joy the child gives at twelve is not open to doubt because of the absolute certainty that it cannot last. One could not, indeed, specify just what man it is—the man of twenty-five, of forty, or of seventy—that one's joy in a child might be in anticipation of, were that to be thought its source; and if later reflection suggests that what one saw, when the child of twelve glowed before one and one responded then and there, was something more than what must pass and did pass, then there is the thought that it is only the whole person over his whole lifetime, glimpsed all at once, or the things still of the present that a child before one permits one to see again in one's adulthood, that one can be seeing and, on reflection, conceive of oneself as having reference to. And of the identity of a whole person over his whole lifetime, and of identifications and mergings between oneself and such whole persons of one's vision that reveal also who one is oneself, we have talked a bit in this book.

Neither lawyer nor theologian may like any suggestion that they are brother and sister. Theologians may not like it, thinking that lawyers are individuals peculiarly without belief of any kind. Lawyers may not like theology's other-worldliness and claim of universal domination. Turning to theology may seem a failure, a giving up of the reach to become a science like the other disciplines that escaped the domination of theology hundreds of years ago. But law that has not become a science may, if it recognizes the fact, teach a thing or two to the life sciences and the science of man. Law may indeed be a science of man. And it may be necessary to look into a mirror that leaves nothing out if law is to see itself for what it is. Theology may not be law any more than any metaphor is the same as that which it reflects. But it has the perhaps unique advantage that, like law, it leaves nothing out, not person, nor present, nor freedom, nor will, nor madness, nor the individual, nor the delight of a child, nor the eyes of a fellow human being, nor our sense of the ultimate, in its effort to make sense of our experience and make statements that are consistent and understandable in light of it all.

EPILOGUE

Dark woods in early morning light
Open round the traveler sleeping.
Horizontal light bathes tall straight trunks
Till each glows light golden from within;—
A vision brief—
Choirs have no time to sing before it goes.

These woods recall a columned temple; that is their beauty
And the reason why the eye dwells upon them
Rather than upon the flower underfoot
Or the rushing stream that stays the same.
But oh, temple columns:
Have we not read that they began
As trees set up by man?
And when we see them set up now,
Or look upon arches set together row on row,
Columns with their branches on and joined together overhead,
What do we see?
The forest?

Is this where the temple's beauty lies
And what we recognize when we see the beauty in it?
Those rows of long straight cylinders set on end:
Why do they grip us glowing golden from within,
Ruined even, on an acropolis,
Or barely lit, in a shady hush?
Why does man respond and gaze reflectively upon columns
Collected together, arched or linteled, with or without a roof?
Why is this beautiful? Why does not the eye pass on?

Is it, oh, recollection, of the forest?
And if it is, where are we,
Forest recalling temple, temple the forest?

No. Listen: Temple columns process along.
Trees in forests lead nowhere.

AMPLIFICATIONS

Chapter 2

1. A Small Example of the Elision of Time

What Mr. Justice Marshall wrote in 1803 is subtly changed when it is treated as authority, that is, when it is examined by lawyers rather than by antiquarians or historians. Its punctuation may be changed, its capitalization and spelling are changed, its rather liberal use of italics may be toned down, and it is reprinted without the fuffy S's characteristic of late eighteenth- and early nineteenth-century orthography and printing. *Marbury v. Madison* (1803) in the original leaves a different impression. It seems antique, the voice speaking a voice from long ago. Asked why the opinion is not printed today as it originally appeared, a scholar of constitutional law will reply that small liberties are taken with the text so that the impression upon the modern ear—the impressionable student of law—of what Mr. Justice Marshall says for the Court (and the present tense is often used) will be more like the impression made upon the contemporary ear in 1803. This is a small example of elision of time. In this connection readers may find helpful the sensitive discussion of translating an authoritative text into contemporary idiom in the translators' introductions to the *New English Bible*.

2. Word Definition

What do we mean by "mind"? To try to specify in a prior definition what we mean by mind would be to fall into the very way of thinking and talking that it should be our purpose above all to bypass.

Much speculation about the relation between mind and brain suffers from inattention to the whatness of mind. Mind is defined, and once defined it is evident that mind is not what is being talked about. I shall not try to specify in this way. What good would it do? What good would it do to try to define what we mean by "tragic"? Our meaning will come clear only in discussion. If the word "mind," when I use it, does not rightly convey to you what I have in mind, I am confident that communication will emerge, for I shall be drawing on experience and knowl-

205

edge I believe you already have. I shall not in any event confine myself to the one word "mind." Readers will find such other words used in conjunction with it or in lieu of it as seem natural in the circumstances.

3. POINTS OF DEPARTURE

Readers need not share the same empirical base to pursue our question. I do not think there is likely to be any error of substance in the basic facts I have set forth; but if, as an empirical matter, either pole is thought to be exaggerated here— either, with regard to the Court, the novelty of the situation and the present potential for further bureaucratization; or, on the other side, the degree of bureaucratization in the production of legal texts by American administrative agencies— readers will still have the point of departure in mind. That point is in the contrast, in having before us that of which there can be a greater or lesser degree. If the bureaucratization of the Supreme Court were not a problem at all, we should urgently want to know what has prevented the problem from arising in a world of steadily increasing numbers, systemization, and division of labor.

Chapter 3

1. THE PROPOSAL OF A HEAVEN WITHOUT LAW

Grant Gilmore's *The Ages of American Law* (1977) is the most accessible summary of this history, saying out loud that great numbers of lawyers have often thought to say at least since the 1950s.

A fine book by a great man of the law, enlightening and freeing, *The Ages of American Law* nonetheless poses a most difficult problem for its readers. Gilmore does not want to think of law as a brooding omnipresence in the sky, and he says so. At the very end of his book he wants to think of law as hardly real at all, only a reflection of a reality, which he denominates by the term "society." "In Heaven there is no law," he concludes. Presumably in Heaven there is only reality. "In Hell there is nothing but law." Presumably in Hell there is nothing real, and that is a reason, if not the reason, why Hell is Hell.

But if one examines Gilmore's sentences throughout his book, one cannot escape the suspicion that what Gilmore wants to think law is, is not what Gilmore actually thinks law is. Rather it appears quite possible that, for him, law is indeed a brooding omnipresence in the sky.

Gilmore defines what he means by "law" twice in the course of discussion. He does not define law at the beginning. His introduction starts by noting that from age immemorial various dispute-settling organs "excreted law" or "something like law." In referring thus to "law" he does not speak as if he were using a pure term of art or a foreign word: "law" is meant to evoke a response from the general reader.

Later in the book comes a definition. "The process by which a society accommodates change without abandoning its fundamental structure is what we mean by law." This is repeated elsewhere. The function of law is to provide a mechanism, and "the function of the lawyer is to preserve a skeptical relativism." But from beginning to end no definition of law as process, which this seems to be, is actually *used* by Gilmore. Though he states it, it cannot be taken as his definition. It seems almost to be the interpolation of another voice, at war with the implication of the rest of his discussion.

Take his discussion of an example from his own field, commercial law:

> Without going into the merits of the question, it suffices to say that no student of negotiable instruments law, from the time that law began to take its modern shape in the late eighteenth century down to the present time, has ever doubted that antecedent debt and new value should, for this purpose, be treated as functional equivalents. . . . The obvious solution to *Swift* v. *Tyson* was to have pointed out that the only authoritative statement of New York law on the pre-existing debt question had been by Chancellor Kent in *Coddington* v. *Bay* (as well as in his *Commentaries*). Careless dicta in the Court of Errors and subsequent confusion of a few lower court judges were entitled to no weight. Thus the law of New York coincided with that of the rest of the civilized world and there was no need to go any further.

He speaks with confidence when stating the law from the inside, as a lawyer. When speaking of it somewhat from the outside, as a historian, he is no less confident. He says, for instance, of Justice Story, that Story was

> preaching what would be somewhat barbarously referred to a hundred years later as a policy-oriented approach to law. . . . We did cut ourselves loose from the English tradition. We did set out to create a rationally organized system of law. . . . Thus in Rome in the third century, as in the United States in the nineteenth century, a stable, wealthy, and powerful society found both the need and the opportunity to create a rational system of law.

And he is confident in his criticism—against a standard of living law—as in his comments on institutional practices after the Civil War:

> This predisposition of the judges reflected itself in the style of opinion writing which came into vogue. This became the age of the string citation . . . and the judges, like the professors, rarely, if ever, bothered with the facts of the cases they cited or with the reasons why the cases had been decided as they had been. Nor did the judges make any attempt to explain the reasons for their decisions. It was enough to say: the rule which we apply has long been settled in this state (citing cases). Indeed it was improper, unfitting, unjudicial to say more. The juice of life had been squeezed out; the case reports became so many dry husks.

and in his comments on the law review articles of Wesley Sturges in the 1920s

> which were of an almost unbelievably narrow scope and focus. . . . The point of the study was to demonstrate that the North Carolina law of mortgages made no sense and could most charitably be described as a species of collective insanity on the march. . . . [His] casebook [on credit transactions] consisted principally of the most absurd cases, along with the most idiotic law review comments, which he had been able to find. The law, as Wesley Sturges conceived it, bore a striking resemblance to the more despairing novels of Franz Kafka.

In contrast, Gilmore praises Karl Llewellyn's "encyclopedic knowledge of the law," and his casebook that was followed by a

> series of magisterial articles on sales law. In both the articles and the casebook he traced, in meticulous detail, the development of sales law in the United States from the 1800s to his own time.

What could this *law* be to which Gilmore so constantly refers throughout his book? What would he have had social scientists study, when he comments, "Few lawyers ever bother to study any of the social sciences (any more than the social scientists, even those who join the law faculties, ever bother to study law)"?

There is more to law for him than process, though his definitions and his final images of it say not. We may conclude that even Gilmore never completed his thinking about legal method or what he meant by law. He despairs at the end of his book, caught between an authoritarian source of law outside man, brooding omnipresence, and Hell. That was the end of his career. The rest of us cannot despair while we live, and our situation is such today that I think we cannot avoid thinking seriously about legal method and law.

2. Positivism in Social Science

There is a standard tradition in social science which seeks to turn the subject-matter of its study into fact that exists apart. This, the positivist tradition, is the background against which disputes about what social science is take place.

An influential contemporary defense of positivism in social science can be found in Herbert Simon's *Administrative Behavior* (1976). The difficulties posed, for those seeking knowledge of society, by positivism and by the analogy to the physical sciences from which it flows, have been explored at length by Richard Bernstein in *The Restructuring of Social and Political Theory* (1976). Such is the force of the desire to be like the hard sciences, that fields and modes of analysis not based on positivistic assumptions tend to lose the title "scientific" and slip into the humanities. Historians, cultural anthropologists, and psychiatrists are among those students of society who have remained ambiguous about their assumptions, and in the future positivism may cease to be vital to scientists in any field. But full debate about what should be called "scientific" is not warranted here. To emphasize the appropriate distinction and to avoid any implication that the experimental method or quantification is essential to science, I have used the term "naturalist" as an alternative, by which I mean to include sciences that operate with a theory as well as sciences (such as anatomy) that operate without theory.

Readers interested in the possibility of bridges between disciplines will find discussions particularly pertinent to the consideration of legal analysis in Michael Polanyi's *Personal Knowledge* (1958) and Geoffrey Vickers' *The Art of Judgment* (1965); with them should be compared Roger Scruton's *The Aesthetics of Architecture* (1979). Each is "postcritical" or "postmodern"—in physical science, public administration, and art—addressing directly the conceptions of the self that have pervaded disciplined work through most of the century.

3. Sociobiology

This is the great difficulty of sociobiology when it is extended to human affairs. Words such as "value," "ethical," "choose," "law," "property," "eschatology," "language," "love," "time," "brutality," or "culture" leap out from the pages of Edward O. Wilson's *On Human Nature* (1978) as if printed in red ink, or as if italicized because from a foreign tongue. They have almost nothing to do with what he is talking about, and appear in his sentences and paragraphs odd and out of place. It is clear that in his usage they do not have the meaning they ordinarily have.

The evolutionary consciousness from which sociobiology grows, however, can be sensitive to the complexity of things. The evolutionary consciousness is the historical consciousness, and biologists seeking to advance evolutionary perceptions might well turn outside their field, perhaps (for example) to Fernand Braudel's, for guidance.

4. Paradigms in Thinking about Law

Do you wonder at this as the first question faced by lawyers? The reason may lie in the fact that so much discussion of law and lawyers begins with a simple court case of tort or contract between two individuals represented each by a lawyer charging a fee, to whom a judge will eventually speak as one individual to another, giving orders, with the army at his back, to pay something or do something.

But that is not the place to begin if one wants to think about law and lawyers in the world as it is. It would be helpful as an antidote to begin instead with a case of an administrative pronouncement or regulation that is being analyzed, explained, and litigated by lawyers in groups, who can and do routinely change, rearrange, and create the very entities and units of reference of law and legal discourse, who act for organizations, and who often have sufficient time, resources, and persistence to bypass, or to delay, or to read and litigate a reading of a regulation to the point where it is a dead letter in the life of the client or anyone else. That is closer to the reality of what lawyers and law students face from the moment they enter legal training. It is connected indeed with the reality officials face as they ask themselves what they are to do under the law to those who appear before them who do not have such resources of combat, and the reality industrial workers face in a society in which "working by the rule book" is a recognized form of disobedience.

One may of course bring into one's thinking the simple case of two lawyers arguing on behalf of individuals in court, but such a case is best brought in as a special instance, not as a paradigm.

5. Public and Private Purposes

The ends of which we speak here may be separate, secret, purely private. They may also be recognizable, known, and shared, but one may be uninformed and unaffected by what the law defines is to be taken into account in thinking about them and moving toward them.

In either case—the secret end of value only to the individual, or the public value defined idiosyncratically—there is a loss of integration. Wholeness, organization, order, understandability flicker and dim as experience flows on.

Whether any particular instance of this is a harbinger of chaos, instead of a newly created meaning newly shared, must be known to us in some way, however slightly; for we do feel we know for ourselves, and can judge in others, when going a separate way is right. Integration is not an unalloyed good. It may in the end be a mystery—as time is a mystery—that full meaning and complete order must lie beyond our grasp. In much religious discourse full life lies only in death, an observation that has something of a double edge to it. If there were no private definition of public roles, if everyone did just as he should, the result might be perfect, and also static and still.

I talk, however, as if public roles, the definition of what is to be sought and taken into account, the law's commands, were sufficiently clear and well-developed that such choices—between the separate or new way, and the shared way—are actually possible. Roles, commands, public values are never so clear or well-developed. It is, after all, we who make them. They are not ready-made and presented to us from the outside, and we have never come close to eliminating the need for individual definition of what floats between us and gives us a sense of who we are and what we are to do. We live in a clamor of suggestions from all sides about what public values are, what it is to *be* a mother, a father, a scholar, a carpenter, a sportsmanlike athlete. That a perfect world might not be perfect—or might have no place for us individually in it—is not a problem we have ever faced. Law presents only an opportunity to move toward meaning or away from it.

6. FORMS OF THE AUTHORITARIAN

Many in the United States have experienced, in a special context, the exercise of power without recognition of its legitimacy by those subject to it:

> A middle-class Negro informant said . . . that he would not show any undue deference, smile in a servile manner or scratch his head or the like. He followed the main forms because he had to, but he would not add to them by a jot and he carried them out in a cool and reserved manner. The aggressive element is quite obvious in this, the more so when one thinks that whites expect Negroes not only not to be aggressive, but to be positively ingratiating at every turn.
>
> Lower-class Negroes seem to make few reservations with regard to carrying out deference forms toward white people. . . . We have already noted that their sabotage is more passive and takes the form of slowness, awkwardness, and indecision about their work. After all, this is a slavery accommodation; the slave may not show his resistance by stopping work altogether, but he can at least slow up. It may also be that the carelessness of white time and goods often attributed to lower-class Negroes is another evidence of resistance. (John Dollard, *Caste and Class in a Southern Town* [1937])

Slavery is a polar form of the authoritarian.

7. AMBIGUITIES OF FREE ENTERPRISE

Concern for the consumer, as anything more than a means to profit, sits uncomfortably with classical economic theory and the premises of strict or ideal free enterprise. But if the customer cannot trust the corporation, why should the corporation assume that it can trust the customer? There are other common examples of tricking the telephone system, in use as I write, such as the making of collect long-distance calls to fictitious names which are in fact coded messages, with assertion that the person is not home leading to no charge for the call. How this is to be condemned, except by assuming that the consumer ought to internalize the telephone company's purposes, is most difficult to see. Yet such an assumption cannot be made in the war of all against all that a regime of pure competition envisages. Economists generally assume that the law of property (or crime) will take care of such problems for them, but it does not.

Contradictions are rife. Businessmen object to judicial or administrative review under legal standards, or what is called government regulation, and vigorously ask to be trusted. Then they turn around and vigorously object to any legal definition of their role that would make it anything other than the strictest profit maximization, and wonder why evidence of lack of trust mounts up. The problem is not concentrated power, though that may be bad enough. The problem is power in the hands of men who cannot be trusted, who make irresponsibility and the irresponsible use of power a virtue. Benevolent despots can be borne, but not despots without a trace of benevolence. Pressed on this, businessmen do have an answer. What power? they ask. We have no power. We are the slaves of the consumer, the ministers of the market. But any demonstration that the market in this sense does not exist outside the bazaar is met with evasion, for the market is only a ploy. It must be: if they were slaves of the market businessmen would not care whether they were trusted or not, regulated or not. Their whirring, mechanical obedience to signals would be the same. Their desire for trust, and quite human it is, betrays their belief in their autonomy. The difficulty actually lies in their glorying in selfishness, as street-gang members might glory in gore; and taking all in all, one cannot believe they mean it.

Chapter 4

1. THE NAME OF SCIENCE

Natural scientists, including men and women of distinction whose claim to the title "scientist" is sure, do sometimes talk in the literary, legal, or religious way that their discipline historically has set its face against, and say they speak still as scientists. But the scientific remains a recognizable cast of mind notwithstanding. We have noted the standard background against which current disputes over method in social science take place. A wave of a wand does not change it, though a wave of a wand will allow an individual to depart from it. When he does, and continues to call himself a scientist, no doubt he incrementally changes the notion of science, as does a court when it works with a word; but if in his departure he moves to another cast of mind that has another name and a different spirit, he cannot very well cling to the name of that from which he has departed and refuse to recognize the name for what he has become. Eventually he may be able to use the old name again, or, since these things take generations, we should say that eventually one in his position may. The name he likes can in time detach itself from the old allegience and merge with the new, squeezing out the name that was there before. But if there should be a change in what is meant by the name "scientist," the cast of mind that was science before will not necessarily disappear; and in the period of transition the contention will be as much over the name of one or another cast of mind as over loyalty to it. The word "science," with its root in the word for knowledge itself, is a formidable prize.

2. A Note on Observations about Legal Analysis
Because we are engaged in making observations *about* legal analysis, and not engaged here in the practice of it, it may be useful to underline a point implicit in what we have said and will say. To understand law or legal method one must see it from the inside. Since law is not the property of lawyers only, there is no exclusion of the uninitiated in insisting upon this. Indeed in law the outside becomes the inside, as doing becomes saying, the is becomes the ought, or process becomes substance. If what a man does is search for meaning, that "is" of what he does is not separated from the "ought" of our lives by such an impassable chasm. Who are we, lying deep within ourselves, but the selves (in part) that we want to be and wish we were? One half views law from the outside, perhaps, when one lays it side by side with other similar phenomena to help place it in one's mind. But when we say law is or authority is, it is never clear that we distinguish or can distinguish the existence of what we have in mind from its effective normative claim upon us.

3. The Literary Canon
Keats is a nice example of canonization. Critics in his lifetime were quite divided about him, but now he comes, like Shakespeare, as a voice to be responded to and talked about. His place in the canon could be called, objectively, a presupposition of excellence. From the point of view of the young *coming upon* Keats or Shakespeare, an event happening every day, what is demanded is either faith that it is worthwhile talking about these particular texts, or simple acceptance of them as language is accepted—and in Western society it is more faith than simple acceptance that is called for.

4. Majority Rule
The modern conceptual comfort in analogizing individuals to the atomic units, integers, or molecules of natural science has nothing to do with legitimacy. The special legitimacy of majority rule as a deadlock-breaking device in political democracy is rooted in individual human dignity—the sense of and belief in individual human dignity. It is recognition, for instance, of the importance of being in a position to make a difference, even if infinitesimal, and especially the importance of having the powerful come to you periodically to beg for something, however small.

Majority rule is also supported by the belief, which sometimes grows out of a sense of individual dignity, that on matters to be put to a vote there is no right or wrong, and one man's or woman's opinion is as good as any other. But the premise that there is no right or wrong, and therefore one individual's view is as good as any other, does not obtain at all in legal analysis beyond the formal recognition of an electoral or legislative act.

And one may question whether such a premise obtains in politics either. If we really believed that one view is as good as any other, we would not have speeches and discussion before voting. We would not try to persuade one another. We would just vote. Our underlying disbelief in relativism, however much we may still be convinced of individual dignity and the importance of tolerance is one reason why so many accept with such surprising equanimity demonstrations that the political system is structured in such a way that majority rule is more an impossible ideal than an actuality.

We shall have more to say about majority rule as something other than a deadlock-breaking device in Chapters 9 and 10.

5. HERMENEUTICS
Hermeneutics, the body of reflections arising from the long scholarly effort to put together correct versions of ancient texts (and thus make possible reading for understanding and debate about their substance) will be found pertinent in many ways to this description of what legal analysts typically do. For an introduction see Zygmunt Bauman, *Hermeneutics and Social Science* (1978).

6. A NOTE ON THE OBJECTIVITY OF LANGUAGE
We say "words mean" or "words meant." Language is objective not because *it* means anything but because it is part of the world each individual faces. In law, when we ask why someone decided to use a word or turn of phrase we are interested in what he knew when he made his decision, and language is evidence of what he knew, like any other evidence of his situation that we would take into account in deciding what he meant.

As we shall see in Chapters 6, 7, and 8, legal hierarchy may be of some help in handling the linguistic evidence, for speaker and listener alike.

7. CONNECTION TO THE PAST
The addition of dinosaurs to our companion animals, which occurs at some point in the typical Western childhood, is much the same. They expand our present world with wonderful new gigantic shapes, but they are still familiar, and we can drowse easily, thinking either of a brontosaurus grazing on mesozoic reeds or a cow in a summer pasture.

8. LEGAL METHOD AND CLEAR MEANING
I do not want to suggest that method is straightforward and agreed-upon in its particulars. To take but one example, putting limitations on the materials that may be looked to in ascertaining the meaning of a statement of law is a perennial difficulty, indeed a matter of continuous dispute. Furthermore, unresolved methodological problems are often at the root of substantive disputes. To use the same example, many of the questions that can be raised about the meaning even of simple traffic regulations can be traced to the unresolved problem of drawing lines around that to which one can look.

It may be helpful to elaborate briefly here on traffic regulation, by way of illustration. Show an American automobile driver a sign "Speed Limit 55 Miles Per Hour" and he may well tell you, quite seriously, that he is not sure of its meaning. What is happening is that, in reading the law, he is looking at materials of which the sign is a part but only a part.

He may be looking behind the sign at the steady flow of traffic at sixty-five miles per hour and at the headlights turned on to warn fellow motorists of speed traps. He may also have before his mind half-hearted enforcement, suggesting what lawyers call desuetude in the law; or reports of the imposition of fines on a quota system with revenue as its purpose or signs along the highway setting out the posted tariff for each additional five miles per hour above fifty-five, suggesting that the law is more a tax than a safety measure; or reports of administrative or judicial allowance of various excuses and justifications for higher speeds, suggesting that a number of concerns and values beyond saftey are legally pertinent to his own decision about how fast to drive. He may have heard that signs saying, "The 55 Mile-per-Hour Speed Limit is Strictly Enforced by This State," are erected not for motorists but for an audience of Federal Highway Administration inspectors (who may cut off highway funds to a state if they conclude the speed limit is not being enforced). And he may have kept abreast of resistance in the state legislature to the outlawing of sale or use of so-called fuzz busters or radar detectors, or he may know of various judicial opinions raising doubt about such laws in states where they have been passed, suggesting that the field of activity he is about to enter has more of the elements of sport in it than is usual in legal regulation, more even than tax practice.

The motorist does not have to agree that law is merely a prediction of what officials will do, or that what law is is revealed by the actual behavior of citizens, before he can question the meaning, in these circumstances, of the apparently clear command "Do Not Exceed 55 Miles Per Hour." The questioning citizen or lawyer is still reading the traffic law, but there is more to read than the words on the sign.

The problem of the relative clarity of legal commands thus points to the problem of the relative clarity of legal method. Nothing is clear in law except that method makes it so.

To the extent there are unresolved problems of method, there are unresolved problems of meaning, and following on these are unresolved problems of authority, obligation, and obedience. One cannot enter on a critique of law, Marxist or otherwise, without asking what the law is, and in asking that, one must be prepared to ask and answer the prior question, how one decides what it is. Similarly, one cannot ask whether there is an obligation to obey the law without asking what the law is that is to be obeyed; and if someone says, "Well, let us ask whether there is any obligation to obey a clear command," then the question must be, "How did you arrive at such a clear command?" Any lawyer will shudder at the *legal* use of the word "clear" once he has dealt with tests for judicial jurisdiction that bring in the notion of clarity as an operative part of legal doctrine, those tests that turn on whether an administrator has acted "in clear excess of his jurisdiction" or with "blatant lawlessness" (as opposed to simply going beyond his authority or committing mere legal error). Legal use of the term "clear" presupposes clarity in that which is not clear, the self-interpreting, the obvious, words which themselves speak.

We may add that whatever position one may take on the possibility of dividing statements of law into those which are "clear" and those which are not, or of viewing rules as having "clear" cores and "ambiguous" penumbras, one would still be left with the question of what general view of the legal situation is to provide the basis for lawyers' rumination about the authority of law. Suppose it is the case that not all law need be thought complex. If it be admitted that not all law need be what is called clear, then there is no reason whatever to choose the so-called clear as the paradigm, or the representative, or what obtains "in most cases." It would be quite impossible to set out numerical criteria for determining whether enough of law is complex or, for that matter, clear: it is enough that the complex is the focus of lawyers' activity. This is the law the lawyer sees, and which therefore raises for him his dilemmas. The paradigm is the complex and the complex offers rich and often complete opportunities to lawyers to reduce it to a dead letter without any choice on their part so gross as to disobey. The choice to be made by lawyers in action is the adult one of attitude toward a command, not the child's choice to obey or else to defy and hide.

9. AN EXAMPLE OF LEGAL METHOD OUTSIDE LAW

Lawyers are known to take their method with them even when they work outside law. Joseph Sax's book *Mountains without Handrails* (1980) is an example. Sax's object is to answer the question why preservationists should be the recipients of deference in a democracy—why, for example, when demands for packaged commercial recreation in the public parks conflict with the preservation of wilderness for those who seek to experience nature on their own, the preservationist should be heeded and followed.

In the course of his answer he develops a number of themes, putting forth the experience of wilderness as redemptive, suggesting the moral basis of the preservationist ethic, and questioning the capacity of consumers, alienated by the nature of their daily work from any strong sense of self-direction, to demand what they want from wilderness. But Sax wants more than merely to stimulate or even to persuade. He wants authority for the preservationist—or to explain why the preservationist does have authority, though it is clearly not grounded in a majority, in the eyes of legislator and administrator.

Thus he does what seems at first a curious thing: he spends much time exploring the literature of the preservationist tradition. What he says may be new and is certainly his own, but what he says appears, as the book progresses, more and more interstitial, between quotations from texts. He does not give his reasons for this procedure. But it is clear that he has chosen to work with texts not simply because it is congenial to him as a lawyer but for a further purpose; what is more, he is seeking to arrange these texts into a coherence. He works with texts, but he also seeks a whole. "[The preservationist] rests his case on the evidence presented by Olmstead and Thoreau, Cotton and Ortega, Faulkner, Hemingway, Leopold, and the myriad others for whose view of man's relationship to nature he claims to speak. To the extent they are persuasive in stating a general philosophy, he asks the public to accept him as a spokesman before the Congress and the administrative officials who will give these views official status." And legislators and administrators act as carriers, not as sources of authority.

Sax's reference to authority explicitly contemplates the limits a set of texts (though he does not call the preservationist ethic a set of texts) places upon individual speakers of authoritative statements: "[T]he preservationist boldly asks the public to vest a similar power in him—to the extent that he remains within the bounds of his tradition. . . . [I]f we are willing to give any authority to teachers, as we routinely are, what we give is a freedom to operate within a professional tradition, recognizing that the bounds of that tradition are themselves a significant protection against purely personal or capricious judgments." We may note here for future reference, however, it is not *limits* that give authority, when there is conflict between the commands of a speaker acting within those limits and the other urgings experienced by a listener. The existence of limits raises the possibility of heresy and loss of authority, but authority itself is derived from something far more forceful, as to which the very notion of limits is in fact problematical. It is what is not "purely personal or capricious," but what that is must be constructed. It is constructed, as we shall see in the next chapter, upon a presupposition of authenticity composed of seriousness and belief. In another connection, speaking of advertisements that play upon the ambivalence of individuals toward the wild, Sax remarks, "To confound these competing strains so as to purport to serve longings for independence in the form of packaged entertainment is to dull the very qualities of personal engagement that give the river experience authenticity." The presupposition of authenticity is indeed clear throughout Sax's work.

Chapter 5

1. Critics' Choices

Critics may be wrong in their initial determinations. They are known to turn away with some frequency from writing which comes later to be seen worthy of close reading. Writing from which they turn away may later be seen to have enlarged the very idea of poetry or the novel. Critics may also change their classification of a work and later see it as less parasitic than they thought.

Obviously too there are many reasons why critics focus initially on a text. They may for instance read a text closely precisely to show that it is a waste of time to read it closely. But they cannot do much of that, for they cannot read everything closely. They operate in an economy of time and effort. They cannot escape choosing what they read. They begin work generally assuming a difference between what may turn out to fail after close reading and what does not begin to sustain such attention.

2. Games

Of course we all play games with one another, all the time. Games are fun. We tease, test and are tested. And games merge into ritual, dance, form itself. Life may be a game at the highest level, but, if so, it is a game played with death and nature.

When games are dance and ritual, they become serious and important: an arbitrary step, a false step, a wrong step, destroys the form and the meaning of the form. At that point trickery disappears. In important affairs people living together do not trick each other. In important affairs people are engaged in tricking nature, or their enemies.

3. A Note on Constitutional Free Speech
It may be useful, particularly for lawyers in the United States, to contrast this aspect of ordinary legal analysis with constitutional analysis under the First Amendment of the United States Constitution.

To be protected by the First Amendment speech does not have to be truly meant, or sincere. We are all insincere at one time or another. Freedom of speech is, in a way, testimony to the strength of our belief in the everyday techniques of authentication we constantly use in listening to others. We are reasonably confident that we can and do sift out the manipulative from the meant. But the question here is not freedom of speech. The question is not whether a speaker of legal statements is to be allowed to speak or whether noises that have the appearance of speech can be muffled. The question is whether speaker or speech is going to be heard. There is in fact a live issue whether a speaker of law, who purposes to be authoritative, is to be allowed to say certain things; there is a concept of heresy in law. But here we ask a different question, which is what the listener to a statement of law is to do with what is said.

It should be added that there is no absolute barrier between the legal thinking that goes on under the First Amendment and the response in law to inauthentic legal statements. For instance, First Amendment doctrine contains a distinction between protected speech and speech that is conduct, which is not protected. There can be found today, moreover, judicial expression of the view that speech of a profit-maximizing entity, the extreme example of manipulative speech, is not fully protected.

4. Monumentality
Someone's word must be taken too for the fact that an original is the original. But there is protection in the monumental surroundings of the original, the naves and transepts through which one walks to reach it, whether in law or in art.

5. Legal Rules
This is one reason why legal rules are so often general and, in a sense, unclear.

Even if a decision presented to a citizen or judging official is an easy one—the decision of a driver on a clear road to swerve rather than run over a child might be an easy one to make—there may be no clear rule involved: the rule applicable to the driver (after the situation is characterized) is "no unjustifiable killing" or "no negligent homicide." Decision making by citizen or official does not always or even often bump up against anything solid. The question presented by legal rules is less likely to be "I know what this means, shall I obey?" than "How shall I read this and with what attitude?"

Decision making consists of weighing purposes, values, factors, channels of thought. Rules are not self-executing, in law. There is always, in law, a decision maker, and what are called rules in law are expressions of considerations to be taken into account by a decision maker. They focus not on themselves as a self-contained system but upon decision-making activity pointing forward. Talk of rights and rules of a static kind, projecting an image of law standing off by itself, obscures the focus that legal rules have in fact, always a decision that must be made, at the edge of lives that have not been lived before, in a world that has not been seen before.

We may note here that what makes rules distinctively *legal*, among all the various expressions of considerations for human decision making, is that the decisions upon which they focus are to be accompanied by a claim to the respect of others. Such decisions are not private. Part and parcel of them is a proposition that they are to be carried out and realized by and through others' action and forbearance, paid attention to in others' own lives, enforced we sometimes say, respected we say when enforcement does not yet enter our heads. Decisions that make no claim to respect and do not ask to be taken into account by others in their lives—a decision of the kind that might follow the question, Shall I eat a peach?—are not legal decisions (at least not legal if in a wilderness with an abundance of peaches and the eating of a peach raises no question of property), but it is surprising how many ordinary and daily decisions are legal.

6. The Relation between Obedience and Understanding

There is often a distinction made between the question of the meaning of a statement of law and the question of what one does with it. Can such a distinction be made? I have thought so, not because law is a thing outside us but because there is always a center of choice within us where *we* reside. But it is not clear to me that true or full understanding, on the one hand, and, on the other, obedience in the sense of taking into account what another wishes one to take into account, are different. I conceive it possible that understanding and obedience are very much the same, though the truly authoritative may be blinding. Therefore a dichotomy between meaning and obedience, and the related conception of understanding *followed by* the choice to obey or disobey, perhaps ought not to be points from which we start in our thinking about the authority of law.

The reader may want to consider this as we proceed. It is not clear, for instance, that one can dissociate oneself from the beauty of an object once one has perceived its beauty. We speak of the power—or even authority—of a work of art. The two situations may be found much the same: the beauty of an object is a question, as is the meaning of a statement of law; the answer—the beauty itself—is something with which the perceiver has much to do, and we know this to be the case also in law.

7. Movies

Joan Didion makes a similar observation, which may pedantically be called methodological, about the possibility of criticism of the modern moving picture. She notes the "almost queasy uneasiness with pictures:"

To recognize that the picture is but one by-product of the action is to make rather more arduous the task of maintaining one's self-image as . . . "a critic of new works." Making judgments on films is in many ways so peculiarly vaporous an occupation that the only question is why . . . anyone does it in the first place. A finished picture defies all attempts to analyze what makes it work or not work: the responsibility for its every frame is clouded not only in the accidents and compromises of production but in the clauses of its financing. *The Getaway* was Sam Peckinpah's picture, but Steve McQueen had the "cut," or final right to edit. . . . Nor does calling film a "collaborative medium" exactly describe the situation. To read David O. Selznick's instructions to his directors, writers, actors and department heads . . . is to come very close to the spirit of actually making a picture, a spirit not of collaboration but of armed conflict in which one antagonist has a contract assuring him nuclear capability. . . . About the best a writer on film can hope to do, then, is to bring an engaging or interesting intelligence to bear upon the subject. . . . "Motives" are inferred when none existed; allegations spun out of thin speculation. Perhaps the difficulty of knowing who made which choices in a picture makes this airiness so expedient that it eventually infects any writer who makes a career of reviewing; perhaps the initial error is in making a career of it. (*The White Album* [1979])

8. The Law of Agency
The law of agency is a law that allocates monetary gains and losses from joint endeavor among participants, and turns far less on actual mind and intent—indeed in much of the law of agency it is acknowledged that the principal did not wish the agent to do that which is being held against the principal—than on factors appropriate to the allocation of wealth and the risks of loss of wealth in particular kinds of situations.

9. Intimations in Action
One of the presuppositions associated (as responsibility is associated) with the presupposition of authenticity is what may be called the presupposition of intimations. That too is impossible with the imitative. The same phenomenon can be found in theology, where church practice is deemed relevant to serious theological work and there is thus a belief that truth can be perceived before it can be fully articulated and placed. Without doubt legal analysis proceeds on this premise also, if legal truth be taken for what it is. But analysis that proceeds in this way, in theology or in law, assumes that the practitioner being looked to is authentically engaged.

10. Statements as Things
A thing said is also a thing done. That is one reason why we can speak of a thing said as a thing. We will discuss this in Chapters 6, 7, 8, and 10 in connection with the structure of mind and the function of focus in authoritative speech.

11. Ghostwritten Philosophy
While giving a public lecture of some importance John Rawls once spent much

time minutely analyzing whether what he was saying was inconsistent with what he had said in A *Theory of Justice* (1971). Panel speakers afterward did the same, and questioners from the floor quoted and requoted from his lecture and the book. If, in the course of picking over the language of first one and then the other, it had been revealed that the lecture or the pertinent paragraph in the book had been written by a research assistant or an editor, would the participants using this method of speaking about the matters that were of concern to them (which were not of course what Rawls the individual himself meant at some point in time, or whether he had committed the sin of inconsistency) have continued using the method—or using these texts?

Chapter 6

1. Closed Systems and Relativism

The methods of what is sometimes called positivism (see Amplification 2, Chapter 3) fail here because their use assumes not only that meaning is entirely relative but that it is determinable only in a system less than the whole and closed off from it. The two, arbitrariness or relativism, on the one hand, and its methodological or definitional location within a closed subsystem, on the other, may indeed be virtually interchangeable.

The fact is that lawyers operating in the United States or the European Community, or on the multinational and international plane, are not in closed subsystems, and they are always taking side glances at the whole.

2. A Further Note on Hierarchical Statements

Consider how much *chance* there is in discourse in fields that are not hierarchically structured.

I say something in a book. To whom? Necessarily to the world. I conceive a lecturer picking the book up during a lecture, reading a passage out loud with disdain, and saying, "How ridiculous!" To whom is he speaking? The world.

Why is he quick to refute? Because what I say is a text, evidence sitting there. He no more wants it there than any of us wants a misstatement of our own to stand uncorrected. The lecturer wants to organize, to make sense and meaning. To make sense he must extirpate this, if this is being heard and paid attention to.

His alternative is to ignore me. Hundreds of millions of people speak. Tens of thousands write books, and there are millions of pages in their books.

Each does of course have some influence. Even the idiosyncratic accent of one individual will change the accent of the group ever so slightly. Causes are delicate. For want of a nail a kingdom is lost. But beyond this slow, incremental movement that reaches past our time most speech can be deprived of significance and effect by the simple expedient of ignoring it. It need not enter the organized canon. Most speech will not enter; it cannot. There is too much of it.

On the other hand, this lecturer must have a place to start—a foil, a text. And he doesn't know whether what I have said might not come to occupy the field, or part of the field. Although he gives me force by noticing me, he is loath to take a chance that others will though he does not. He may take the chance. Then again he may not.

3. Superior Texts of Inferior Authors

An example of such replacement can be found in the much-publicized constitutional litigation over the landmark designation of the Grand Central Terminal in New York City. This produced an extraordinarily rich opinion from Judge Breitel on the New York Court of Appeals (the state supreme court) and something rather rigid and mechanical from the Supreme Court of the United States. While the reason for the evident difference may have been that the Supreme Court wished to shift the basis of decision and avoid addressing the questions opened by Judge Breitel, an analyst wishing to probe the law of takings will end with Judge Breitel's opinion, and treat the Supreme Court opinion for what it is, a cautionary note.

4. The Theory of a Case

In the old common law, a theory of the case (as it was called) had to be chosen at the beginning. The lawyer then asked for a particular writ, into the requirements of which he shoehorned his case. He kept it squeezed in even if his initial request for the particular writ turned out to be ill-advised. Modern procedure allows multiple alternative theories and the emergence of theories along the way, but the requirements of the logic used, and the necessities of building one thing upon another, tend to seal in theories nonetheless at a rather early stage in argument.

Chapter 7

1. Counterthrusts toward Irresponsibility

There is a counterthrust toward irresponsibility in legal thinking, perhaps a necessary shield and excusable, but counterthrusting nonetheless. The strategic lawyer comforts himself that the consequences he foresees will not be his fault but the system's (the system including the duty of persons deemed "others" and outside to protect themselves). The counselor and the judge comfort themselves that it is not their decision that will bring about consequences but rather the decision of the "law" which is outside them.

Certainly the weight of lawyers' and judges' words is supplied by their office and their method, their method above all. There is a sense in which they transmit what they say. The responsibility for what they say, *if* they are serious enough, work hard enough, argue vigorously enough and get it right, is not theirs.

But, though this might release them into irresponsibility and callousness, and does in fact dispose them in that direction, *they* must first get it right. They are held back from the mechanical and the irresponsible by the demands of their method.

Chapter 8

1. A Note on Limits to Infinite Regress

We have spoken of reducing or elevating through analysis the immediacies of present experience, and have used an analogy (the problem of the rock in Chapter 7) from the realm of science. But, in science, moving to the more particular and reducing a phenomenon to its components as a rock is reduced to its molecules is also moving to a more general and abstract level, since the components are all of a relatively few kinds in contrast to the infinite variety of the products of their postulated combination.

In contrast, in analyzing a process of choice it is not necessarily true that one moves to the more general as one moves to the more particular. It seems at least possible to proceed toward infinite regress because there are choices at each level and the factors taken into account in making a particular decision may be resolvable into further factors, and those factors into factors, for each decision, without reaching abstraction. Remaining in the concrete and individualized world one finds more than enough novelty and variety to occupy the mind.

It is possible that some or even most such factors are unities—some readers may recall G. E. Moore's simples—that glow and respond and are not at all built up from ingredients. And even if they are built up, outside science the product is not necessarily reducible to its ingredients. Whatever one may think of the validity or usefulness of the notion of emergence in biology or physics, in law wholes may be greater than the sums of their parts, and it may be necessary to respond to them as they are and not as if they were merely gateways to their parts.

2. OBJETS TROUVÉS

A landscape is a form of objet trouvé, selected from all the possible prospects for the eye, to be gazed at over and over again. A particular landscape may be grand without any sign of human cultivation in it. But then it is not one within which we feel at home. And in any event landscapes of wilderness (apparently untouched by human hand) that are selected to be gazed at are often chosen because they resemble the landscapes of the mind's eye, which are gardens.

Some mountains have more majesty than others, the shapes of some rocks make the eye return to them. The curve of a particular line of hills or the juxtaposition of gnarled tree and gleaming lake may be chance, but it is not chance that the human eye selects it and celebrates it.

3. A FURTHER NOTE ON CONVERSATION AND CONSISTENCY

We shall note at another point the fact that the author is rather more of a joining of different people than is the conversationalist, because the author works on his writing at different times and over a greater stretch of time, during which he himself changes.

This, and not the tour de force of it, is the excitement of good talk—the immediacy of it, the peculiar if evanescent consistency of it, which fades upon analysis when laid beside the joint work of one man's efforts at different times or several men's efforts at one time, but which nonetheless speaks to us of present existence and makes Samuel Johnson still a figure to be reckoned with.

Chapter 9

1. Commitment and Acceptance in Joint Writing

The degree to which this kind of negotiation, or what might better be called calibrated mutual deference, separates the outcome of a drafting process from the actual beliefs of any of the individual participants is most difficult to measure. An individual looking back on a joint product must be in some doubt about how he would have proceeded each step of the way if the journey had been left to him alone, and thus must find it difficult to say that the statement does *not* represent what he actually believes. Unsatisfactory though the statement may be on many counts, conceiving of an immediate replacement for it as a whole, and thus creating a hypothetical outcome for purposes of comparison with the one at hand, is perhaps impossible. The same is very largely true of any particular thing one produces by oneself.

But there must be the sense of joint endeavor, or trust—as there naturally seems to be between oneself in one mood on one day and oneself in another mood on another day, however different a person one may seem to oneself to be at the one time and at the other—before one can ever disregard the difference between what one *can* say one *does* believe, and what one *cannot* confidently say one does *not* believe. Only then will the difference between the outcome one might have achieved through one's own intellectual processes, and the outcome at hand, not matter much.

Indeed, with regard to the outcome of the process of joint work there will be much the same kind of predictability as with one's own work, in the sense that there will at least not be *surprise*. In the absence of trust one is on guard, and when one is on guard one is ready to counter the unpredictable move, as in a game, because one is seeking to avoid a surprise that matters. But a surprise that does not matter is hardly a surprise. One is not surprised to see an ant crawling across the sidewalk, although that event is unpredictable. It is surely not just that we are at a higher level of generality, at which ants crawling on sidewalks might be predictable. the particular of that ant crawling does not evoke in us the feelings of surprise. The occurrence and the fact do not matter.

So, if the outcome of joint work is one that was sought by all in the same spirit (as we do say) and, being only an instant in time, will be handled and responded to in the future in the same spirit, it is an outcome whose difference (if any) from what one might have expected may not matter; and then there is really no surprise. For those things in which we are truly interested, we are far more likely to be able to predict in the sense of avoiding suffering surprise if we can assume that others are moving as we would move and that we move along together—if we look at the future from the inside rather than the outside, knowing that in our unpredictable encounters with the world (and with the various results of our own past actions) we will be seeking and wanting the same, so that the results that emerge, though not predictable in the strict sense, or necessarily what we might produce alone (which would not be so very predictable either), may be quite acceptable, their acceptability indistinguishable from the acceptability of what we might produce alone.

Now acceptance is quite different from commitment. But commitment is to what is sought and what lies behind the particulars that are the outcomes of processes. Lawyers, being so aware of processes, are prone to making the mistake of thinking that since outcomes are contingent there is only process left to hold onto, and that commitment to law is commitment to process, or, as it is called in law, procedure. Law *is* procedure, it is sometimes said. But since there can be no real commitment to process—when one embraces one's child, husband, wife, or lover one does not fold one's arms around a process—the result is that there is no real commitment to law. Lawyers' mistake in thinking contributes greatly to the relativism and emptiness they so often espouse and suffer so needlessly. Process is not all that is left when particular outcomes are seen to be contingent.

The scientist in his professional capacity may think so, if, as one school has it, scientific proof through rigorous experimentation is never of a positive but always disproof of an alternative to a positive: for scientists there may *only* be the state of not being able to say that he does not believe a thing. But then a scientist assumes nature outside, and the constancy, at some level, of natural processes he does not himself fashion. The lawyer knows that the processes with which he deals are designed and chosen—"molded" is perhaps the better word. They too are the outcome of striving and seeking, and they too are contingent as all outcomes are. But they do not dissolve into the process of their making any more than *statements* made, jointly or singly authored, dissolve just into the process that produced them when they are criticized and seen to be incomplete and inadequate and not final in themselves. Chosen statements and chosen processes take their place in the pattern of particulars that come before—and are evidences to be used in the making of—the next choices. Of this we shall have more to say in a later chapter.

Commitment is to what one is seeking to express, not to the outcome of the process that seeks to express it or to the process itself. Belief is in what guides and animates. One does not believe in the words themselves that are the outcome, but in the meaning of those words.

2. COURT AND ADMINISTRATIVE AGENCY

The administrative agency is often approached in the same way, as we saw in our first chapter. Contrast these two passages by Louis Jaffe. The first, a view of courts and statements of law made by courts, was written in 1955 in the middle of Jaffe's long career as a scholar of administrative law:

> A judge may say: "There is more than one sensible construction of this statute, but this construction appears to me to be the correct one." If this is what he thinks, he should not defer either to his colleagues or to the agency. Such a view better explains the decisions, particularly those in which majority and minority judges both write persuasive opinions concerning which *reasoning* men disagree. Such a view comports better with a confident and responsible judiciary; if a judge may vote as he sees the law only on condition that he first conclude that the opposition is "unreasonable" he, if sensitive or modest, may be finally reduced to mere deference or frustration.

The second, a view of administrative agencies and the statements made by administrative agencies, was written in 1973 at the end of Jaffe's active life:

> I would propose a view of administration which recognizes the peculiar political process which provides the milieu and defines the operation of each agency. The elements of this political process are common to all potential law making activity—the intensity of a given problem, the degree to which it is felt throughout an organized and stable constituency, and the representation (or lack thereof) of varying interests within and without the law making body. The significance of each of these elements and the manner of their interaction are unpredictable, and likely to vary with each successive problem. Often the outcome will be determined not by the abstract merits of the situation, but by the character of certain interests which are cohesive and vociferous. . . . It makes little sense to criticize an administration for failure to meet a critic's judgment of what the "public interest" requires. The action or inaction of an agency acting under a broad delegation is often the result of the political process operating on the agency, and is, after all, all that can be expected. Indeed, the criticisms of administration must be recognized as themselves a component of the political process, and critics' invocation of the "public interest" as a standard with readily discoverable content should be viewed as but a useful tactic in the political debate.

The title Jaffe gave to this late reflection on agencies, "The Illusion of the Ideal Administration," though unexceptionable in itself, reflects a movement in his thought. It is not a coincidence that as he reduces more and more to process, his mind turns to the problem of illusion.

Students of Jaffe's work cannot fail to note its increasing cynicism. But even at the end he continues to use terms that counter his cynicism and rise above process, the term "Ideal" in this title, for one, or, in the body of the same piece, terms such as "Congress," "congressional intent," "abstract merits," or "a strong and persistent public opinion." He did not complete the thrust of his thought and feeling, until, perhaps, he fell silent and wrote no more.

3. An Example of the Demand for the Actual
It may be that any demand in law for the actual raises a question of this kind.

For example, federal judges in the United States reviewing the legality of challenged administrative decisions—in contrast to legislative action—do not accept from lawyers what are called "post hoc rationalizations," reasons and factors thought up after the fact which might have been relied upon, but which there is no evidence were actually relied upon. Any notion produced by the phrase "were actually relied upon" is pregnant with a question. Relied upon by whom? The invocation of actuality removes analysis from the realm of abstract reason—where the persons actually making decisions are those engaged in discussing Reason—and pushes however uncomfortably toward the perception of persons, other than critic and reviewing judge, who must have a connection to the concerns that animate the decision in question and whose connection with those concerns gives life to the concerns themselves.

Of a piece is the troubled judicial treatment of ex parte representations in situations where hearings or other set procedures are used to reveal and channel the concerns that will bear upon a decision. The legal difficulty is not just that those who were unaware of (or did not engage in their own) ex parte representations are being treated unfairly, in the sense that their treatment is inconsistent with rules of an adversarial game. The legal difficulty is couched also in terms of actuality. For example, in administrative adjudication the concerns spread upon the public record are meant to form the basis of the administrative decision. Ex parte submissions and arguments are by their nature not part of the public record. An opinion of an administrative agency will necessarily refer only to the arguments and factors placed in the public record. But to a reviewing court this is a "fictional account of the actual decision-making process" if there were ex parte submissions—an account of an empty procedure.

In either situation the question is not "*Could* a decision like this be justified by reference to concerns like these?" but rather "*Was* this decision justified in the mind of the responsible decision maker by these concerns?" Speaker and spoken are not to be separated. The drive toward the actual is a drive toward the connection between speaker and spoken. The drive toward the actual is ultimately toward perception of a speaker. It is perception of a speaker that makes the spoken actual and saves the spoken from being mere appearance, deception, fiction.

4. JOKES

Jokes are tricks. The *world* plays tricks on men. Humor is a reflection of the world, a way of absorbing and mastering it in its reality, as any successful description, in art or science, is a mastery.

Humor is, over and over again, a playing with the best laid plans of mice and men. Things are not what they seem, things do not turn out the way they are supposed to, and if one can just relax about it, says humor, it is terribly funny. But there is another kind of mastering than the descriptive. What of the suffering?

The world is really better the way it is perhaps: If things were always what they seemed, they would be prosaic, would they not? If things always turned out the way they were intended to, there would be no adventure, no surprise, no excitement, no laughter, no *jokes*. The unintended consequence is a very large part of life. It is not at all clear that we would wish to rid ourselves of the unintended consequence entirely, and our ambivalence toward this central fact of our existence is, naturally, one of the root dilemmas of legal doctrine. For what of the suffering?

Chapter 10

1. LAW AND POLITICS

There is more to the legality of the field of politics than the involvement of courts and judicial opinions, important as they are.

Consider political parties: If you want to study the law of the National Labor Relations Board, you would begin by going to a law library (though you would not end there). You would find an organic statute, substantive rules, administrative cases, hearing examiners' and commissioners' opinions, procedural rules, and descriptions of institutional structures. You might also look at hearings, study commission reports, and legislative history generally. The same materials can be found, in the law library or in some other collection, for the national political parties, with the exception of organic statutes, which are to be found addressed instead to state parties at the state level. The Democratic National Party indeed has a permanent judiciary with jurisdiction over some party matters, especially delegate selection and affirmative action.

This is a wealth of obviously legal material, obviously legal although it may never get into court. Poring through the rules of procedure for credentials challenges to convention delegates may not be gripping, but it is the legally trained who ultimately must do it, and great issues, such as whether a "liberal" or a "conservative" will be the party nominee, may turn upon small points in those rules.

The legal structure of politics exists even though the political has been identified by lawyers as having a special quality that makes it untouchable by organized institutions, the kind of magic, perhaps, that attends any creative process. For instance, a "political question" in American constitutional jurisprudence or a "political development" has been thought to lie very deep in the life of society. It is mysterious, religious—vox populi, vox *dei*—and mere mortals do not touch it or interfere with it. But despite what lawyers say, lawyers do touch it and handle it.

2. Organizing Mechanisms and the Process of Speech

Some readers may be unsettled by the thought that there are also processes within any speaker that shear away alternatives and produce bipolar choices in the course of building up a statement. After all, saying is action too. To say something one must act. One must choose between words and then between phrases. One cannot use two words or phrases at the same time. Therefore speech is sequential like action.

But there is a distinction. The distinction is that if a word is not right one can use another word to make it right. One can almost eliminate the word, phrase, or sentence previously used (that is, the action that was taken), by contradicting it or retracting it. Of course with speech or published writing it is never fully possible to take back the previous word, for it remains as evidence of the meaning of the speaker. But with unpublished writing it does seem that one can erase, except in one's own memory of oneself. At the least, the speaker or the author colors previous words with words subsequently used, adds to them, and reformulates what was said before, all in the continuing effort to create meaning. And the listener looks at the whole, or what there is so far, to take the meaning of the entity which is not itself a succession of events.

With action, on the other hand—what is done—the acts that are the product of processes designed to produce bipolar choices and thus permit *something* to be done cannot be so retired into insignificance, precisely because the search for meaning is not there. Actions, events, are causes with ramifications in the world that are mysterious beyond man's measure even today. There is no perception of an entity behind the sequence, certainly insofar as the sequence is not thought to be communicative. The sequence of events is there, cold, fixed in history, and each part of it may be as important as any other.

Now, of course, in action we do try to counteract, eliminate the effect of a previous act, trace down causal chains and stop them, correct, adjust, and make the total outcome right. But this is never so possible as with meaningful speech, again because with action and the world there are not two persons, a speaker and a listener, trying to define themselves and come together.

Thus the committee structures and the voting and amendment rules for large groups of participants, which are designed to produce bipolar choices and build up a statement that is not gibberish, might seem to be perfect analogs of processes within the individual designed to make the choice of a particular word or phrase possible. But if a speaker is missing (as may be true far more often in the former case than in the latter), the outcome is not at all the same. If the human body is equated with the processes that eliminate alternatives and produce its organization, we say immediately, "Yes, they are marvelous, but they are not me." The same is true of the organizing processes that permit speech. The structures do not produce a speaker and the speaker cannot be equated with and reduced to the structures.

3. THE EFFECT OF SIZE

The mere size of the decision-making body may make irrelevant whether individuals are acting as strategists in secret or as joint adventurers in candor. Then the distinction between what one believes and what one cannot say one does not believe cannot be relaxed. In such situations, insofar as the statements produced are expressions of mind they are expressions of those who have power to choose words by reason of their strategic positions in the process. What can be hoped is that the statements produced have behind them the belief of those persons, and that they are seeking to express, like any other public official, the meaning of the whole. But whether they do seek to express vox populi depends on their sense of their role as legislators, to which we have adverted, as well as on what the situation allows.

4. VETOES

There is an argument that in a democracy the people may veto what they cannot stand. Granted, it is said, that the outcome of the democratic process does not have its source and origin in the will of the people: the people are given frequent enough opportunity to reject it. There is acquiescence to be found in failure to veto when one has the power and opportunity to do so; and, as any lawyer knows, acquiescence by silence can be viewed as ratification.

But this has its limits, and notions drawn from the allocation of money claims through agency law are not fully transferable. Actual assent, true acceptance, focusing, comparing are involved in ratification by a mind. Formal acquiescence is never a substitute. Formal acquiescence is quite consistent with treating what is said as a formality, ignoring it where possible. It is a far cry from saying that a decision is not such as to rouse the electorate to action, to saying that it is the electorate's own decision, and this remains true even if it were not the case that what may be designated a veto after the fact is itself an outcome of factors feeding into the workings of the system through which alone an outcome can be produced.

Chapter 11

1. System and Process
We may note that *system* is an alternative term but not a redundant one. It presents a mechanical version of process. All process has parts, linked in ways to one another, and thus is organized. The word system holds process for a moment against time, for a process is also changing and is itself an outcome of a process, as that further process is also the outcome of a process.

2. Examples of Legal Method
I have chosen examples from what are generally regarded as among the best of American legal analysts. Contributions that emerged from their analyses have been important and regarded as important. Professor Fiss's monograph, for instance, which begins by taking apart a forty-one-year-old footnote, is a penetrating statement of the modern judicial function. His work reaches out to the legal mind with sympathetic imagination and engages assent by uncovering conviction. There is nothing dry about it. Nonetheless it uses lawyers' method.

Similarly, it is Professor Regan's clarity and candor that make his work useful material for the study of legal method. In his comment on the authority of the Supreme Court's 1973 abortion decision he inquired whether state laws against abortion fit an integrated whole. He chose an analysis guided by current equal protection doctrine, which provides particular verbal and conceptual paths to take in the course of work devoted to the seeking of integration. Acknowledging that the question of abortion is one of moral philosophy as well as law, and that he himself was a moral philosopher (that is to say, a professional moral philosopher, conversant with the modes of argument and the texts of what is denoted moral philosophy in particular), he confined himself as a lawyer to the statements of judges, including an unpublished opinion of a Pennsylvania judge at the lowest hierarchical level, an intermediate appellate Louisiana decision, and a fifteen-year-old Restatement and a treatise on torts which relied upon such statements at all times and places. Eventually he argued from a principle in the spirit of the law, but he had to construct that law from legal texts, which were evidence of the integrated mind he presupposed.

After arguing that there was in the law a principle against *required* good samaritanism, he compared state abortion laws with that principle. The abortion laws themselves were, of course, evidence of a contrary principle, and there were no devices such as quantity or age by means of which one side might be weighed in a calculating manner against the other. What Professor Regan was doing instead was seeking to understand, and in passing he remarked that the degree of deference to be given legislators depended in some measure upon the degree of reflection and deliberation behind a statute. He concluded that if he were making an argument in moral philosophy, he would shift analysis to the definition of persons (and might indeed approach good samaritanism differently). It should be clear from what we have seen that Professor Regan was already engaged in the definition of persons in his more strictly legal analysis.

3. LEGISLATION AND LAWYERS

Even when a legislature passes a statute, the text is heard through lawyers. Only a tiny fraction of statutory utterances are new; the vast bulk are buried in the great mass voted upon by individuals who are gone. And if a legislator is alive and in office he can tell no more than what he thought a statutory utterance meant when he voted on it, and what he thought it meant to some others who voted on it.

4. IMPERSONAL CRITERIA

An appeal to objective, rational, or impersonal criteria, in the giving of reasons to do or think something, is possible (whether or not it is effective) only if a person hears and attends to what the reason giver is saying.

Thus an appeal to objective criteria cannot, from the very beginning, be independent of a relationship between the speaker and listener, nor can who makes the appeal be irrelevant. This the experience of legal method allows its practitioners to see rather more easily than is the case for practitioners of other disciplines.

And thus lawyers can decline to accept that law is objective or rational—in the sense that it is impersonal—without thinking themselves pushed to the view that law is merely the mask of power, for lawyers know they continuously decide to whom and how attentively they should listen, as they go about making legal judgments on the basis of the materials of law spread before them.

Chapter 12

1. CONSEQUENCES OF METAPHOR

If we substitute the metaphor for the animal consequences follow. If we think an animal is a species of clock (to move away from the motorcar) that makes a peculiar noise—a squealing noise—when it is kicked, rather than the usual ring or grinding clatter that ordinary clocks make when kicked, we may not kick an animal wantonly anymore than we would go about kicking clocks. But we might very well kick a clock if it served our purposes to do so and we could easily replace it. And certainly a clock would not worry about cutting *our* finger if we stuck a finger in its gears (or perhaps I should say, would not worry about shocking us if we put a finger onto its circuits). In fact we shrink from inflicting pain on animals, even when it serves our purposes and there is a reserve of available replacements. That is because we believe animals feel and that pain is not simply a signal transmitted from one part of a system to another. (On the question whether animals are like man, instead of what is often presumed, that man is like an animal, see Donald R. Griffin, *The Question of Animal Awareness* [1981].)

2. ANTI-SUMMARY

A book by a physicist on space and time will be found full of equations, each an elegant summary. We would not want to cast aside our discussion and offer up formulaic theses to take its place, but we also can play with equations of a sort.

Who a person says he is, and whether to start paying attention to what he says, may be the same.

Whether a person is who he says he is, and whether to continue paying attention to what he says, may be the same.

Whether to obey and whether to continue paying attention, may be the same.

Therefore, who a person is, and whether to obey, may be the same.

We could go on:

Whether to continue paying attention, and whether there is a mind perceived, may be the same.

Whether what appears to be a person is believed to be a person, and whether there is a perceptible mind, may be the same.

Whether there is mind, and whether the person speaking is greater than the individual, may be the same.

And so on.

Now the very making of such statements of equivalence as these involve the presuppositions we have discussed, of the existence of mind, of the responsibility of speakers, of the authenticity of statements, of intimations in action, of entities beyond individuals, even of the transcendence of space and time.

But all this is play. These equations do not summarize, and we should not make statements in this form to be taken seriously. They go too far, they do not go far enough. The form suggests a closed system, whereas the system of law, if system it is, is open. The form is ultimately static, and does not take into account the phenomenon of change. Discussion does point to change. It contains change, and it is open. So let us resume discussion.

3. OTHER INSTITUTIONS

We should emphasize that institutions beyond courts, legislatures, and administrative agencies speak or appear to speak to citizens in daily life. These are beyond our subject, but the texts they produce are linked through legal doctrine to texts produced by legal institutions, and we should note them here. They often pose similar problems.

Consider the example of the phone box again. The instructions on it read, "Put in a quarter, wait for the dial tone, and make your telephone call." The instructions do not go on to say, "Do not take your quarter back out." If it occurs to you to tie a thread around your quarter so that you can lift it back out after it has done its work as an input into the system, you have to engage in some interpretation of the words you read before you can think that you are violating a command in pulling your quarter out.

Looking at the situation quite objectively, like an engineer, you might observe that a quarter rather than a fingertip is necessary to activate the system because that is simply the way the machine happens to be built. Coin return lockers do exist. There is the notion of fair exchange in the situation (the notion of exchange alone is not very helpful in guiding conduct); but then it is certainly possible to see the public telephone as a Trojan horse—a gift with an ulterior purpose, a habit former—or as a ploy to build goodwill. The notion of property, in its division of things into things that are yours and things that are not, does not help. (You are not proposing to smash the box.) Words are involved in your encounter with the box, as they are in encounters everywhere in daily life. The necessity of interpretation is pervasive and real.

Now of course there is more than the written from which you can begin your interpretation. There is the lock on the box which prevents you from easily extracting your quarter.

But is it only inconvenience that leads the ordinary person not to report a malfunctioning machine which supplies free calls or gives back a cascade of change? Why should you concern yourself with what the telephone company would want you to do when you discover you can pull your quarter back out? The telephone company may not be capable of intent. It may be merely a system, as a large bureaucracy is a system. It may be like the box itself.

Furthermore, insofar as you do personify the telephone company and ascribe intent to it, you might reasonably conclude that its intent is not a very attractive one. If you believe what is said in some standard accounts of the American business corporation, the telephone company would really like to have not just your quarter but all of your money if it could, and all of everyone else's money too.

That is the profit maximizer's intent, and any subsidiary or more specific intent is a means to that general end. It does not care about you? It sets no limits on itself, it respects only limits that are imposed from without? It is playing a game with you? Then you have no reason to interpret the words it causes to be written on its telephone boxes in light of its purpose. Its purpose ultimately is to do you in. In a game there is no reason to inquire truly into the desires of the other side and seek to accommodate them in your own thinking and behavior. The other side would not do that for you.

Could some outside source of authority order you to pay this kind of attention to the words of the opposite side in a game? No; it could direct some words to you but nothing that would have meaning for you.

If such a source of instruction beyond you and the company—call it the law—did tell you to pay such attention, you would have to interpret what *it* said to you as presupposing that you are not involved entirely in a game, that you are misconceiving the other side and the other side is misconceiving itself as profit maximizing. Then you will ask whether that presupposition of the law's command is realized, whether, that is, the other side is listening to the law.

Otherwise, whatever source is instructing you to pay such attention to the other side is itself only playing a game with you, and you can only calculate. Can you get away with pulling your quarter out? No one is telling you specifically not to take your quarter out. Why play their game for them? If those on the other side want you not to do something, let them tell you quite specifically. Indeed, let them tell you so to your face, in a court. After all, everything is *action* in a game, even words spoken. See whether they move against you. Unless they do, you are free—free, that is, to listen to real voices.

Thus you might think. Many people have. This is the problem generally where there is no distinction between what is said and what is done, in theory, or in fact.

Chapter 13

1. DOING AND SAYING

We cannot say that the outcome, or the result, of decision making and what is called the "application" of statements of law is not important. Of course the result is important. Our hopes are realized in results. Results feed into the physical world and constitute the material with which each of us and all of us together wrestle. But when we speak of results in law, it is really not the result *itself* that is important. It is rather something about the result. This is why, when one is inquiring into what the law is, one cannot even know what a court does without looking at what a court says about what it does.

Suppose the actual result of the deliberation in a case, the concrete outcome, is that $100,000 flows from one pocket to another, either through order of a court after litigation, or through a decision by someone not a judge who decides, at least in part, on the basis of what he conceives the law to be on the matter. Is the movement of $100,000 from one pocket to another interesting in itself to the law? Of course not. Units of $100,000 move electronically from pocket to pocket innumerable times a day inside banks around the world. In itself the event, the result, is of no more interest to the law than a bloody arm, without more, is of interest. A bloody arm could be the result of a surgeon's incision or a storm-blown tree branch. Only if the bloody arm, what *happens*, is connected to something beyond it is it of any significance or interest to the legal mind. Money may pass between individuals, but we could not distinguish that event from identical events happening in banks without connecting it to something more, to something about the event that makes it of legal interest.

This is not so very peculiar. Even an individual's loss of money must be associated with something more before the individual, from his purely individual point of view, can think about it. He loses a thousand dollars, he is unhappy, and he wishes the outcome had been different or that he had been insured. But then he also wishes he had not been born with such a homely face or large ears. If the loss is the result of a storm, he picks up and goes forward in the changed circumstances, and perhaps recalls that he might not have had that thousand dollars in the first place if things had not turned out so well before. He points into the future because he must, and there is nothing in the loss of the thousand dollars itself that *says* anything. It does not even say anything about the future, though it most certainly affects the future.

His world without the thousand dollars is simply the world as it presents itself to him to be worked with, in the same way that the world presents itself to him with the force of gravity included. What happens is always rather contingent, even what happens as the result of legal decision making, contingent, that is, in presenting a new world for the future to be worked with, always surprising, still a place for adventure. What need not be contingent is what we say about the result, what interests us. We do not have to accept that in the way we have to accept the world. It is not just what happens.

The difference between results in themselves and what makes them of interest is often seen in the treatment of pain. There is ambiguity in the notion of pain. Is pain inflicted upon a robot when its arm is twisted off, if the robot is equipped with an electronic sensor that sends to a central computer a signal containing the information that the arm is being twisted off, and the central computer precipitates, according to its program, a response designed to prevent the twisting or to repair the aftereffect? Or is pain inflicted on a rabbit when an experimenter cuts into it without anesthetic and the rabbit cries out?

We know we ourselves treat sensations traveling in from nerve endings in different ways, depending upon what we know and think about the neurological event occurring within. The hurt caused by the surgeon who must scrape a wound without anesthetic in an emergency, or by the rescuer who must release our leg pinioned under an automobile, is different from hurts caused in other ways and for other purposes by other persons. The sensations in the first sort of case do not arouse our emotions, or we can see to it, through the exercise of the virtues called bravery or fortitude, that they do not arouse our emotions for long. What arouses emotion is that *about* the event, the sensation, the neurological, the chemical or electronic message, that about it which has meaning for us and which we judge and criticize. In itself it is an event that will pass in time and that we will put behind us because it has no meaning for the future. We grit our teeth, try to think about something else, and let the neurons fire.

Similarly, to the extent our conception of robots has not crossed the line between that which is and which happens, on the one hand, and that which judges and is judged, criticizes and is criticized, endows and is endowed with meaning, *not according to some set of rules and responses reducible to that which is, but in a living way pointed toward the future and the largest consistency*, to that extent the electronic message triggered when a robot's arm is twisted off is not in itself of any interest at all to us.

With regard to rabbits, most of us are in sufficient doubt to hold back. We hear the rabbit's cry, as a *cry*, of a *rabbit*. It is not the ringing of a bell in a system, not even a bell in a system of rabbits. We still believe in the sacred, even we in the modern secular world. We hold back and want to hold others back from cutting into the rabbit without anesthetic, just because of the rabbit's pain, whatever our reasons may be for wanting to cut the rabbit. There is something sacred about the rabbit. To speak of its life is not to speak in metaphor as we do when we speak of the life of a motorcar or a robot. We try to find some other way to achieve what we want. We accord the rabbit some dignity.

2. COMMANDS AND CATEGORIES

Categorization is the operative form of much legal ordering. Animals we order, or categorize, without regard to what they may think about it—those with good fat over here, those with good hair there, those with good bones over there. Human beings are different. Human beings classify themselves, betake themselves into categories. An official might bark to men and women on a truck, blacks over here, Hispanics over there, and it rises up in the breast of the man or woman on the truck to say I am not only that, or even that at all. The official might just as well be saying good bones here, good skin there, good fat over there. How would a human being react in going about categorizing himself in response to such orders as these? Pushed and prodded and grouped from the outside like an animal he might be, but never from the inside. Black I am not only, or black I am but not what that person has in mind by black. I am not a bone to be eaten.

3. A Note on Escape and the Problem of Punishment

Even today escape from prison in the United States is defined as an independent crime. It is a useful exercise to read the discussion of the Supreme Court of the United States in 1980 about just how to define a condemnable state of mind— or mens rea—in an escapee from prison; just what degree of intention to give oneself up would affect a judgment of the heinousness of that crime of escape; what the timing of the expression of such an intention is required to be; and which side has the burden of proof on whether such an actual, good faith intention existed. It is a striking discussion, odd, Swiftian, extraordinary in that men engaged in it at all.

There is indeed a peculiarity in punishment generally, whether or not for escape, which is that the losses and gains involved are not matched. The gain to the punisher is less than his own loss; the loss to the punished is far greater than his illicit gain. The gap can be ignored, if we pretend that human beings as such mean nothing to us. But the problem is starkly put if one shifts to the punishment of a child, one's own child (and childless or not, we were all children once).

"Don't leave the attic door ajar. It's winter, heat escapes. If you do it again you can't go into the attic." But the attic is enormous fun for a child (just as freedom from the horrors of prison may be thought enormously important to the adult). Do we really so calculate gains and losses that the lifetime memories of attics are less than a few dollars of heat? The assumption has to be that the punishment will not be necessary, that the child will learn and that parent and child can have both heat conservation and fun. But what must the child think of the parent who lays down the rule—or we of ourselves as we threaten prison? There is an air of oddness about all discussions of punishment, and this oddness is one of the constant sources of the drive toward the authoritative. Theorists of deterrence are often unwilling in the end to distinguish between the deterrent and the condemnatory or retributive aspects of criminal law, because in their view deterrence works by securing a change of heart. If fear were the reason for pursuing the law's commands, the enforcement costs of policing would be unimaginably high and quite unacceptable.

One does run across discussions of deterrent punishment that are more or less mild versions of that set out by some economists in their consideration of criminal penalties for economic crimes. Drawing out the logic of calculation, they suggest that in setting fines the wrongful gain to the offender be multiplied by the inverse of the likelihood of detection. This seems to treat the potential defendant as a pigeon, on the tenets of strict behaviorism. Blame seems out of place; the actor himself seems just a learning mechanism, simply an intermediary between external stimuli and external behavior. However, when addressing the argument from fairness (the argument that imposing such a drastic penalty on the one detected in the act is to engage in disproportionate punishment), the position of these same analysts is that on the average the actor has gotten away with the act a number of times before and salted away a nearly equivalent gain over time. The avoidance of all blame, which is one of the hallmarks of social engineering, appears then to be premised upon the most total blame. Either this is to be taken as the loss of the individual from sight and his merger into some other entity (a loss of the individual in what is commonly considered a most individualistically based mode of thought); or it says much about what is assumed to be the attitude of the calculating actor toward law, and especially toward law that calculates with respect to him.

4. Contractual Relations and Relations of Duty
In view of the difficulty of telling when a person doing something for another is an agent-fiduciary, and when he is himself a principal merely contractually related to a customer, it is not surprising that there is an element of duty-to-customers running through legal texts setting out the definition of business proprietors or corporate business managers. One might think that corporations should exploit customers on a profit-maximization theory, but the application of that theory presumes what is most difficult to establish, which is the capacity in which a person is doing something for another. It seems easy to accept that when a customer orders the Ford Motor Company to make a particular car, and selects his color, upholstery, radio, transmission, and other details, and that particular car is put together especially for him by the company, that he remains a customer and not a principal for whom the Ford Motor Company is an agent and fiduciary. But in fact it is not easy to distinguish this case from the case of one individual hiring another.

5. A Further Note on Form and the Recognition of Entities
Problems of form and substance often end as problems of recognizing entities apart from their formal definitions; and these problems in turn are connected to the problem of recognizing the outcome of defective procedure as legitimate, or, to say the same thing, as the act of the entity, which someone is claiming it to be the act of. Harmless error is one doctrine under which this recognition routinely takes place. There are others, often lurking in the definition of scope of review in judicial inquiries preceding the use of judicial enforcement powers to aid some individual who says he is acting on behalf of an entity. The question whether the decision is to be enforced or, to the contrary, reversed as not being on behalf of the entity is often translated, and can be seen in opinions to be translated, into a question of what a decision maker on behalf of an entity did or did not take into account. There is often then a further translation or, if you will, change in the object of search. Very often in deciding to recognize the outcome of a defective process—the substance of a thing beyond its form—it is good faith, sincerity, authenticity, belief in the identity being adopted, on the part of those adopting it, that is of as much interest as any precise or ever more detailed definition of what is or is not to be taken into account.

Seriousness, or sincerity, is not at all a subjective thing only. We do not rely on another to tell us whether he is sincere or not. We are satisfied of that, or we are not, or we rest somewhere in between believing and disbelieving. We do not utterly put ourselves in his hands. And much administration of law comes down to a determination of sincerity. Fraud, lying, misleading, withholding information are specialized areas of law, but beyond them running throughout the law is the search for good faith. There is nothing so subtle in law as the constant struggle for authenticity. Highly elaborate structures of wholly objective rules can melt into the warm connection of a satisfied inquiry into good faith. Man can be made to turn square corners and do other such things by rules that have nothing to do with state of mind, but on important matters there is usually a giving and demanding of faith.

6. DEATH

Money, blood, and pain were our examples in our discussion (Amplification 1, this chapter) of the difference between doing and saying. We did not mention the outcome death there. What of death? Is it contingent? Does it have to be accepted? Does it say anything?

Death is a special kind of fact, hardly a fact at all, more a parting, which is a fact yet the *parting* in it has nothing to do with event, fact, what is, what exists outside: it has more to do with time, which is not a fact but a mystery, in us as well as beyond us. If in considering money, blood, and pain the thought occurred to you that you could not put the death of your child or your friend behind you like the loss of a thousand dollars, then it may also occur to you that death is not a fact. You may think death is not a fact. That may be in fact what you know or what you believe: death does not *just* happen—or *happen* at all, not the *death* in it. Or should it be said that it *does* just happen, and so does not involve us really?

Death is certainly not the electronic and chemical event. That we could put behind us, like anything else that happens, and continue on. Death is the something about that event, and, more, it has to do with a person, which goes beyond the about, to what the about is about. The person we part from, *if* a person, is inside us in part—at least in part—and that is why we cannot put the parting or the person behind us. After all, we part from ourselves every instant. Does a person die as he changes?

The question is the reality of death. The question is also the reality of life. There seems to be one or the other. We may actually believe in one, or the other, not both. And we ask ourselves which one we believe in. We can ask only ourselves, no one else.

WORKS QUOTED IN TEXT

Adams, Henry, *The Education of Henry Adams: An Autobiography* (London: Constable & Co., 1918).

Bakke: See *Regents of the University of California v. Bakke.*

Barfield, Owen, "Poetic Diction and Legal Fiction," in *Essays Presented to Charles Williams,* ed. C. S. Lewis (Oxford: Oxford University Press, 1947; reprint, Grand Rapids, Mich.: William B. Eerdmans, 1966), p. 126.

Barzun, Jacques, *Darwin, Marx, Wagner: Critique of a Heritage,* 2d ed. rev. (Garden City, N.Y.: Doubleday & Co., 1958; reprint, with a new preface, Chicago: University of Chicago Press, 1981), p. 322.

Bate, W. Jackson, *Samuel Johnson* (New York: Harcourt Brace Jovanovitch, 1977).

Bauman, Zygmunt, *Hermeneutics and Social Science* (New York: Columbia University Press, 1978).

Berlin, Isaiah, *Vico and Herder: Two Studies in the History of Ideas* (New York: Vintage Books, 1977).

Bernstein, Richard J., *The Restructuring of Social and Political Theory* (Philadelphia: University of Pennsylvania Press, 1978).

Bishin, William R., and Stone, Christopher D., *Law, Language, and Ethics: An Introduction to Law and Legal Method* (Mineola, N.Y.: Foundation Press, 1972).

Bishop, Joseph W., Jr., "Sitting Ducks and Decoy Ducks: New Trends in the Indemnification of Corporate Directors and Officers," *Yale Law Journal* 77 (1968): 1078.

Blackmun, Harry A. (Justice), *Chiarella v. United States,* 445 U.S. 222, 247–48 (1980).

Braudel, Fernand, *Afterthoughts on Material Civilization and Capitalism,* trans. Patricia Ranum (Baltimore: Johns Hopkins University Press, 1977).

Breitel, Charles D. (Chief Judge), *Penn Central Transportation Co. v. City of New York,* 366 N.E.2d 1271 (N.Y. 1977), affirmed, 438 U.S. 104 (1978).

Bunyan, John, *The Pilgrim's Progress,* ed. Roger Sharrock (Harmondsworth: Penguin Books, 1965).

Calder v. Bull, 3 U.S. (3 Dall.) 386 (1798).

Carolene Products Co.: See *United States v. Carolene Products Co.*

Carroll, Lewis, *Alice's Adventures in Wonderland* (New York: Macmillan Co., 1923), chap. 9, "The Mock Turtle's Story," pp. 137–40.

Chadwick, Owen, *The Secularization of the European Mind in the Nineteenth Century* (Cambridge: Cambridge University Press, 1975).

Chatterton, Thomas, *The Rowley Poems of Thomas Chatterton*, ed. Maurice Evan Hare (Oxford: At the Clarendon Press, 1911).

Chiarella v. United States, 445 U.S. 222 (1980).

Coleridge, Samuel Taylor, *The Rime of the Ancient Mariner*, in *Coleridge: Select Poetry and Prose*, ed. Stephen Potter (London: Nonesuch Press, 1950), p. 19.

Commission on the Third London Airport, *Report* (London: Her Majesty's Stationery Office, 1971) (Roskill Commission), pp. 120, 133, 152, and 261; *Papers and Proceedings*, vol. 5 (1969), pp. 1299–1306; *Papers and Proceedings*, vol. 7 (1970), pp. 27–28, 39–41, and 414–23.

Dahl, Roald, "The Great Automatic Grammatisator," in *Someone Like You* (New York: Alfred A. Knopf, 1969), pp. 250–76.

Dewey, John, *Human Nature and Conduct* (1922; New York: Modern Library, 1930), p. 261.

Dicey, A. V., *Lectures on the Relation between Law and Public Opinion in England during the Nineteenth Century*, 2d ed. (1914; London: MacMillan & Co., 1954).

Didion, Joan, *The White Album* (New York: Simon & Schuster, 1979), pp. 164–65.

Dollard, John, *Caste and Class in a Southern Town*, 3d ed. (Garden City, N.Y.: Doubleday & Co., 1949), p. 304.

Dostoyevsky, Fyodor, "The Grand Inquisitor," bk. 5, chap. 5, in *The Brothers Karamazov*, trans. Constance Garnett (New York: Vintage Books, 1950), pp. 292–314.

Dred Scott v. Sandford, 60 U.S. (19 How.) 393 (1857).

Eliot, Valerie, ed., *T. S. Eliot, The Waste Land: A Facsimile and Transcript of the Original Drafts Including the Annotations of Ezra Pound* (New York: Harcourt Brace Jovanovich, 1971).

Ely, John Hart, "On Discovering Fundamental Values," *Harvard Law Review* 92 (1978): 5; "Constitutional Interpretivism: Its Allure and Impossibility," *Indiana Law Journal* 53 (1978): 399.

Fiss, Owen M., "The Forms of Justice," *Harvard Law Review* 93 (1979): 1.

Frazer, James George, *The Golden Bough: A Study in Magic and Religion*, abridged ed. (1922; New York: Macmillan Co., 1963), pp. 826–27.

Gilmore, Grant, *The Ages of American Law* (New Haven: Yale University Press, 1977).

Griffin, Donald R., *The Question of Animal Awareness* (New York: Rockefeller University Press, 1981).

Hadley v. Baxendale, 9 Exch. 341 (1854).

Hegel's Philosophy of Right, trans. T. M. Knox (Oxford: At the Clarendon Press, 1958).

Hohfeld, Wesley N., *Fundamental Legal Conceptions as Applied in Judicial Reasoning and Other Legal Essays*, ed. Walter Wheeler Cook (New Haven: Yale University Press; London: Humphrey Milford, Oxford University Press, 1923).

Holmes, Oliver Wendell, Jr., "The Path of the Law," *Harvard Law Review* 10 (1897): 457.

"Introduction to the Old Testament," pp. xvii–xviii, and "Introduction to the New Testament," pp. v–viii, in *The New English Bible, with the Apocrypha*, std. ed. (New York: Cambridge University Press, 1970).

Jaffe, Louis L., "Judicial Review: Question of Law," *Harvard Law Review* 69 (1955): 239, 264; "The Illusion of the Ideal Administration," *Harvard Law Review* 86 (1973): 1183, 1188–91.

James, William, *The Letters of William James*, vol. 1, ed. Henry James (Boston: Atlantic Monthly Press, 1920), p. 220.

Johnson, Samuel, Dr.: See Bate.

Keats, John, "Lamia," *Endymion*, and "Ode to a Nightingale," in *The Poems of John Keats*, ed. Jack Stillinger (Cambridge, Mass.: Belknap Press of Harvard University Press, 1978).

Knight, Frank H., *Freedom and Reform: Essays in Economics and Social Philosophy* (New York: Harper & Row, 1947; reprint, Port Washington, N.Y.: Kennikat Press, 1969).

Machiavelli, Niccolo, *The Prince*, trans. Luigi Ricci (New York: Modern Library, 1950).

Macpherson: See Ossian.

Manning, Bayless, "The Stockholders' Appraisal Remedy: An Essay for Frank Coker," *Yale Law Journal* 72 (1962): 223, 245 n.37.

Marbury v. Madison, 1 Cranch (5 U.S.) 137 (1803).

Marvell, Andrew, "The Garden," in *The Poems and Letters of Andrew Marvell*, ed. H. M. Margoliouth, 3d ed., vol. 1, rev. by Pierre Legouis with E. E. Duncan-Jones (Oxford: At the Clarendon Press, 1971), p. 52.

Moore, George Edward, *Principia Ethica* (1903) (Cambridge: Cambridge University Press, 1959).

Murray, K. M. Elisabeth, *Caught in the Web of Words: James A. H. Murray and the Oxford English Dictionary* (New Haven: Yale University Press, 1977).

The New English Bible, with the Apocrypha, std. ed. (New York: Cambridge University Press, 1970).

Noonan, John T., Jr., *Persons and Masks of the Law: Cardozo, Holmes, Jefferson, and Wythe as Makers of the Masks* (New York: Farrar, Straus & Giroux, 1976).

Orwell, George, *Nineteen Eighty-Four* (London: Secker & Warburg, 1955), pp. 255–66.

Ossian, *The Poems of Ossian, Translated by James Macpherson, with Notes and with an Introduction by William Sharp* (Edinburgh: John Grant, 1926).

Polanyi, Michael, *Personal Knowledge: Towards a Post-Critical Philosophy* (Chicago: University of Chicago Press, 1962).

Radin, Max, "The Endless Problem of Corporate Personality," *Columbia Law Review* 32 (1932): 643, 647.

Rawls, John, *A Theory of Justice* (Cambridge, Mass.: Belknap Press of the Harvard University Press, 1971); "The Basic Liberties and Their Priority," in *The Tanner Lectures on Human Values*, vol. 3, ed. Sterling M. McMurrin (Salt Lake City: University of Utah Press; Cambridge: Cambridge University Press, 1982), p. 1.

Regan, Donald H., "Rewriting *Roe v. Wade*," *Michigan Law Review* 77 (1979): 1569.

Regents of the University of California v. Bakke, 438 U.S. 265 (1978).

Rehnquist, William H. (Justice), *First National Bank of Boston v. Bellotti*, 435 U.S. 765, 823 (1978).

Rosberg, Gerald D., "The Protection of Aliens from Discriminatory Treatment by the National Government,"*Supreme Court Review* (1977): 275, 298–99.

Sax, Joseph L., *Mountains without Handrails: Reflections on the National Parks* (Ann Arbor: University of Michigan Press, 1980).

Scruton, Roger, *The Aesthetics of Architecture* (Princeton: Princeton University Press, 1979)

Simon, Herbert A., *Administrative Behavior: A Study of Decision-making Processes in Administrative Organization*, 3d ed. (New York: Free Press, 1976), pp. 45–60.

Taine, Hippolyte: See Chadwick, pp. 204–11.

United States v. Carolene Products Co., 304 U.S. 144 (1938).

United States v. Hartford Empire Co., 46 F. Supp. 541, 606 (N.D. Ohio, 1942).

Vermont Yankee Nuclear Power Corp. v. Natural Resources Defense Council, Inc., 435 U.S. 519 (1978).

Vickers, Geoffrey, *The Art of Judgment: A Study of Policy Making* (London: Chapman & Hall, 1965).

White, James Boyd, *The Legal Imagination: Studies in the Nature of Legal Thought and Expression* (Boston: Little, Brown & Co., 1973).

Wilson, Edward O., *On Human Nature* (Cambridge, Mass.: Harvard University Press, 1978).

INDEX OF WORDS
AND PHRASES

Abraham, and the sacrifice of Isaac, p. 169; Genesis 22:1–18, *New English Bible*, p. 22. The Moslem feast of Id al-Adha celebrates the story.

Administrative agencies, opinions issued by, p. 12: Bureaucratic writing of administrative opinions has been a subject of empirical study and lively debate in the United States at least since the enactment of the federal and state Administrative Procedure Acts. See, e.g., H. R. Rep. No. 2711, 85th Cong., 2d Sess. 41 (1959); Administrative Procedure Act: Hearings on S. 1663 Before the Subcomm. on Administrative Practice and Procedure of the Senate Judiciary Comm., 88th Cong., 2d Sess. 47–63, 282–88 (1964) (statement of Robert M. Benjamin); Administrative Procedure: Hearings on S. 674, S. 675, and S. 918 Before a Subcomm. of the Senate Comm. on the Judiciary, 77th Cong., 1st Sess. 816 (1941) (statement of Dean Acheson); Special Message of President Kennedy to the 35th Congress on the Regulatory Agencies, 13 April 1961, *Public Papers of the Presidents, John F. Kennedy 1961* 267, 271 (1962) (based upon the Landis Report); President's Advisory Council on Executive Organization, *A New Regulatory Framework: Report on Selected Independent Regulatory Agencies* 49–50 (1971) (the Ash Report); Louis B. Hector, "Government by Anonymity: Who Writes Our Regulatory Opinions?" *American Bar Association Journal* 45 (1959): 1260; Bernard Schwartz, *The Professor and the Commissions* (New York: Alfred A. Knopf, 1959), pp. 189–92; Howard Westwood, "The Davis Treatise: Meaning to the Practitioner," *Minnesota Law Review* 43 (1959): 607, 617; Frank E. Cooper, "Administrative Law: The Process of Decision," *American Bar Association Journal* 44 (1958): 237.

Descriptions of agency practice may be found in Martin Shapiro, *The Supreme Court and Administrative Agencies* (New York: Free Press, 1968), pp. 131–33; Joseph C. Palamountain, Jr., "The Federal Trade Commission and the Indiana Standard Case," in *Government Regulation of Business: A Casebook*, ed. Edwin A. Bock (Englewood Cliffs, N.J.: Prentice-Hall, 1965), p. 156; David M. Welborn, "Assigning Responsibility for Regulatory Decisions to Individual Commissioners: The Case of the ICC," *Administrative Law Review* 18 (1966): 13; Richard O. Berner, *Constraints on the Regulatory Process: A Case Study of the Regulation of Cable Television* (Cambridge, Mass.: Ballinger Publishing

NOTE: Full references for titles in short form will be found in WORKS QUOTED IN TEXT.

Co., 1976), pp. 61–83; William K, Jones, *Licensing of Domestic Air Transportation by the Civil Aeronautics Board: Report to the Committee on Licenses and Authorizations of the Administrative Conference of the United States* (1962), pp. 170–74; William L. Cary, *Politics and the Regulatory Agencies* (New York: McGraw-Hill, 1967), pp. 84–86 (Securities and Exchange Commission); William F. Pedersen, Jr., "Formal Records and Informal Rulemaking," *Yale Law Journal* 85 (1975): 38, 51–65 (Environmental Protection Agency); Peter L. Strauss, "Rules, Adjudications, and Other Sources of Law in an Executive Department: Reflections on the Interior Department's Administration of the Mining Law," *Columbia Law Review* 74 (1974): 1231, 1245–47; Archibald Cox, Derek C. Bok, and Robert A. Gorman, *Labor Law: Cases and Materials*, 8th ed. (Mineola, N.Y.: Foundation Press, 1977), pp. 117–18.

In American administrative law the issues are litigated under various rubrics—"institutional decision making" or "the one who decides must hear," "post hoc rationalization," "ex parte communication," "adequacy of record." See, e.g., Daniel J. Gifford, "The Morgan Cases: A Retrospective View," *Administrative Law Review* 30 (1978): 237; *T.S.C. Motor Freight Lines, Inc.* v. *United States*, 186 F. Supp. 777 (S.D. Texas, 1960), affirmed sub nom. *Herrin Transportation Co.* v. *United States*, 366 U.S. 419 (1961); *Mazza* v. *Cavicchia*, 105 A.2d 545 (N.J. 1954); *KFC National Management Corp.* v. *National Labor Relations Board*, 497 F.2d 298 (2d Cir. 1974).

American Law Institute, on law of future interests, p. 139: See *United States Law Week* 48 (1980): 2833–34.

Ancient Mariner, p. 14: Coleridge, Samuel Taylor, *The Rime of the Ancient Mariner*, in *Select Poetry and Prose*, p. 19.

Anderson, John, What good would it do, p. 137: Associated Press and United Press International Reports, Ann Arbor News, 15 September 1980, p. A6.

Authentic texts, without Supreme Court, p. 64: Annotations to Staff (q.v.) and Studies (q.v.) include materials on the extent of the internal bureaucratization of state courts and federal courts inferior to the United States Supreme Court.

Bad man, p. 39: See Oliver Wendell Holmes, Jr., "The Path of the Law"; *American Banana Co.* v. *United Fruit Co.*, 213 U.S. 347, 356 (1909). For an example of Lon L. Fuller playing with the Bad Man who must predict what a good man will do, see *The Law in Quest of Itself* (Chicago: Foundation Press, 1940), pp. 92–95.

Bakke decision, p. 152: *Regents of the University of California* v. *Bakke*, 438 U.S. 265 (1978).

Berlin, Isaiah, writing on Tolstoy, Marx, or Vico, p. 154: E.g., Berlin, *Vico and Herder*.

Bishop, on liability for negligence, pp. 150–51: Bishop, "Sitting Ducks and Decoy Ducks," pp. 1100–1101.

Bishops, Catholic, super-majority rule in Conference of, p. 135: New York Times, 15 November 1979, p. A24; 16 November 1979, p. A13.

Blatant illegality, p. 164: e.g., *Oestereich* v. *Local Board #11*, 393 U.S. 233 (1968). There are, in addition, accepted reasons to reverse a decision maker (as a remedial matter) for taking into account a wrong factor even if its decision still seems to be supported by other independent grounds ("seems," because there is always a question whether a decision maker does or can consider grounds separately and independently; see, e.g., *Clay* v. *United States*, 403 U.S. 698 [1971]). A reversal may be symbolic, or a form of deterrent punishment, if, for instance, race or political party is taken into account today in a situation where such discrimination is clearly inappropriate.

Braudel, Fernand, field of, p. 209: A short introduction is Braudel, *Afterthoughts*.

Caligula's horse, p. 134: This is the story. The evidence may suggest only that Caligula planned to award a consulship to Incitatus (the horse) and assassins intervened. See Suetonius, *Caligula* 55.3–55.4, in Suetonius, *The Twelve Caesars*, trans. Robert Graves, rev. by Michael Grant (Harmondsworth: Penguin Books, 1979), p. 181.

Caseload, increase in, p. 10: See, e.g., Paul A. Freund, Alexander M. Bickel, Peter D. Ehrenhaft, Russell D. Niles, Bernard G. Segal, Robert L. Stern, and Charles A. Wright, "Report of the Study Group on the Caseload of the Supreme Court," 57 F.R.D. 573 (1972); Gerhard Casper and Richard A. Posner, *The Workload of the Supreme Court* (Chicago: American Bar Foundation, 1976); *Brown Transport Corp. v. Atcon, Inc.*, 439 U.S. 1014 (1978).

Challenge no longer heard, p. 93: This is a standard point in the teaching of American administrative law. For a particularly elegant brief statement of it, see J. R. Lucas, "On Not Worshipping Facts," *Philosophical Quarterly* 8 (1958): 144–56.

Chatterton, Thomas, poems of, presented as written by Rowley, p. 55: See Chatterton, *Rowley Poems*. For an example of a work by Chatterton (1752–1770) in a standard modern anthology, see Helen Gardner, ed., *The New Oxford Book of English Verse 1250–1950* (Oxford: Oxford University Press, 1972), p. 471.

Chiarella, Is this course relevant after, p. 152: *Chiarella v. United States*, 445 U.S. 222 (1980). In part the dispute to which *Chiarella* spoke was over means to a common end, the realization of a capital market efficient by current economic standards. In part the dispute was over the nature of legal obligation, whether it could ever have its source in system rather than person. Cf. *Dirks v. Securities and Exchange Commission*, 463 U.S. 646 (1983). On crystallization of axiomatic change, my discussion in Part I of *Legal Identity: The Coming of Age of Public Law* (New Haven: Yale University Press, 1978), pp. 13–64, may be found pertinent.

Children, figures in American law without, p. 49: See Noonan, *Persons and Masks of the Law*, p. 143.

Choice of law, law of, p. 66: For a discussion of the example used here, see Alfred F. Conard, "Company Laws of the European Communities from an American Viewpoint," in *The Harmonization of European Company Law*, ed. Clive M. Schmitthoff (London: United Kingdom National Committee of Camparative Law, 1973), pp. 55–62.

Clear, legal use of, in tests for judicial jurisdiction, p. 214: See, e.g., on sovereign immunity, the writ of mandamus, statutory preclusion of review, and scope of review of jurisdictional fact: *Larson v. Domestic and Foreign Commerce Corp.*, 337 U.S. 682 (1949); Louis L. Jaffe, *Judicial Control of Administrative Action* (Boston: Little, Brown & Co., 1965), p. 181; *Leedom v. Kyne*, 338 U.S. 184 (1958), and *Clark v. Gabriel*, 393 U.S. 256 (1968); and *Gudmundson v. Cardillo*, 126 F.2d 521 (D.C. Cir. 1942).

Clip an angel's wings and empty the haunted air, p. 5: John Keats, "Lamia," in *Poems*, p. 452.

Clock, as metaphor for animal, p. 230: The clock metaphor, still in use today, may be traceable to Descartes.

Coldness and hardening of hearts, p. 178: Detlev F. Vagts, "Legal Opinions in Quantitative Terms: Lawyer as Haruspex or Bookie?" *Business Lawyer* 34 (1979): 421, 425–27; Laurence H. Tribe, "Trial by Mathematics: Precision and Ritual in the Legal Process," *Harvard Law Review* 84 (1971): 1329.

Commentators, responding to Supreme Court opinion, p. 38: E.g., Richard B. Stewart, "*Vermont Yankee* and the Evolution of Administrative Procedure," *Harvard Law Review* 91 (1978): 1805; William H. Rodgers, "A Hard Look at Vermont Yankee: Environmental Law under Close Scrutiny," *Georgetown Law Journal* 67 (1979): 699.

Common mind, p. 65: For an example of exploration of such connections, see Barzun, *Darwin, Marx, Wagner*. Risking a degree of circularity, some trace recognition of a common mind to the influence of Vico, see Chadwick, *Nineteenth Century*, p. 198.

Comparativist, p. 65: A brief essay on the method of the comparativist is Eric Stein, "Uses, Misuses—and Non-Uses of Comparative Law," *Northwestern University Law Review* 72 (1977): 198.

Computer administered examination, example of p. 24: Detroit Free Press, 7 May 1979, p. 1A.

Computerize legal analysis, efforts to, p. 28: E.g., Charles M. Harr, John P. Sawyer, Jr., and Stephen J. Cummings, "Computer Power and Legal Reasoning: A Case Study of Judicial Decision Prediction in Zoning Amendment Cases," *American Bar Foundation Research Journal* (1977): 651; James A. Sprowl, "Automating the Legal Reasoning Process: A Computer That Uses Regulations and Statutes to Draft Legal Documents," *American Bar Foundation Research Journal* (1979): 3. In the 1980s the giving of legal advice was viewed as an "expert system" in the field known as "Artificial Intelligence." See generally Herbert A. Simon and Allen Newell, "Heuristic Problem Solving: The Next Adventure in Operations Research," *Operations Research* 6 (1958): 8; Pamela McCorduck, *Machines Who Think: A Personal Inquiry into the History and Prospects of Artificial Intelligence* (San Francisco: W. H. Freeman & Co., 1979); Herbert A. Simon, *The Sciences of the Artificial*, 2d ed. (Cambridge, Mass.: M.I.T. Press, 1981).

Contours, decision characterized as having, p. 45: E.g., Boris Bittker, "The Case of the Fictitious Taxpayer: The Federal Taxpayer's Suit Twenty Years after *Flast v. Cohen*," *University of Chicago Law Review* 36 (1969): 364, 374.

Corporate law, and legal analysts, p. 120: See, e.g., William L. Cary, "Federalism and Corporate Law: Reflections Upon Delaware," *Yale Law Journal* 83 (1974): 663; Ernest L. Folk III, "State Statutes: Their Role in Prescribing Norms of Responsible Management Conduct," *Business Lawyer* 31 (1976): 1031, 1052–60.

Craftsmanship, criticism of, p. 10: See, e.g., Henry M. Hart, Jr. "The Time Chart of the Justices," *Harvard Law Review* 73 (1959): 84. Compare Thurmond Arnold, "Professor Hart's Theology," *Harvard Law Review* 73 (1960): 1298. See also Herbert Wechsler, "Toward Neutral Principles of Constitutional Law," *Harvard Law Review* 73 (1959): 1.

Criminal antitrust, as source of conspiracy analysis, p. 98: See, e.g., by an opponent of the development, Francis A. Allen, *The Criminal Law as an Instrument of Economic Regulation*, International Institute for Economic Research Original Paper no. 2 (Ottawa, Ill.: Green Hill Publishers, 1976).

Critics, choosing what they read, p. 41: Lionel Trilling works with the problem of authenticity in *Sincerity and Authenticity* (Cambridge, Mass.: Harvard University Press, 1972). The work is itself an example of a critic choosing texts to read closely.

Death of the motor car, p. 162: Joseph McCabe, *Haeckel's Critics Answered*, rev. ed. (London: Watts & Co., 1910), p. 113, in Chadwick, *Nineteenth Century*, p. 180.

Democratic National Party judiciary, p. 227: Descriptions may be found in *Cousins v. Wigoda*, 419 U.S. 477 (1975), and *O'Brian v. Brown*, 409 U.S. 1 (1972).

Design of democratic process, some in position to block change, p. 138: The standard example in the United States is apportionment of representatives to geographical and other voting units. See, e.g., *Baker v. Carr*, 369 U.S. 186 (1962). Compare *Ripon Society, Inc. v. National Republican Party*, 525 F.2d 567 (D.C. Cir. 1975) (en banc), certiorari denied, 424 U.S. 933 (1976) (apportionment of delegates to political party conventions). A useful discussion of some of these problems may be found in Alexander Bickel's defense of the Electoral College as part of the process of choosing the president of the United States,

Reform and Continuity: The Electoral College, the Convention, and the Party System (New York: Harper & Row, 1971).

Deterrence, theorists of, p. 235: E.g., Franklin E. Zimring and Gordon J. Hawkins, *Deterrence: The Legal Threat in Crime Control* (Chicago: University of Chicago Press, 1973), pp. 70–83.

Discomfort, with postulation of profit-maximizing man, p. 116: For examples from the history of economic thought, see Alfred Marshall, Preface to First Edition (1890), *Principles of Economics: An Introductory Volume*, 9th (Variorum) ed. (New York: Macmillan Co., 1961), 1:vi; Tibor Scitovsky, "A Note on Profit Maximization and Its Implications," *Review of Economic Studies* 11 (1943): 57; Kenneth J. Arrow, "A Difficulty in the Concept of Social Welfare," *Journal of Political Economy* 58 (1950): 328, reprinted in *Collected Papers of Kenneth J. Arrow: Social Choice and Justice* (Cambridge, Mass.: Belknap Press of Harvard University Press, 1983), p. 1.

Dissatisfaction, murmur of, p. 10: What is said privately is stronger than what is written. Some criticism is a reflection of special concern for constitutional law, some is not; the Supreme Court is by no means exclusively a constitutional court. For examples of what is written (from the decade 1971–81), see James B. White, "A Response to 'The Rhetoric of Powell's *Bakke*,'" *Washington and Lee Law Review* 38 (1981): 73; Note, "Plurality Decisions and Judicial Decisionmaking," *Harvard Law Review* 94 (1981): 1127, 1127–28; Wayne R. Lafave, *Search and Seizure: A Treatise on the Fourth Amendment*, vol. 3 (St. Paul, Minn.: West Publishing Co., 1978), 1981 Pocket Part, pp. 106–15; Christina B. Whitman, "Constitutional Torts," *Michigan Law Review* 79 (1980): 5, 27; Henry P. Monaghan, "Taking Supreme Court Opinions Seriously," *Maryland Law Review* 39 (1979): 1; Vincent A. Blasi, "*Bakke* as Precedent: Does Mr. Justice Powell Have a Theory?" *California Law Review* 67 (1979): 21; Philip B. Kurland, Book Review, *University of Chicago Law Review* 47 (1979): 185, 197–98; David L. Shapiro, "Mr. Justice Rehnquist: A Preliminary View," *Harvard Law Review* 90 (1976): 293; John F. Davis and William L. Reynolds, "Juridical Cripples: Plurality Opinions in the Supreme Court," *Duke Law Journal* (1974): 59; John Hart Ely, "The Wages of Crying Wolf: A Comment on *Roe v. Wade*," *Yale Law Journal* 82 (1973): 920: Alan M. Dershowitz and John Hart Ely, "*Harris v. New York*: Some Anxious Observations on the Candor and Logic of the Emerging Nixon Majority," *Yale Law Journal* 80 (1971): 1198. See also the eloquent but guarded comments of Paul A. Freund, Alexander M. Bickel, Peter D. Ehrenhaft, Russell D. Niles, Bernard G. Segal, Robert I. Stern, and Charles A. Wright in "Report of the Study Group on the Caseload of the Supreme Court," 57 F.R.D. 573, 582–83 (1972).

Double taxation, as term of argument, p. 97: E.g., Charles E. McLure, Jr., *Must Corporate Income Be Taxed Twice?* (Washington, D.C.: Brookings Institution, 1979).

Dred Scott, pp. 152, 193: *Dred Scott v. Sandford*, 60 U.S. (19 How.) 393 (1857), holding descendants of Africans who were enslaved at the time of adoption of the Constitution could not be citizens of the United States even if emancipated, and denying them standing to argue the merits of questions of emancipation in federal courts invoking diversity jurisdiction.

Drowning, and scope of employment, case involving, p. 84: The example builds upon *O'Keefe v. Smith, Hinchman and Grylls Associates, Inc.*, 380 U.S. 359 (1965).

Dynamo, as image, p. 162: Henry Adams, *The Education of Henry Adams*.

Economist, story of, p. 118: I have the story from my colleague William James Adams.

Ejectment, early nineteenth century action of, p. 157: "If A brought an action of ejectment against X to establish A's title to land of which X was in possession, the whole proceeding was based on a purely fictitious or imaginary action brought by a plaintiff, John Doe, who had no existence, against a defendant, Richard Roe, who had no existence, for an assault committed against the said John Doe on the land claimed by A, which assault had never been committed by anyone, either on such land or elsewhere." Dicey, *Law and Public Opinion*, p. 92. The passage goes on (pp. 93–94), "These long labyrinths of judge-made fictions . . . seem to a lawyer of to-day as strange as the most fanciful dreams of *Alice in Wonderland*"—Dicey not at his best, for the dreams in *Alice* are not strange. They are no escape through fancy. They retain their grip.

Elision of time, small example of, p. 205: Compare, e.g., *Marbury v. Madison*, 1 Cranch (5 U.S.) 137, 178 (1803), with *Marbury v. Madison* in William B. Lockart, Yale Kamisar, and Jesse H. Choper, *Constitutional Rights and Liberties: Cases and Materials*, 5th ed. (St. Paul, Minn.: West Publishing Co., 1981), p. 1 at 6.

Ely, on Calder, Dred Scott, Bakke, Carolene Products, pp. 151–53, 154–55: "Discovering Fundamental Values," pp. 26–27 n.95 (*Calder*); "Constitutional Interpretivism," p. 417 (*Dred Scott*); "Discovering Fundamental Values, pp. 9–10 n.33 (*Bakke*); "Discovering Fundamental Values, pp. 5, 5–6, 6 n.7 (*Carolene Products*). "Constitutional Interpretivism" and "Discovering Fundamental Values" are incorporated into *Democracy and Distrust: A Theory of Judicial Review* (Cambridge, Mass.: Harvard University Press, 1980). The judicial review in Dean Ely's subtitle is review of the constitutionality of legislative action.

Employee, obedience of, p. 193: Following the use of the terms "power" and "authority" through the opinion in *Whirlpool Corporation v. Marshall*, 445 U.S. 1 (1980), is an exercise in tracing the various involvements of lawyers with the authoritarian. At issue in the case was the validity of refusal to obey as a remedy to enforce the law in a modern American factory. The most useful background for a consideration of the conceptual and perceptual problems now associated with obedience in the hierarchical settings of economic life is to be found in historical work, particularly of a kind which is helpfully focused upon but not narrowly concerned with what is called economic history. See, e.g., E. J. Hobsbawm, *The Age of Revolution: Europe 1789–1848* (London: Weidenfeld & Nicolson, 1962); *The Age of Capital: 1848–1875* (New York: Charles Scribner's Sons, 1975).

Equal dignity rule, p. 120: See, e.g., Melvin A. Eisenberg, *The Structure of the Corporation: A Legal Analysis* (Boston: Little, Brown & Co., 1976), pp. 218–23.

Equations, legal, of Hohfeld, p. 27: See Hohfeld, *Fundamental Legal Conceptions.*

Escapee from prison, mens rea of, pp. 183, 235: *United States v. Bailey*, 444 U.S. 394 (1980).

Fictional account of the actual decision-making process, p. 226: *Home Box Office, Inc. v. Federal Communications Commission*, 567 F.2d 9, 54–55 (D.C. Cir. 1977).

Fictions, legal, in A. V. Dicey, p. 10: See, e.g., *Law and Public Opinion*, pp. 91–94.

Finger of God, written by, p. 56: Exodus 31:18, *New English Bible*, p. 96.

Fiss, inquiry into the American judicial function, pp. 154, 229: Fiss, "The Forms of Justice," pp. 6, 6 n.19, 10, and 10 n.26 (*Carolene Products* footnote four); pp. 1–58 (example).

Footnote, short, in a 1938 opinion, p. 154: *United States v. Carolene Products Co.*, 304 U.S. 144, 152 n.4 (1938).

Force of law, p. 52: *Abbott Laboratories v. Gardner*, 387 U.S. 136, 150 (1967), is an example of the use of the term.

Ford Motor Company, criminal prosecution of, p. 174: I have drawn this account from the trial transcript, *State of Indiana v. Ford Motor Company*, no. 11–431, Pulaski Circuit Court, Annual Term, 1979, and contemporary reports in the *New York Times* (1978–80), the *Wall Street Journal* (1978–80), the *American Lawyer* (April 1980), and *Mother Jones* (September/October 1977). See also Lee P. Strobel, *Reckless Homicide?* (South Bend, Ind.: and books, 1980).

Foreign law, attitude toward, p. 180: E.g., American Law Institute, *Principles of Corporate Governance*, Tentative Draft no. 2, 13 April 1984, p. 34.

Forlorn! the very word is like a bell, p. 151: Keats, "Ode to a Nightingale," in *Poems*, pp. 371–72.

Form of discussion, p. 29: Each reader must search his own experience for the example that strains the form and thus brings it to consciousness. In my case it was Frederick Engels' *Anti-Dühring: Herr Eugen Dühring's Revolution in Science* (Moscow: Foreign Languages Publishing House, 1959). For vindicating examples in contemporary philosophy and literary criticism, see Stanley Cavell, *Must We Mean What We Say?: A Book of Essays* (Cambridge: Cambridge University Press, 1976).

Four fingers, as five fingers, in imagined authoritarian system, pp. 72, 85: Orwell, *Nineteen Eighty-Four*, pp. 255–66.

Freedom, and acceptance of restraints, Knight on, p. 94: Knight, "Freedom as Fact and Criterion," in *Freedom and Reform*, p. 10.

Freedom and emptiness, in Hegel, p. 94: E.g., *Philosophy of Right* § 207, pp. 133–34. I refer to this passage in particular—which includes a remark about growing up to the importance of the concrete—because the remark leaps out to the reader (at least to the reader not grown up) and strengthens resolve to push on through Hegel's text.

Gilmore, proposal of heaven without law, p. 206: Passages quoted will be found (in order of quotation) on pp. 111, 1, 14, 110, 31–32, 34–35, 39, 62–63, 81, 82, and 88 of *The Ages of American Law*.

Gods, and atavistic remnants, p. 149: The social engineer might say these remnants need still to be preserved for the sake of those men, perhaps the mass of men, who are still not adult enough. For an intriguing exploration of the possibility that individuals did once quite literally *hear* such voices, see Julian Jaynes's much criticized *The Origin of Consciousness in the Breakdown of the Bicameral Mind* (Boston: Houghton Mifflin Co., 1976).

Golden calf, p. 46: Exodus 32:1–35, *New English Bible*, pp. 96–98.

Grand Central Terminal, opinions in constitutional litigation over landmark designation of, p. 221: *Penn Central Transportation Co. v. City of New York*, 366 N.E.2d 1271 (N.Y. 1977) (Breitel, C. J.), affirmed, 438 U.S. 104 (1978).

Grand Inquisitor, pp. 145, 198: Dostoyevsky, *Brothers Karamazov*, bk. 5, chap. 5, "The Grand Inquisitor," pp. 292–314.

High Court of Parliament, p. 114: Charles H. McIlwain, *The High Court of Parliament and Its Supremacy* (New Haven: Yale University Press, 1910).

I AM, p. 199: Exodus 3:13–14, *New English Bible*, p. 63.

In analyzing the likelihood he coldly weighs, p. 178: *United States v. Hartford Empire Co.*, 46 F. Supp. 541, 606 (N.D. Ohio, 1942).

Inequality of rights and of power, p. 193: *Quod Apostolici muneris*, Actae Sanctae Sedis, 11:370–72 (1878) (Leo XIII).

It took almost twenty-five years, p. 35: Gerald D. Rosberg, "The Protection of Aliens," pp. 298–99.

Jaffe, Louis, two passages by, p. 224: "Judicial Review: Question of Law" (1955), p. 264, incorporated into *Judicial Control of Administrative Action* (Boston: Little, Brown & Co., 1965), p. 576; "The Illusion of the Ideal Administration," (1973), pp. 1188–91.

Jury trial, in corporate law, p. 99: See *Ross v. Bernhard*, 396 U.S. 531 (1970).

Keats's *Endymion*, as example, p. 48: See Walter Jackson Bate, *John Keats* (Cambridge, Mass.: Belknap Press of Harvard University Press, 1963).

Law school, and systematic discussion of purpose, p. 192: I am indebted to my colleague Philip Soper on this point.

Lawyers' signals, p. 37: See the Columbia Law Review, the Harvard Law Review Association, the University of Pennsylvania Law Review, and the Yale Law Journal, *A Uniform System of Citation*, 13th ed. (Cambridge, Mass.: The Harvard Law Review Association, 1981).

Legislation, made into game, p. 124: A discussion and review of approaches (in disciplines other than law) to concerns arising from this problem will be found in Charles E. Lindblom, *Politics and Markets: The World's Political-Economic Systems* (New York: Basic Books, 1977).

Letters of opinion, p. 39: See, e.g., Special Committee on Legal Opinions in Commercial Transactions, "Legal Opinions to Third Parties: An Easier Path," *Business Lawyer* 34 (1979): 1891; Morgan Shipman, "Professional Responsibilities of the Corporations Lawyer," in *Professional Responsibility: A Guide for Attorneys* (Chicago: American Bar Association Press, 1978), pp. 271–309.

Liberation in theology, p. 193: Modern Western theology of course has its roots in earlier work. Much of it today is distinguished by an ecumenical reach, embracing not just the Catholic, Protestant, and Judaic traditions but (in some small measure) the Eastern and the Islamic also. See, e.g., Hans Kung, *On Being A Christian*, trans. Edward Quinn (New York: Simon & Schuster, 1978).

Life is but a day, p. 34: "And it comes strangely over me in bidding you goodbye how a life is but a day and expresses mainly but a single note." William James, *Letters*, 1:220.

Lower courts, responding to Supreme Court opinion, p. 38: See, e.g., Antonin Scalia, "Vermont Yankee: The APA, the D.C. Circuit, and the Supreme Court," *Supreme Court Review* (1978): 345, 371–75, and 400.

MacArthur, General, p. 175: William Manchester, *American Caesar: Douglas MacArthur 1880–1964* (Boston: Little, Brown & Co., 1978), p. 339.

Macpherson, James, poems of, presented as written by Ossian, p. 55: See *The Poems of Ossian, Translated by James Macpherson*. Schiller and Herder admired them; Goethe (a lawyer once) translated them; Napoleon is said to have carried them with him during his campaigns. The scope of the controversy over what was called their authenticity and the attention Macpherson (1736–96) achieved may be surveyed in George F. Black, *Macpherson's Ossian and the Ossianic Controversy: A Contribution towards a Bibliography* (New York: New York Public Library, 1926).

Manipulative speech, speech by profit-maximizing entity as example of, p. 217: See, e.g., the discussion and references in the various opinions in *First National Bank of Boston v. Bellotti*, 435 U.S. 765 (1978) (reversing a state supreme court decision upholding a statute regulating involvement of business corporations in political debate on matters legislatively defined as unrelated to their business or property). A reader giving the close reading to the opinion of the Court that has been usual in legal practice, on the assumption such a response is appropriate to the text, may possibly conclude that, in disagreeing with the position of the dissents (White, Brennan, Marshall, JJ., and Rehnquist, J.) the majority may have been disagreeing with one or more of their apparent premises: that business corporations are to be viewed as profit-maximizing entities, or that business corporations may be reduced to the holders of equity shares in them.

Mark out a little island, p. 105: Dewey, *Human Nature and Conduct,* p. 261 (published 1922).

Marshall, John, in 1803, p. 9: E.g., Marshall, C. J., *Marbury v. Madison.*

Mathematics, as ideal, Radin on, p. 27: Radin, "The Endless Problem of Corporate Personality," p. 647. Radin, like others of his time who were called legal realists, found it difficult nonetheless to move away from the scientific analogy.

Mechanical deliberation, and British Commission, p. 127: Commission on the Third London Airport, *Report* (London: Her Majesty's Stationery Office, 1971) (Roskill Commission), pp. 120, 133, 152, and 261; *Papers and Proceedings* (1969), 5:1299–1306; *Papers and Proceedings* (1970), 7:27–28, 39–41, and 414–23. David McKie, *A Sadly Mismanaged Affair: A Political History of the Third London Airport* (London: Croom Helm, 1973), pp. 18–19, 180–81. (The church [A.D. 1150] was well-known, one of three of its kind in the country that had not been substantially altered. The fire insurance was £51000 and could provide shelter from the elements. Eventually the value of the church was omitted entirely, as was the value of wildlife at other sites. The calculation pointed to an airport over Stewkley.)

Mind, that Ocean where each kind, p. 173: Andrew Marvell, "The Garden." The lines quoted are in anthologized form, modernized in spelling and capitalization. Helen Gardner, ed., *The New Oxford Book of English Verse 1250–1950* (Oxford: Oxford University Press, 1972), p. 336. For the original text, see *Poems and Letters,* 1:52.

Mock Turtle, p. 47: Lewis Carroll, *Alice's Adventures in Wonderland,* chap. 9, "The Mock Turtle's Story," pp. 137–40.

Models, of process of deliberation, p. 146: C. H. Waddington, *Tools for Thought* (New York: Basic Books, 1977) (posthumously published; see Eric Ashby, "Thinking about complexity," *Nature* 267: 377–78 [1977]), is a useful introduction to the problem of perceiving processes (particularly those now known as complex systems) without means of describing them.

Mormon, Book of, p. 56: An account of the central text of the Mormons may be found in John W. Welch, "Chiasmus in the Book of Mormon," in *Chiasmus in Antiquity: Structures, Analyses, Exegesis,* ed. John W. Welch (Hildesheim: Gerstenberg Verlag, 1981), p. 198.

Murray, James A. H., and Johnson, Samuel, dictionaries of, p. 86: See K. M. E. Murray, *Caught in the Web of Words: James A. H. Murray and the Oxford English Dictionary;* Bate, *Samuel Johnson,* pp. 240–60.

Necklace, as accoutrement of virility, p. 81: E.g., *New York Times,* 6 February 1980, p. D20.

No man sues with just cause, p. 196: Isaiah 59:4, *New English Bible,* p. 892.

Partners, contrasted with shareholders in business corporation, p. 97: "Partnership," it should be noted, is also an organizing term, in both state and federal law and even in constitutional law. See, e.g., *Bellis v. United States,* 417 U.S. 85, 97 (1974).

Party Convention rules, press analysis of, p. 137: E.g., *Newsweek,* 11 August 1980, p. 23. In the 1980 Democratic National Convention one rule in question was that determining whether elected delegates to the Convention were to be bound on the first ballot to the candidate whom they had originally announced they would support. In the 1972 Democratic Convention the striking example was the rule determining who was eligible to vote, which itself had to be put to a vote. See generally Austin Ranney, "Changing the Rules of the Nominating Game," in *Choosing the President,* ed. J. D. Barber (Englewood

Cliffs, N.J.: Prentice-Hall, 1974), and, I shall suggest also, my own "Delegate Selection Reform and the Extension of Law into Politics," *Virginia Law Review* 60 (1974): 1389.

Party structure, substructure beneath, p. 137: The standard example in American jurisprudence is the series of institutions effectively disenfranchising black voters in the South, see, e.g., *Terry v. Adams*, 345 U.S. 461 (1953). For a comparative discussion of the structure of politics, see Gerhard Casper, *"Williams v. Rhodes* and Public Financing of Political Parties under the American and German Constitutions," *Supreme Court Review* (1969): 271.

Pius IX, universal suffrage opposed by, p. 193: Chadwick, *Nineteenth Century,* p. 113.

Playing fields, images of, p. 115: See Johan Huizinga, *Homo Ludens: A Study of the Play-Element in Culture* (1944; Boston: Beacon Press, 1955).

Popper, Karl, story of, p. 118: Bauman, *Hermeneutics and Social Science,* p. 172, a paraphrase of Popper's longer (and entertaining) telling of it in "The Logic of the Social Sciences," in *The Positivist Dispute in German Sociology,* ed. Teodor W. Adorno et al., trans. Glyn Adey and David Frisby (London: Heinemann, 1976), pp. 93–95.

Post hoc rationalization, rejection of, p. 225: E.g., *Burlington Truck Lines v. United States,* 371 U.S. 156, 168–69 (1962); *Motor Vehicle Manufacturers Association v. State Farm Mutual Insurance Co.,* 463 U.S. 29, 43 n.9, 42–44, 49–50 (1983).

Press access to criminal proceedings, opinion in case concerning, p. 37: *Gannett Co. v. DePasquale,* 443 U.S. 368 (1979).

Privilege, parent-child testimonial, p. 182: See, e.g., discussions and references in *In the Matter of the Application of A. & M.,* 403 N.Y.S.2d 375 (Supreme Court Appellate Division, 1978); *People v. Fitzgerald,* 422 N.Y.S.2d 309 (Westchester County Court, 1979); *In Re Agosto,* 553 F. Supp. 1298 (D. Nev., 1983).

Public lecture, of John Rawls, p. 219: "The Basic Liberties and Their Priority" (delivered 10 April 1981), in *The Tanner Lectures on Human Values,* vol. 3, ed. Sterling M. McMurrin (Salt Lake City, Utah: University of Utah Press; Cambridge: Cambridge University Press, 1982), pp. 1–87, analyzing his *Theory of Justice.*

Punishment, logic of calculation in setting, p. 235: E.g., Richard A. Posner, *Economic Analysis of Law,* 2d ed. (Boston: Little, Brown & Co., 1977), pp. 163–78; Gary S. Becker, "Crime and Punishment: An Economic Approach," *Journal of Political Economy* 76 (1968): 169–217: Ronald A. Coase, "Economics and Contiguous Disciplines," *Journal of Legal Studies* 7 (1978): 201, 210.

Reckless homicide, p. 174: Indiana Code Annotated § 35-41-2-2(c); § 35-41-2-3; § 35-42-1-5 (St. Paul, Minn.: West Publishing Co., 1978).

Regan, discussion of abortion, pp. 153, 155, 229: Regan, "Rewriting *Roe v. Wade,"* p. 1636 ("The most important fact"); pp. 1614–15 ("It is interesting to note"); pp. 1569–1646 (example).

Rules of inference, and metaphorical weighting, p. 82: References to rules of inference as rules of weight are part of the long effort to express the actual function of rules in legal decision making, whether in scholarly or official analysis, e.g., Attorney General's Committee on Administrative Procedure, *Final Report* (Washington: 1941), pp. 87–88, 90–91 (1941), or by authors of the legal opinions on which much of the textual part of legal analysis is focused, e.g., *Citizens to Preserve Overton Park, Inc. v. Volpe,* 401 U.S. 402 (1971).

Scanning other disciplines, and theology, p. 192: Examples of contemporary observation, by American legal scholars, of the connections between the study of law and the study of theology may be found in Roberto Mangabeira Unger, *Knowledge and Politics* (New York:

Free Press, 1975), pp. 106–19, 290–95, and Milner S. Ball, *The Promise of American Law: A Theological, Humanistic View of Legal Process* (Athens: University of Georgia Press, 1981). The recent work of Robert A. Burt, Michael J. Perry, and Sanford Levinson in constitutional law, Harold J. Berman in legal history, and Warren Lehman, Thomas L. Shaffer, and John T. Noonan in legal ethics, suggests that taking the theological analogy seriously is not at all idiosyncratic. I do not think, however, that any of these— or others who would be named in a survey of the moment—considers himself to be singing in a chorus; each comes upon the connection (or the possibility of it) as a personal discovery, as have I, and as, I imagine, will many of those who come to it in the future.

Sects, p. 195: The lawyer may also perceive sects within the discipline of law, and even within the domain of central institutions operating in one or another geographic jurisdiction. In Christian theology alone, the work of David Tracy, e.g., *Blessed Rage for Order: The New Pluralism in Theology* (New York: Seabury Press, 1978), or Edward Schillebeeckx, e.g., *Ministry: Leadership in the Community of Jesus Christ*, trans. John Bowden (New York: Crossroad, 1981), in the Catholic tradition might be pitted against the Protestant work of John MacQuarrie, e.g., *Principles of Christian Theology*, 2d ed. (New York: Charles Scribner's Sons, 1977), or Paul Lehmann, e.g., *Ethics in a Christian Context* (New York: Harper & Row, 1963); both might be pitted against what is called fundamentalism on the one side and what is called liberation theology on the other. But a lawyer reading them for aid in thinking about law is not forced by their terms of discourse to pit one against another, any more than in working through the legal literature of structural remedies the lawyer trained in the common law tradition must give up his sense of what law is about.

Secular, as a descriptive term, question of, p. 191: My principal debts are to David Knowles (e.g., *The Monastic Order in England: A History of Its Development from the Times of St. Dunstan to the Fourth Lateran Council, 943–1216* [Cambridge: At the University Press, 1941]) and Walter Ullmann (e.g., *The Growth of Papal Government in the Middle Ages: A Study in the Ideological Relation of Clerical to Lay Power* [London: Methuen & Co., 1955]). I have been particularly stimulated also by Chadwick, *Nineteenth Century.*

Shining caps, of pyramids, p. 76: I. E. S. Edwards, *The Pyramids of Egypt* (Harmondsworth: Penguin Books, 1952), p. 234.

Simples, p. 222: Moore, *Principia Ethica*, chap. 1 (published 1903).

Social contract, metaphor of, p. 193: I have discussed this point briefly in *Legal Identity: The Coming of Age of Public Law* (New Haven: Yale University Press, 1978), e.g., p. 155.

Speech of business corporations, on political or public issues, p. 97: E.g., *First National Bank of Boston v. Bellotti*, 435 U.S. 765 (1978).

Squeeze-outs and phantom corporations, p. 139: E.g., *Bryan v. Brock and Blevins Co.*, 490 F.2d 563 (5th Cir.), certiorari denied, 419 U.S. 844 (1974); *Singer v. Magnavox*, 380 A.2d 969 (Del. 1977). Compare *Hariton v. Arco Electronics, Inc.*, 182 A.2d 22, affirmed, 188 A.2d 123 (Del. 1963).

Staff, growth and use of, p. 11: John Bilyeu Oakley and Robert S. Thompson, *Law Clerks and the Judicial Process: Perceptions of the Qualities and Functions of Law Clerks in American Courts* (Berkeley: University of California Press, 1980), contains a pioneering description of the growth and use of staff within appellate courts generally and at the Supreme Court, together with an extensive bibliography of published material. See also Gerhard Casper and Richard A. Posner, *The Workload of the Supreme Court* (Chicago: American Bar Foundation, 1976), pp. 72–73, 78–81, 108–109, and 115; Paul A. Freund, Alexander M. Bickel, Peter D. Ehrenhaft, Russell D. Niles, Bernard G. Segal, Robert L. Stern, and Charles A. Wright, "Report of the Study Group on the Caseload of the Supreme Court," 57 F.R.D. 573, 582–83 (1972); *Board of Education of Rogers, Ark. v. McCluskey*, 458

U.S. 966, 971–73 (1982). The publication of Bob Woodward and Scott Armstrong, *The Brethren: Inside the Supreme Court* (New York: Simon & Schuster, 1979), relying more on clerks' than judges' descriptions of the opinion-writing process, and using journalistic rather than scholarly techniques of investigation, evoked a substantial secondary literature of comment and criticism, often by former clerks, which is itself a source of information. See, e.g., John P. Frank, "The Supreme Court: The Muckrakers Return," *American Bar Association Journal* 66 (1980): 161. For a review of that literature and citations to it, see Richard B. Saphire, "The Value of *The Brethren*: A Response to Its Critics," *Texas Law Review* 58 (1980): 1475. A brief but widely circulated discussion of writing by staff at a time when the size of the staff was smaller can be found in John P. Frank, *Marble Palace* (New York: Alfred A. Knopf, 1958), pp. 116–18.

Standing, p. 114: I shall make reference here to my own *Legal Identity: The Coming of Age of Public Law* (New Haven: Yale University Press, 1978), pp. 55–56, and to the references therein.

State parties, statutes addressed to, p. 227: See, e.g., *Marchioro v. Chaney*, 442 U.S. 191 (1979).

Structural remedy, p. 166: On structural remedies generally, see, e.g., Owen M. Fiss, *The Civil Rights Injunction* (Bloomington: Indiana University Press, 1978). The difficulties of which we speak here are prior to those presented by the situation of individuals who may have relied upon the appearance of authority in their own thinking and action. I have discussed other aspects of these matters in *Legal Identity: The Coming of Age of Public Law* (New Haven: Yale University Press, 1978), pp. 80–101.

Studies, of lower court procedures, p. 11: See, e.g., J. Woodford Howard, Jr., *Courts of Appeals in the Federal Judicial System: A Study of the Second, Fifth, and District of Columbia Circuits* (Princeton: Princeton University Press, 1981), pp. 198, 200, 208–9, and 279; John Bilyeu Oakley and Robert S. Thompson, *Law Clerks and the Judicial Process: Perceptions of the Qualities and Functions of Law Clerks in American Courts* (Berkeley: University of California Press, 1980) (examining the Ninth Circuit, the United States District Courts in California, the California Courts of Appeal, and the California Supreme Court); B. E. Witkin, *Manual on Appellate Court Opinions* (St. Paul, Minn.: West Publishing Co., 1977); Wade H. McCree, Jr., "Bureaucratic Justice: An Early Warning," *University of Pennsylvania Law Review* 129 (1981): 777; Alvin B. Rubin, "Bureaucratization of the Federal Courts: The Tension between Justice and Efficiency," *Notre Dame Lawyer* 55 (1980): 648; Harry T. Edwards, "A Judge's View on *Justice, Bureaucracy, and Legal Method*," *Michigan Law Review* 80 (1981): 259; Robert A. Kagan, Bliss Cartwright, Laurence M. Friedman, and Stanton Wheeler, "The Evolution of State Supreme Courts," *Michigan Law Review* 76 (1978): 961, 971–73, and 982; Robert S. Thompson, "One Judge and No Judge Appellate Opinions," *California State Bar Journal* 50 (1975): 476; John Lesinski and N. O. Stockmeyer, Jr., "Prehearing Research and Screening in the Michigan Court of Appeals: One Court's Method for Increasing Judicial Productivity," *Vanderbilt Law Review* 26 (1973): 1211; Paul R. Baier, "The Law Clerks: Profile of an Institution," *Vanderbilt Law Review* 26 (1973): 1125; George R. Smith, "A Primer of Opinion Writing for Law Clerks," *Vanderbilt Law Review* 26 (1973): 1203. See also Paul D. Carrington, Daniel J. Meador, and Maurice Rosenberg, *Justice on Appeal* (St. Paul, Minn.: West Publishing Co., 1976), pp. 45–55; Daniel J. Meador, *Appellate Courts: Staff and Process in the Crisis of Volume* (St. Paul, Minn.: West Publishing Co., 1974).

Successor liability, p. 97: E.g., *Turner v. Bituminous Casualty Co.*, 244 N.W.2d 873 (Mich. 1976).

Such inquiries should not be pushed too far, p. 106: Knight, "The Planful Act: The Possibilities and Limitations of Collective Rationality," in *Freedom and Reform*, p. 335 (emphasis supplied).

Taken into account, translation of questions into question of what was, p. 236: In the law of business corporations (as one example) consider *Zapata Corp.* v. *Maldonado*, 430 A.2d 779 (Del. 1981), and *Auerbach* v. *Bennett*, 393 N.E.2d 994 (N.Y. 1980).

Then said the shepherds, pp. 143: Bunyan, *Pilgrim's Progress*, pp. 160–61. I have reproduced Roger Sharrock's modernization of capitalization and italicization. For the original text (1678–84), see *The Pilgrim's Progress*, ed. J. B. Wharey, 2d ed. rev. by Roger Sharrock (Oxford: At the Clarendon Press, 1960), p. 121–23.

They thought they saw something like the Gate, p. 161: Bunyan, *Pilgrim's Progress*, p. 161.

Tower of Babel, p. 109: Genesis 11:1–9, *New English Bible*, p. 11.

Towering skyscrapers of rusted girders, p. 120: Manning, "The Stockholders' Appraisal Remedy," p. 245 n.37.

Tragic choices, p. 177: See Guido Calabresi and Philip Bobbitt, *Tragic Choices* (New York: W. W. Norton, 1978). For a thoughtful and somewhat anguished discussion of these matters by an economist (rather than a lawyer) writing in the current debate about the placing of a monetary value on a human life for purposes of economic analysis of public policy, see Thomas C. Schelling, "The Life You Save May Be Your Own," in *Problems in Public Expenditure Analysis*, ed. Samuel B. Chase, Jr., (Washington, D.C.: Brookings Institution, 1968), p. 127.

Translating an authoritative text into contemporary idiom, p. 205: See, e.g., G.R.D., "Introduction to the Old Testament," pp. xvii–xviii; C.H.D., "Introduction to the New Testament," pp. v–viii, *New English Bible* (translation prepared 1946–70 under auspices of Joint Committee on the New Translation of the Bible representing the major protestant churches in Great Britain and Ireland—Anglican, Presbyterian, Baptist, Congregationalist, Quaker, Methodist—joined by observers representing the Roman Catholic Church).

Tugboat case, p. 177: *The T. J. Hooper*, 60 F.2d 737, 739–40 (2d Cir.) (L. Hand, J.), certiorari denied, 287 U.S. 662 (1932).

Vocal chords, under construction, p. 138: The problem of construction of course goes beyond the electoral process and beyond the legislative traditionally conceived. The outcome of the political process is not assumed, for purposes of legal analysis, to be connected to the will of the people by reason of the fact alone that it is the outcome of the process. See, e.g., the discussion in the opinion for the Court in *Immigration and Naturalization Service* v. *Chadha*, 462 U.S. 919 (1983) (provision for "legislative veto" of administrative decisions, enacted by Congress and signed by President, unconstitutional).

Waste Land, editorial work by Ezra Pound on, p. 14: See Eliot, Valerie, ed., *The Waste Land: A Facsimile.*

GENERAL INDEX

Acceptance: commitment distinguished, 224; of contingencies, 223–24; of death, 237; not of fear, 135, 194; and freedom, 93–94; and identity, 95–96; by individual, of language, 85, 90, 146–47, 162, 223–24, 234–35; of majority decision, 136; ratification and, 140, 228; resignation contrasted, 135; of structure, 100

Action: affecting thought, 39, 80–86, 89–102; enhancement and, 26, 58–59; function of center and, 78

Administrative law, 17, 19, 22, 50, 225–26; practice of, 11–14, 19, 51–52, 147–48, 209, 225; view of, 224–25

Adolescence, 39, 100, 215

Aesthetic decision, 172–74

Aesthetics, 18, 20, 208, 218; images from, 45, 179

Agency, law of: authorization of signature and, 53–54; and definition of entity, 183–84, 236; distributional questions affecting, 54, 169–70, 219; master-servant relationship in, 169–70; and ratification by silence, 140–41, 228

Angel, Congress compared, 121–22

Animals: analogy to, 230; companion, 213; and dignity, 230, 234; human categorization contrasted, 234–35; metaphors for, 162, 230; and the sacred, 234

Animation of legal thought, 177–79

Anthropology, 118, 208

Art, criticism of, 41, 44–45, 49, 208, 218–19

Assent. See Acceptance

Attention, authority and, 10, 11–12, 13–14, 24, 52, 56–59, 68–69, 148, 230–31, 232

Augury, 49, 85

Beauty, authority of, 20, 218

Behaviorism, 118–19, 158

Bipolar choices: electoral and legislative, 138; in individual speech, 227–28. See also Joint statement

Blindness: associated with authoritarian, 76, 171, 183; associated with authoritative, 143, 161, 192, 210, 218

Canon, 30–31; in literature, 29–30, 37, 212, 216; uncertain, 191, 213–14, 219. See also Limitation of material

Case: common law theory of, 221; and conventions of discourse, 38–39; definition of entity and, 176–77; formation of, 21–22, 74, 176, 209, 217; limitations of, 73–75, 176; organization of legal thinking by, 100, 176, 177

Categorization: central institution and, 85–88; in legal method, 21, 33, 36, 74, 217, 234; open, 74, 107, 234

Chinese texts, 30

Christianity: centers in, 77, 78, 190, 193;

257

Christianity (*contd.*)
  connections in, 87; and democracy, 141, 157; eschatology in, 108; and First Amendment, 191
Clarity: complexity compared, 170, 205–6, 215, 231–32; doctrinal use of, 214–15; and generality in statements of law, 106–9, 217–18; legal method and, 161, 209–10, 213–15; in perception of justice, 143, 161
Classical texts, 30, 64, 68
Clerks, at courts, 10–11, 19, 51–57
Closed systems, 123, 220; equations and, 231; and language, 87, 100; legal rules contrasted, 66, 106–9, 218, 233–34; and understanding, 88, 220
Coldness, 26, 27, 46–47, 129, 178
Commercial law, 17, 184, 207–8
Common law, 9, 17, 65–66, 221, 229
Comparative law, 65–66
Complexity, in legal commands, 170, 194, 209, 213–15, 231–32
Complex systems, 32, 146
Compromise, in writing. *See* Negotiation
Computer, as metaphor for law, 28, 45–46, 188
Consequences of words, legal method and, 112–13, 129, 156, 227
Conspiracy, law of, 180
Constitutional law, review of decisions under, 35, 51, 99, 151–53, 154–55, 217, 221
Contract and promise, 36, 66, 165–66, 184; and freedom, 94, 118, 211; and obedience, 45, 193, 194–95, 211, 231–32; about process, 139–40, 236–37; about words, 90–91, 112–13, 156, 231. *See also* Acceptance; Agency; Negotiation; Representation
Conversation, 101–2, 222, 227
Corporate law: and consumer, 211, 236; courts of equity and, 193; definition of entities in, 176, 184, 236; and law of choice of law, 66; legal method and, 150–51; and obedience, 178, 193, 194, 209, 210–11, 231–32, 235–36; as procedure, 120, 139–40; review of decisions under, 50–51, 151–52, 236–37; statutory interpretation in, 92, 120, 151, 152

Corporation: constituents of, 43–44, 96–99, 176–77, 184, 236; criminal liability of, 165, 174, 176, 178; obedience by, 178, 193–94, 209, 210–11, 234, 235–36; obedience to, 193, 194, 209, 210–11, 231–32; obedience within, 193, 194; and structure of legal thought, 96–97, 99, 176, 184, 236
Councils, 132, 192
Craftsmanship, in legal texts, 10
Criminal justice system, 21–22
Criminal law, dilemmas of, 181–83
Critique of law, assumptions in, 112–13, 155–56, 214

Dead: center, 81, 86; speech, 46–47; weight, 178
Death, 149, 159, 185, 210, 237; degrees of, 23, 80–81, 94, 168
Defective process, and definition of public value, 209–10, 236–37
Delegation, 52–58; with office, 53, 57, 70–73
Democracy, 90–91, 132–41; and denial of authoritarian, 141; Jeffersonian, 87. *See also* Equality; Representation
Demoralization, and institutional design, 81
Description: of entity, 35, 96, 184, 236–37; humor and, 42, 226; in legal analysis, 18–20, 21–22, 25, 34, 172
Design of legal institutions, 10–12, 15, 51–52, 81, 94, 111–14, 117, 124, 126–31, 137–41; as continuing question, 62, 63, 77, 90, 124, 145
Detachment, 47–59
Dictionary: central institution contrasted, 86; and closed system, 86, 199
Dignity, perception of substance and, 234
Disclosure, definition of entity and, 43–44, 103, 183–85, 186, 236–37

Economics: ambiguities of, 25, 115–19, 210–11, 231–32, 235–36, 236; assumption of law in, 155–56, 214; and definition of freedom, 94; and law of property and crime, 152, 176–77, 178, 211, 231–32; profit maximization in, 115, 116, 210–11, 232, 235–36; and public policy analysis, 105–6, 115–19; of punishment, 178, 235–36; scanning of, by law-yers, 192, 193

Editing: of authoritative texts, 17, 205, 213; and bureaucratic process, 14, 53; as translation, 205

Efficiency, in close reading, 66–69, 86

Embodiment, imitation contrasted, 57

Enchantment, and action, 58–59

Equality: hierarchy and, 4, 76; idea of, 32, 36, 141, 161; and institutional form, 76, 77, 89, 90

Escape, 74–75, 80–108, 123–25, 147, 161–86, 194–201; crime of, 183, 235; from relativism, 107–8; from self, 95–96, 123; to self, 95–96, 186, 200–201

Eschatology, 108

Etiquette, in legal practice, 72, 188–90

Factual determinations, and rules of in-ference, 82–83, 84

False marginalism, 172–77

Fashion, 81

Fear, 74, 81, 135, 149, 185, 193–94, 235

First Amendment, 97, 191, 217

Following a decision, 45

Footpad and speaker, 61–62

Force: of law, 52; of nature, 50, 62, 186; of office, 69–73

Foreign law, 180

Formalism, 46, 158, 199–200

Forms of deference, 62, 72, 90, 188–90

Games: analogy to, 199, 232; serious, 124, 217

Generations, splicing of, 82, 90, 103

Geographic: images, 163, 164, 165, 177, 196; jurisdiction, 9, 66, 73, 220

Gravity, images from, in law, 164, 177, 178

Great men, study of, 64–65

Hand, analogy of human being to, 108, 170

Harmless error, doctrine of, 164, 236

Heaven: and Tower of Babel, 108–9; view of, as without law, 206

Heresy, concept of, in law, 216, 217

Hermeneutics, 213

History: as cousin discipline, 28–40, 41–42, 125; dilemmas in practice of, 99, 159,

208; as metaphor for science, 28, 188; metaphors for, 28; replacing substance, 48, 56, 121, 122; scanning of, by law-yers, 193; as source of identity, 36, 47, 54, 100; as speaker, 131

Idolatry, 198–200

Impersonality, of criteria, 230

Incremental steps: in evolution of process, 224; in evolution of structure and value, 82, 98–99, 100, 101, 104; false margin-alism in descriptions of legal analysis contrasted, 172–77; in joint writing, 223; in legal reasoning, 74–75; necessity of, as protection, 104; in speech, 227–28

Individualism: and calculation, 106, 236; and formalism, 158; individuality con-trasted, 62, 106, 121

Inquiry: larger, 200–201; nature of, in book, 14–15; outline of, 5–6

Insanity, legal determination of, 43, 165, 181

Instability: and authoritarian, 171, 194; in precedent, appearance of, 177

Institutionalist, 127–31, 138

Intent of statute, 122, 147–48

International law, 65–66

Internalization, 14, 23, 168, 179–85, 196, 212; categorization and, 234; perception of entity and, 79, 146, 209–10, 236–37

Intimations, 168, 172, 219

Irreversibilities: in consequences of statutory words, 126; and hierarchy, 74–75; in in-dividual speech, 227; in material sys-tems, 125

Islam, 77, 78, 190

Isolation: and silence, 18, 147–49, 159; sto-ries of, 117–18

Joint statement, individual statement com-pared, 111–12, 136, 222, 223

Jokes, 42, 55, 59, 100, 123, 226

Judaism: center in, 77, 78, 190; eschatology in, 108; power and authority contrasted in, 141, 157

Jurisdiction: defined by joint purposes, 196; geographical, 9, 66, 196; of ideas, 66

King: beheading, 90, 110; can do no wrong, 165, 166

Laughter: as betrayal, 55; as evidence, 25, 55, 140; as protection, 55; surprise and, 226
Lawyers, as source of legal texts, 13, 39, 40, 67, 179, 191, 197
Legal equations, 16; in anti-summary, 230–31; of Hohfeld, 27
Legal fiction, 10, 148, 157, 158; ambiguity of, 37, 91–92, 98; and emptiness, 148, 199, 225–26
Legalism, 195, 196, 198
Legal rules, 45, 82, 217–18
Legislative reports, 122–23
Limitation of material for analysis: in history, 64–65, 68; in literature, 28–30, 37, 212, 216; in moral philosophy, 28–30, 219–20, 229; in ordinary discourse, 220–21; problems of clear meaning and, 191, 213–15, 219; in theology, 190–92, 219
Limits of language, 185–86
Literary criticism: assumptions in, 41, 212, 216; as cousin discipline, 28, 41; and forms of discussion, 28–31

Madness: cacophony and, 167; and deletion of statement, 32, 67; fear of, 81, 162; and isolation, 43, 149, 159, 162, 186; legal insanity and, 43, 165, 181; and manipulation, 43; and perception of entity, 79; relativity and, 107; of a society, 4, 147
Majority rule, 135–41; as deadlock-breaking device, 31, 212–13; in legal method, 17, 30–31; in multimember court, 30–31, 113, 152–53
Manipulation, 43, 103, 184, 217; of texts, by courts, 52, 126, 196–200; of texts, by lawyers, 12–14, 39, 196–200, 209
Manner of speaking, 9, 35, 110, 188–89; commitment to, 13
Marxism: canon in, 28, 154; critique of law and, 155, 214; and history, 131
Material evidence, 58
Mathematics, 27, 166
Maximizing and exchange theories, and law, 156

Military, images of, in law, 72, 115–17, 152, 153
Monumentality, in legal architecture, 72, 188, 190, 217
Multinational and multistate organizations, 66, 181, 220

Names, 6, 34–39, 75, 211
Naturalist: lawyer as, 17; scientist as, 208
Negative belief, 88, 173, 201, 223–24, 228
Negligence, law of, 150–51, 176, 177
Negotiation and compromise: in individual writing, 112, 227; in joint writing, 11, 47, 51, 69–70, 112, 117, 156–57, 192, 223–24
Novelist: and forms of discussion, 29, 192; legal analyst compared, 29–30, 34, 80, 192

Obedience: categorization and, 32–39, 234–35; and identification of voice, 104, 166–67, 169, 193; inapplicable, 23, 26, 231–32; and understanding, 218; unnecessary even to oneself, 95–96, 123–25
Objet trouvé, 222; and evolved structure, 100; and gardens, 48, 222; speech as example of, 125
Office: force of, on analyst, 55, 57, 70–73, 221; legal method as check on power of, 104; in legislature, 126, 228; and putative authors, 56; transference of, 53, 56–58
Omnipresence, brooding, fear of, 206, 208
Ordinary language, and law, 85, 199
Organizing mechanisms: and democratic process, 138; and process of speech, 227–28

Pain, recognition of, 230, 233–34
Paradigms, in thinking about law, 170, 209, 215, 217
Passions, 20
Pedigree: of office, 57, 71; of a statement, 57–58
Performance, in art, 48, 57, 59
Philosophy: assumptions in reading, 41–42, 219–20; as cousin discipline, 28–31; and forms of discussion, 28–31, 219–20, 229; view of law in, 155, 195
Political question, doctrine of, 227

Politics, legal structure of, 135, 138, 140, 226–27
Polling, and determination of law, 31, 214
Positivism: closed systems and, 220; legal practice and, 17, 39–40, 118; tradition of, in social science, 208, 211–12
Precedent: apparent instability of, 177; doctrine of, 30, 54; weight of, and internal disagreement, 30, 114
Prediction, in legal method, 39–40
Prison, pathology of, 182, 183, 235
Probation, law of, 19, 22
Procedure, judicial and administrative, 180; and commitment, 224; design of, 38, 127, 163, 226
Profit maximizing, 39, 43, 77, 115, 116, 178, 210–11, 232; entity, definition of, 210–11, 236; entity, statements of, 12, 217, 231–32
Pronoun, referent of, 95
Property, 196, 211, 218; as category, 36, 231–32; real, in images of law, 163–66, 196
Psychiatry, 112, 208; understanding in, 87, 95; scanning of, by lawyers, 193; therapeutic compared, 159; therapeutic distinguished, 34
Public policy analysis, 116
Punishment, anomalies of, 181–83, 235–36
Pyramid, 63, 76, 89, 100, 186

Quantification in deliberation, 4, 27, 127, 174, 178, 235

Race, distinctions based on, 32, 234 35
Ratification: in law of agency, 53–54, 219; of outcomes of democratic process, 140–41; by silence, 228–29
Rationalism, 105–9
Rationalization, 180–225
Recharacterization, 72, 73–74, 221
Relativism, 105–6, 117–18, 198; individuality and, 107–8; moral evolution and, 82, 99; in politics, 115–19, 131, 212–13
Repose, doctrines of, 58
Representation, of affected individuals, 102–5, 114–41, 149, 228
Rights, language of, 163–64
Ritual, 216–17

Sacred, secular compared, 191–92, 234
Saving, in legal method, 32–34, 54, 192
Science: analogy to, 3, 16, 19, 27, 152, 208, 222; assumptions in, 37, 91, 93, 122, 192, 208, 224; and history, 28, 159, 188; language of, compared, 91–94; laws in, 21; of man, 201; name of, 211–12
Scope of employment, 83–85
Secret legislator, 125, 134, 197
Separation of powers, 115
Signals, for citations, 37
Size: of collegial body, 69–70, 104; and hierarchy, 69–70, 77–78; of legislatures, 124, 228
Slavery, accommodation, 23, 184–85, 209, 210; to consumer, 211; as form of authoritarian, 49, 85, 89–90, 157, 193, 196, 210; in legal discourse, 196
Social class, comprehensibility of, xvi, 32, 188, 194
Social sciences: positivism in, 17–20, 155, 208, 211–12; scanning of, by lawyers, 193
Sociobiology, 159, 209
Statement by estoppel, 113
Statistical techniques, 30
Stripping, in legal method, 31–32, 50, 191–92
Surprise: ambivalence toward, 125, 226; evaluation and, 223

Testimonial privileges, 181–83
Theater, 48, 55, 57, 59
Theology: religious law contrasted, 195; manipulation in, 196–200; parallels with law, 5–6, 106–9, 188–201; views of, 187, 195, 201
Tone, in legal text, 34, 158
Translation, 31–32, 87–88, 108–9, 199; of authoritative texts, 31–32, 205
Treatises, 65
Tyranny, 76, 157

Veto, as outcome of system, 229

Wilderness preservation, 215–16
Words, definition of, 205–6, 206–7, 213